Adobe InDesign 2024

A comprehensive Mastery Guide to Navigate every facet of Adobe InDesign Interface with Professional Hacks, Shortcuts, and Expert Tricks.

Crystal Gibson

Copyright © 2024 by Crystal Gibson

All rights reserved. This book or any portion thereof should not be reproduced or used in any form whatsoever without the express written permission of the publisher except for the use of brief quotations in the book review.

Printed in the United States of America

CONTENTS

CONTENTS III

INTRODUCTION IX

CHAPTER ONE 10

EXPLORING INDESIGN 2024 NEW FEATURES 10

AUTO STYLING 10
HIDE SPREADS IN INDESIGN 11
ORGANIZE YOUR FILES WITH FILENAME SUFFIXES 12
"PUBLISH AND ANALYTICS" FEATURE 14
DEVELOPING GLYPH RENDERING WITH HARFBUZZ 14
EMPOWER YOUR WORKFLOW WITH UXP PLUGINS 15
PANEL SHORTCUTS 15

CHAPTER TWO 17

FAMILIARIZING WITH INDESIGN CC 2024 17

STARTING INDESIGN CC 18
STARTING A NEW PUBLICATION 18
ACCESSING AN EXISTING WORK 21
NAVIGATING THE INTERFACE 22
EXPLORING THE TOOLS PANEL 23
THE MENU OPTIONS 25
EXPLORING THE PANELS 26
UTILIZING THE CONTROL PANEL 26
USING CONTEXT MENUS 27
THE PAGES PANEL 28
CONFIGURING THE WORKSPACE 29
TOGGLE THE VISIBILITY OF GRIDS AND GUIDES 29
ENABLING THE SNAP FEATURE TO A GUIDE OR GRID 30
EXPLORING SMART GUIDE 31
PERSONALIZING AND ADJUSTING THE MENUS 31

PERSONALIZING INDESIGN INTERFACE APPEARANCE 33
SAVING A CUSTOMIZED WORKSPACE 33
GETTING STARTED WITH DOCUMENTS 34
IMPORTING CONTENTS TO YOUR DOCUMENT 35
VARIOUS WAYS TO VIEW INDESIGN CONTENTS 37
SAVE YOUR INDESIGN DOCUMENT 37

CHAPTER THREE 39

GETTING STARTED WITH TEXT AND TEXT FRAMES 39

WHAT EXACTLY ARE TEXT, FONTS, AND FRAMES 39
CREATING AND UTILIZING TEXT FRAMES 40
GENERATING TEXT FRAMES USING THE TYPE TOOL 40
CREATING TEXT FRAMES USING THE FRAME TOOL 41
CRAFTING TEXT FRAMES FROM A SHAPE 42
IMPORTING TEXT TO YOUR PUBLICATION VIA OTHER APPLICATIONS 42
HANDLING TEXT FLOW 43
INSERTING PLACEHOLDER TEXT 44
TEXT COPYING AND PASTING 45
OBSERVING TEXT FRAME OPTIONS 45
MODIFYING TEXT FRAME OPTIONS 45
EXPLORING AND ADJUSTING COLUMNS 47
ADJUSTING AND LINKING TEXT FRAMES ACROSS PAGES 50
ADJUSTING THE SIZE AND POSITION OF TEXT FRAMES 51
THREADING OR LINKING TEXT FRAMES 52
HOW TO ADD A PAGE JUMP NUMBER 55
FAMILIARIZING WITH PARAGRAPH CONFIGURATION 57
ADJUSTING TEXT INDENTATION 58
FORMATTING TEXT FRAMES WITH ALIGNMENT AND JUSTIFICATION 59
SAVE YOUR PARAGRAPH STYLE 60
EXPLORING THE STORY EDITOR 62
GETTING HAND ON STORY EDITOR 63
VERIFYING ACCURATE SPELLING 64
EXPLORING CUSTOM SPELLING DICTIONARIES 65
WORKING WITH TABLES 66
CRAFTING TABLES: 66
ALTERING TABLE SETTINGS 68

CREATING TABLE STYLES 71
EXPLORING TEXT ON A PATH 72

CHAPTER FOUR 75

GETTING FAMILIARIZED WITH PAGE LAYOUT 75

IMPORTING PICTURES 75
IMPORTING YOUR PDF FILES 77
IMPORTING INDESIGN DOCUMENTS INSIDE ANOTHER 78
CONNECTING AND EMBEDDING IMAGES 80
CONFIGURING IMAGE QUALITY AND DISPLAY 82
SELECTING IMAGES 83
ALTERING TEXT AND GRAPHICS WITHIN A LAYOUT 84
PAGE ORIENTATION AND DIMENSIONS 85
MARGINS, COLUMNS, AND GUTTERS 85
UTILIZING GUIDES AND SNAPPING 86
LOCKING OBJECTS AND GUIDES 88
UNITING TEXT AND GRAPHICS ON A PAGE 89
WRAPPING TEXT AROUND OBJECTS 89
ADJUSTING TEXT WRAPS 92
MANAGING PAGES WITH THE PAGES PANEL 93
SELECTION AND RELOCATING PAGES WITHIN YOUR PUBLICATION 94
INSERTING AND DELETING PAGES 94
PAGE NUMBERING 95
APPLYING PARENT SPREADS FOR PAGE LAYOUTS 96
HOW TO CREATE A PARENT PAGE 97
APPLYING, DELETING, AND REMOVING PARENT PAGES 98
ALTERING PAGE SIZES INDIVIDUALLY 99

CHAPTER FIVE 101

CREATING ARTWORK IN INDESIGN 101

GETTING HANDS-ON DRAWING 101
PATHS AND SHAPES 101
POINTS AND SEGMENTS 102

GETTING ACQUAINTED WITH ESSENTIAL TOOLS 103
HOW TO DRAW SHAPE IN INDESIGN 104
DRAWING A SHAPE WITH PRECISE DIMENSIONS 105
EXPLORING THE POLYGON TOOL 106
MODIFYING BASIC SHAPES 108
USING THE TRANSFORM PANEL TO ALTER SHAPE SIZE..108
USING THE FREE TRANSFORM PANEL TO ALTER SHAPE SIZE 108
CRAFTING OWN CUSTOM SHAPES 109
ALTERING THE (STROKE) OUTLINE OF A SHAPE 110
MODIFY THE SHEAR VALUE 113
ROTATING A SHAPE 114
SKETCHING FREEFORM PATHS 114
EXPLORING THE PENCIL TOOL 114
EXPLORING THE PEN TOOL 115
MODIFYING FREEFORM PATHS 116
ADJUSTING FRAME CORNERS 118
EXPLORING FILLS 120
CREATING BASIC FILLS 120
CREATING TRANSPARENT FILLS 123
GRADIENT FILLS 124
REMOVING FILLS 126
EXPLORING LAYERS 127
GENERATING QR CODES 128

CHAPTER SIX 131

EXPLORING COLOR 131

CHOOSING COLOR WITH COLOR CONTROLS 131
GETTING TO KNOW COLOR MODELS 132
EXPLORING COLOR SWATCHES AND LIBRARIES 133
USING THE SWATCHES PANEL 133
UTILIZING SWATCH LIBRARIES 135

CHAPTER SEVEN 137

CLIPPING PATHS, OBJECT MANIPULATION, AND ALIGNMENT 137
GETTING STARTED TRANSFORMATIONS 137

EXAMINING THE TRANSFORM PANEL 137
MAKING USE OF THE FREE TRANSFORM TOOL 139
ROTATING OBJECTS 141
SCALING (OR RESIZING) OBJECTS 141
SHEARING (SKEWING) OBJECTS 142
REFLECTING OBJECTS 144
GETTING TO KNOW CLIPPING PATHS 144
ALIGNING OBJECTS OVER THE PAGE 146
DISTRIBUTING OBJECTS 147

CHAPTER EIGHT 150

EXPORTING YOUR PUBLICATION 150

PREPARING YOUR DOCUMENTS FOR PRINTING WITH PREFLIGHT 150
PREPARING YOUR DOCUMENTS FOR DELIVERY 152
GETTING TO KNOW FILE FORMATS 154
JPEG (JOINT PHOTOGRAPHIC EXPERTS GROUP) AND PNG (PORTABLE NETWORK GRAPHICS) 155
EPS (ENCAPSULATED POSTSCRIPT) 155
XML (EXTENSIBLE MARKUP LANGUAGE) 155
PDF (PORTABLE DOCUMENT FORMAT) 155
TEXT FORMATS 156
EPUB 156
HTML HYPER TEXT MARKUP LANGUAGE 156
IDML INDESIGN MARKUP LANGUAGE 156
EXPORTING PUBLICATIONS 156
EXPORTING PDF DOCUMENTS FOR PRINTING 156
EXPORTING EPS FILES 159
EXPORTING PNG AND JPEG FILES 161
EXPORTING TEXT FILES 162
PRINTING YOUR PUBLICATION 163
GETTING TO KNOW BLEED 164
SELF-PROOFING AND PRINTING AT THE OFFICE OR HOME 164

CHAPTER NINE 167

USING EPUB TO CREATE DIGITAL DOCUMENTS AND PUBLISH ONLINE 167
SELECTING THE APPROPRIATE DIGITAL FORMAT 167

- STRATEGIZING LAYOUTS FOR DIGITAL DISTRIBUTION 168
- ADAPTING PRINT DOCUMENTS FOR DIGITAL SHARING 168
- CRAFTING LIQUID LAYOUT RULES FOR ALTERNATIVE LAYOUTS 170
- CRAFTING ALTERNATE LAYOUTS..................171
- ADD INTERACTIVITY TO DIGITAL DOCUMENTS 174
- EXPORTING DIGITAL BOOKS AS EPUB 175
- PREPARING EPUB (REFLOWABLE) BOOKS 175
- EXPORTING EPUB (REFLOWABLE) BOOKS 176
- EXPORTING EPUB (FIXED-LAYOUT) 178
- PUBLISH DOCUMENT ONLINE 180
- COLLABORATE AND GET FEEDBACK WITH SHARE FOR REVIEW 181

CHAPTER TEN 183

NAVIGATE YOUR WAY FASTER WITH INDESIGN SHORTCUTS 183

- PANEL SHORTCUTS..................183
- OBJECT SHORTCUTS 184
- CHARACTER SHORTCUTS 184
- TYPE SHORTCUTS 185
- TEXT FRAME OR STORY SHORTCUTS 186
- LAYOUT SHORTCUTS 187
- TOOLS SHORTCUTS..................188

CONCLUSION 189

INDEX..................190

INTRODUCTION

STEP INTO A REALM OF DESIGN ATTRACTION WHERE YOUR IMAGINATION IS UNVEILED

Introducing you to Adobe InDesign 2024 Ultimate User Guide! Whether you're a seasoned design pro or a novice just dipping your toes, Adobe InDesign beckons with its vibrant color and boundless creativity, ready to transport you to new realms of inspiration.

This comprehensive guide comprises diverse lessons grounded in real-life, project-based learning, designed to take you from basics to advanced techniques, packed with invaluable tips and tricks to boost your productivity within the program.

Whether it's for print or online ventures, this guide has you covered: it's skillful at revealing your ideas, whether you're crafting a tangible masterpiece or a digital marvel. Dig into the shades of both print and digital design to elevate your craft

From fundamental concepts like navigating InDesign CC to more advanced topics such as layer management and text flow, this guide leaves no stone unturned in equipping users to craft breathtaking visual structures.

Say goodbye to tedious theory. We believe the best way to learn is by diving in and doing. Begin your journey with step-by-step instructions that will guide you through every design concept. This guide is your steadfast companion, from setting up your initial project to adding those final touches that leave people in admiration.

We understand the value of time. That's why this guidebook is filled with tips and tricks to simplify your workflow. Discover hacks, shortcuts, and expert tricks to breeze through your projects effortlessly.

Embark on your journey to Adobe InDesign mastery today and unveil your creative potential with Adobe InDesign 2024 essential user guide.

CHAPTER ONE
EXPLORING INDESIGN 2024 NEW FEATURES

InDesign's October 2023 Version (**19.0**), introduces an array of innovative features designed to elevate your design and layout capabilities.

AUTO STYLING

At the recent Adobe MAX 2023 event, InDesign unveiled a significant feature known as **"Auto Style",** which is supported by Adobe Sensei – a cutting-edge combination of AI and machine learning technologies. This powerful tool empowers users with the capability to craft their personalized style packs or choose from a library of 20 pre-defined style packs. These style packs are essentially collections of paragraph styles that can be readily applied to various text frames. To explore the prowess of the Auto Style function, follow these steps:

1) Open InDesign and navigate to the "**Style Packs**" panel. To locate this panel, go to **Window** > **Styles** > **Style Packs**.
2) Once the **Style Packs** panel is accessible, you can then select the **text frames** that you wish to format.
3) Within the panel, you have the choice of applying a pre-existing preset style pack or the one you methodically created to suit your specific design requirements.

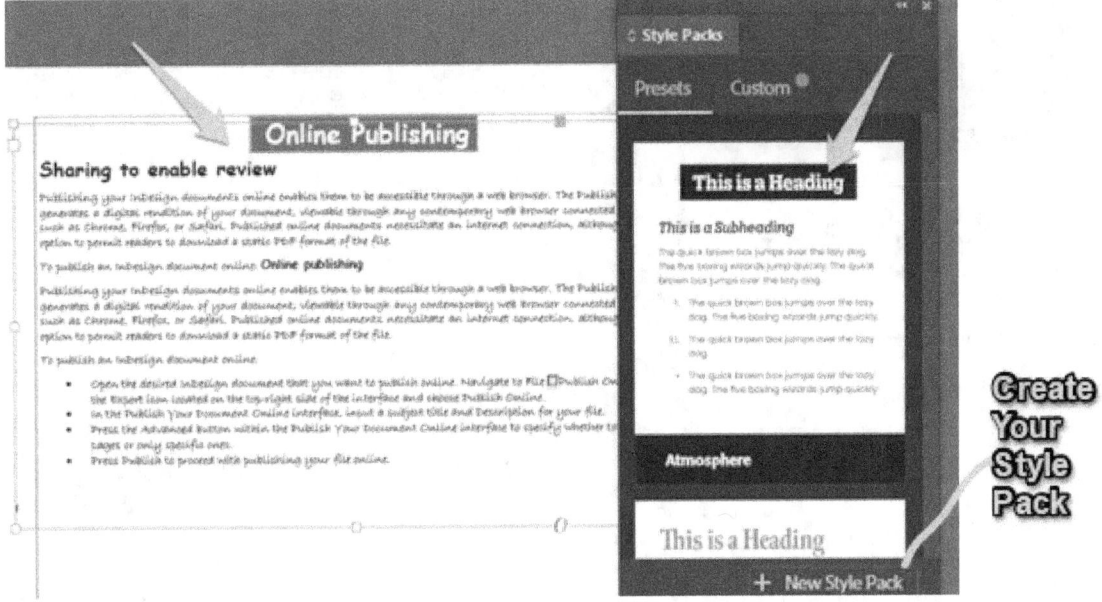

Note : This flexibility allows for a wide range of design customization and simplifies the process of applying consistent styles to text elements within your project.

HIDE SPREADS IN INDESIGN

After you've meticulously styled all the text frames in your InDesign project, you might find it necessary to selectively conceal certain pages for specific purposes. InDesign now facilitates this with a convenient "Hide Spreads" feature. Follow these steps to make the most of this functionality:

1) Locate and access the "**Pages**" panel on the **Window** menu. This panel is essential for managing the visibility of your spreads.
2) Within the "**Pages**" panel, identify the **spread** that you wish to hide from view. Simply click on the spread to select it.
3) Once your target spread is selected, right-click on it. A context menu will appear, and within it, you'll find the "**Hide Spread**" option. Click on "**Hide Spread**" to conceal the selected spread.

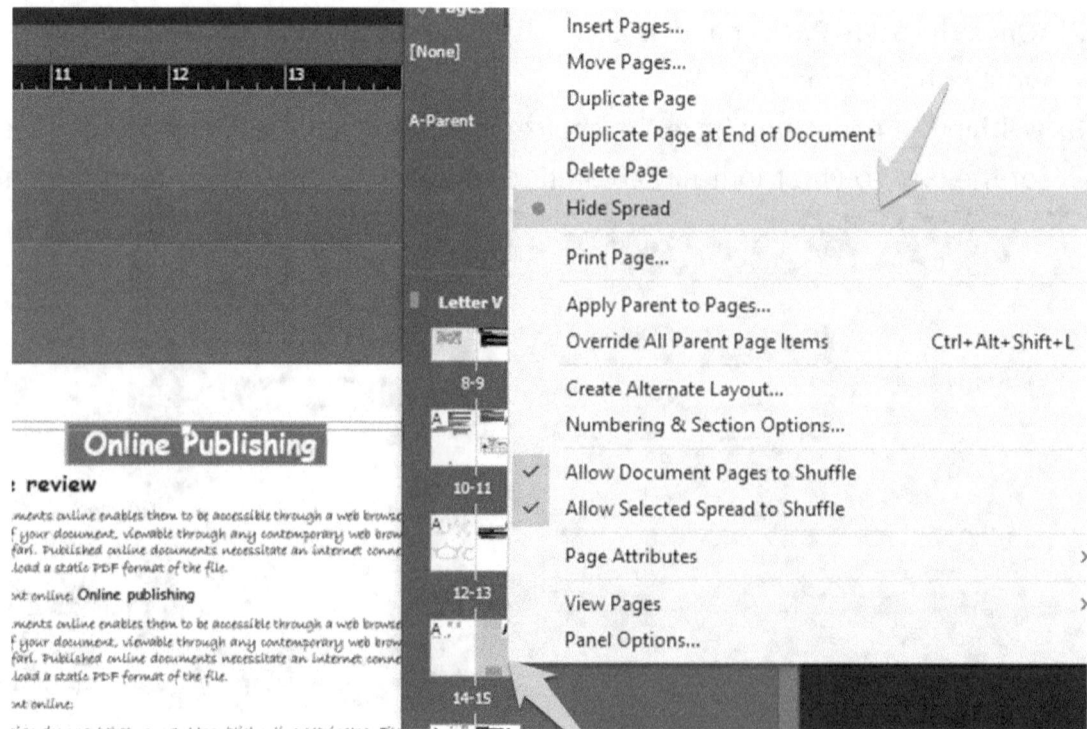

Note : This action is particularly valuable for various scenarios, such as preparing for export or optimizing presentations. Here's why:

When you opt to hide spreads, you gain precise control over which content is visible when you export your document or present it to others. Only the unhidden, or visible, pages will be included or displayed. This feature proves invaluable for tailoring your content presentation, ensuring that your audience views only the material you intend them to see, thereby enhancing the overall user experience.

ORGANIZE YOUR FILES WITH FILENAME SUFFIXES

Adobe has introduced a game-changing feature in InDesign – the "Filename Suffixes." This innovative addition is designed to help you maintain impeccable file organization by enabling the attachment of meaningful suffixes to your filenames. These suffixes can encompass various elements like incremental numbers, page numbers, and page sizes.

The benefits of incorporating suffixes into your file names are substantial. They allow you to quickly identify and categorize your exported images according to their intended purpose. For instance, if you're creating images for social media, you can easily differentiate between sizes meant for various platforms by leveraging these suffixes.

Here's how to make the most of this feature:

1) Open your project in InDesign. Navigate to the "**File**" menu and select "**Export**."
2) Within the **Export** dialog, under the "**Format**" section, choose either "**JPEG**" or "**PNG**" as your desired file format for export and click Save. This prompts the opening of another dialog box.

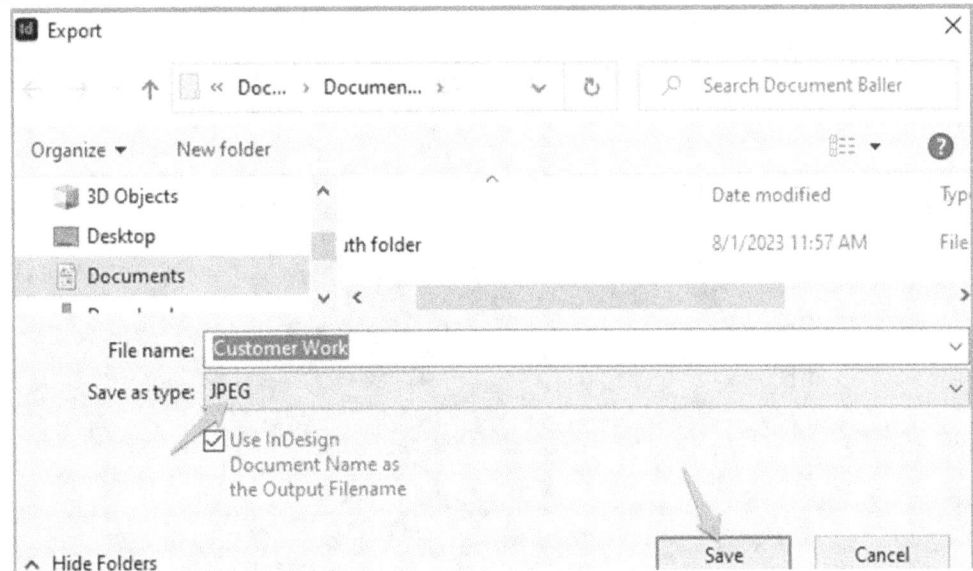

3) In the Export PNG or Export JPEG dialog, find the "**Suffix**" field located under the "**Export**" section. Click on the "**+**" sign within the "**Suffix**" field. This action enables you to start adding your chosen suffixes to the filename.

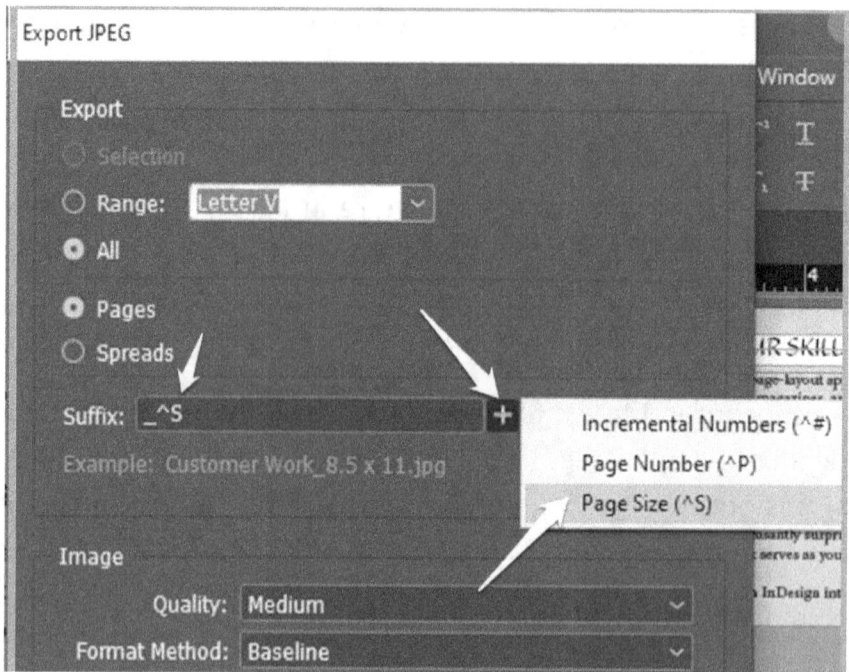

4) Once you've configured the desired suffixes, click "**Export**" to generate the file with the modified filename.

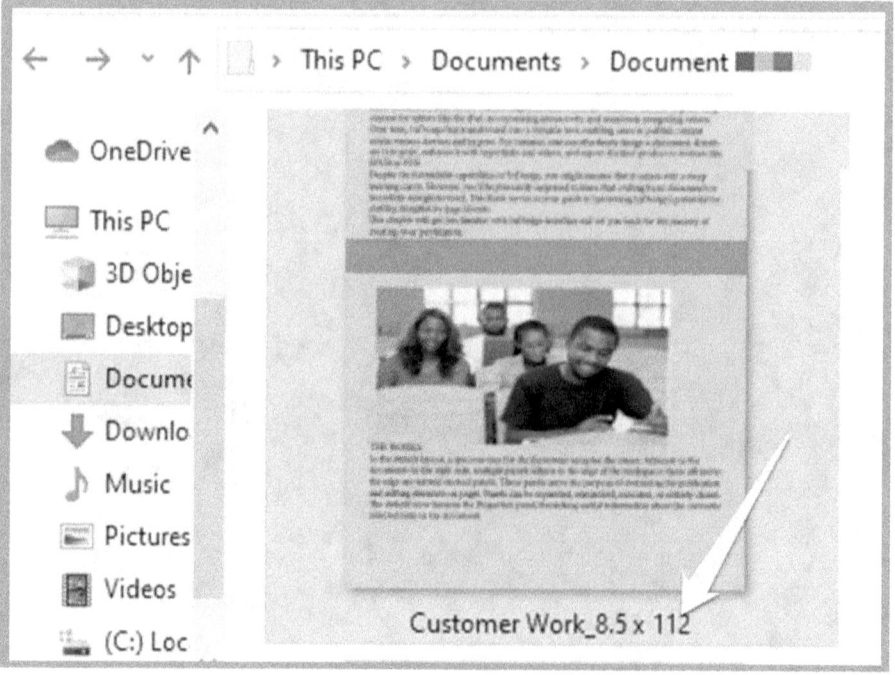

"PUBLISH AND ANALYTICS" FEATURE

"Publish Online" emerges as a powerful feature that empowers designers to effortlessly share their methodically crafted designs and publications with a global audience. This function provides the capability to transform your content into engaging digital versions, complete with comprehensive tracking metrics to gauge its reach and impact. But what truly enhances this feature's potential is the integration of **Google Analytics**, enabling you to gain profound insights into the traffic and engagement surrounding your published documents.

Another notable aspect of this feature is the ability to search text within your published documents. This functionality ensures you can quickly and effectively locate specific information from any device. However, please note that text searching is exclusively available on touch devices.

Desktop and laptop users, on the other hand, enjoy added benefits. They not only have the ability to search for text but can also copy text directly from published documents, making the retrieval of relevant content a seamless process.

Here's how you can access and leverage the "**Publish Online**" feature:

1) Open your project in Adobe InDesign 2024.
2) Navigate to the "**File**" menu and select "**Publish Online.**

DEVELOPING GLYPH RENDERING WITH HARFBUZZ

Harfbuzz represents a substantial leap forward in the software's shaping engine. By adopting Harfbuzz as the default shaping engine within the World Ready Composer, InDesign delivers an exceptional experience marked by enhanced glyph shaping and precise rendering, particularly for Indic and MENA (Middle East and North African) languages.

Here's how the inclusion of Harfbuzz elevates InDesign's capabilities:

Harfbuzz integration equips InDesign with the capacity to impeccably manage intricate scripts, such as Arabic, Hebrew, Hindi, and many others. This signifies a remarkable advancement for designers working with these languages, promising an elevated level of precision in how their glyphs appear both on screen and in print.

The implications of this breakthrough are profound. It means that designers and typographers can now craft documents, publications, and designs in Indic and MENA languages with an unprecedented degree of accuracy and aesthetic quality.

EMPOWER YOUR WORKFLOW WITH UXP PLUGINS

A standout moment at Adobe MAX was the grand revelation of UXP plugins, an innovation that has the potential to revolutionize the design and publishing realm. In the world of creatives, plugins are similar to indispensable tools, boosting productivity and streamlining workflows. The introduction of the Unified Extensibility Platform (UXP) signifies a monumental leap, providing developers with the means to leverage the full gamut of modern JavaScript capabilities, enabling them to construct powerful controls not only for Adobe InDesign but also for a spectrum of Creative Cloud desktop applications.

Here's why UXP plugins are set to redefine your Adobe InDesign experience:

UXP plugins grant you the power to tailor your InDesign environment according to your unique needs and preferences. This opens the door to automating tasks, introducing novel tools, and crafting personalized user interfaces that align precisely with your workflow requirements.

The integration of UXP empowers you to harness your expertise in JavaScript, HTML, and CSS, offering you the creative freedom to fashion customized solutions.

As a result; UXP plugins don't just enhance your productivity; they redefine it. By offering the ability to weave intricate and tailored functionalities into your InDesign experience, these plugins are a game-changer for designers, publishers, and content creators. They pave the way for more efficient and bespoke workflows, where your creative and technical skills harmoniously converge to produce remarkable outcomes.

PANEL SHORTCUTS

Here's a handy guide to essential shortcut keys enabling rapid adjustments to effects, strokes, swatches, links, and layers without the need to constantly reach for the mouse. With these shortcuts at your fingertips, achieving desired effects becomes a breeze, saving you valuable time otherwise spent searching through menus and options.

Note : Complete shortcut keys are in chapter (10) of this book.

USES	WINDOWS	MACOS
Swatches	F5	F5
Pages	F12	F12
Stroke	F10	F10
Preflight	Ctrl + Alt + Shift + F	Command + Option + Shift + F
Align	Shift + F7	Command + Shift + F7
Links	Ctrl + Alt + Shift + D	Command + Shift + D
Layers	F7	F7
Info	F8	F8
Control	Ctrl + Alt + 6	Command + Options + 6

CHAPTER TWO

FAMILIARIZING WITH INDESIGN CC 2024

InDesign stands out as an advanced page-layout application, offering the capability to craft refined documents such as newsletters, magazines, and books. Its versatility extends to generating content for tablets like the iPad, incorporating interactivity, and seamlessly integrating videos. Over time, InDesign has transformed into a versatile tool, enabling users to publish content across various devices and in print. For instance, one can effortlessly design a document, distribute it in print, enhance it with hyperlinks and videos, and export the final product to formats like EPUB or PDF.

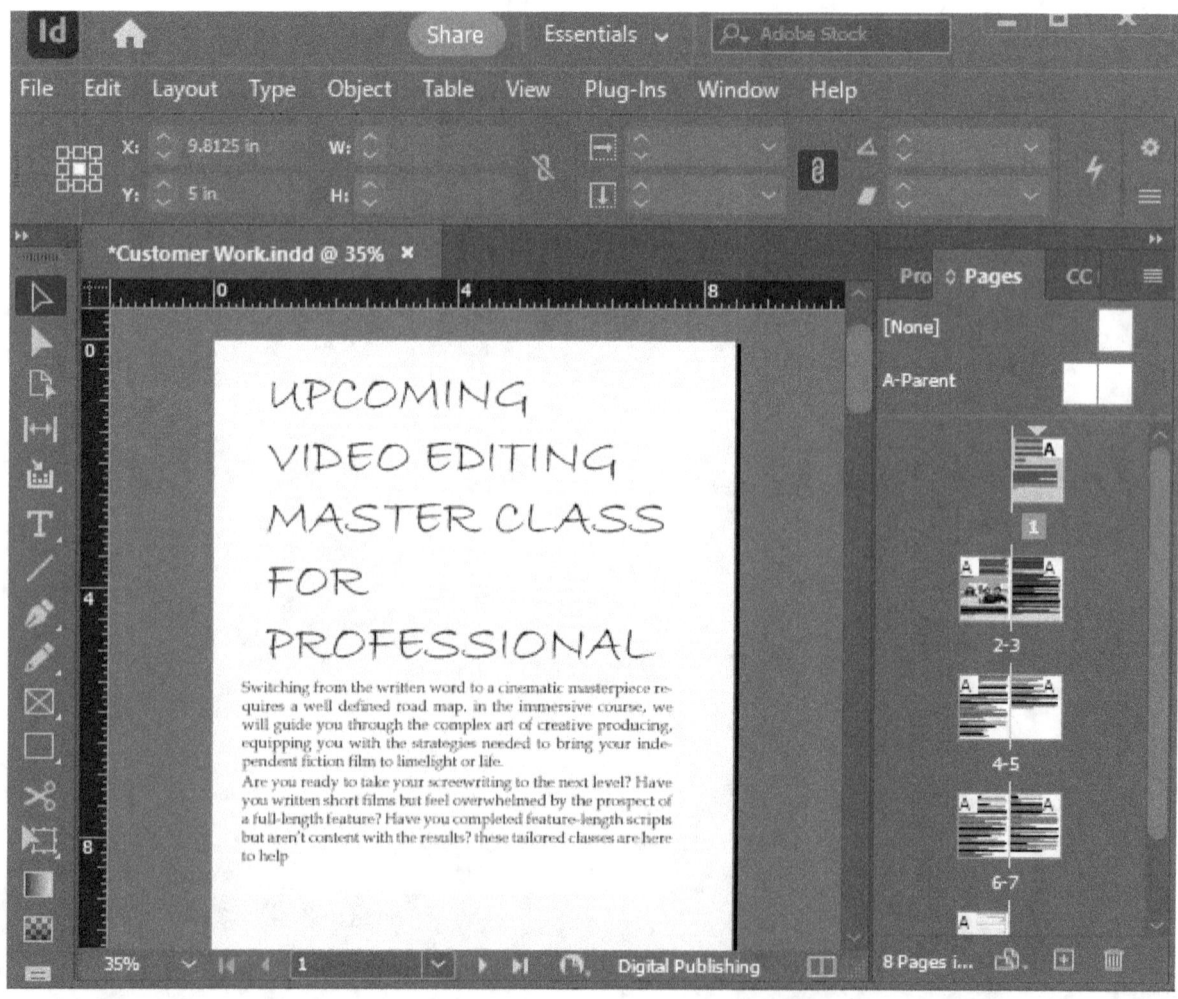

Despite the formidable capabilities of InDesign, you might assume that it comes with a steep learning curve. However, you'll be pleasantly surprised to learn that crafting basic documents is incredibly straightforward. This Book serves as your guide to harnessing InDesign's potential for crafting imaginative page layouts.

This chapter will get you familiar with the InDesign interface and set you on track for the journey of creating your publication.

STARTING INDESIGN CC

InDesign serves the purpose of crafting page layouts enriched with graphics, typography (including **fills** and **strokes**), and images. This application has the potential to incorporate video or interactive buttons to enhance its multimedia capabilities. You can also import images from Photoshop and logos from Adobe Illustrator to Adobe InDesign, this collaboration makes work more effective.

STARTING A NEW PUBLICATION

Upon launching InDesign, the process of creating a new document can be easily undertaken. Simply adhere to the following steps to start a new publication. It's important to note that various methods exist for creating a new document, and their appearance may differ based on individual preferences. Throughout this book, references are made to the default preferences for clarity.

1) To ensure a uniform experience, click the "**Home**" button located in the top-left corner of the InDesign interface.

2) Proceed by selecting the **New File** button on the left side.

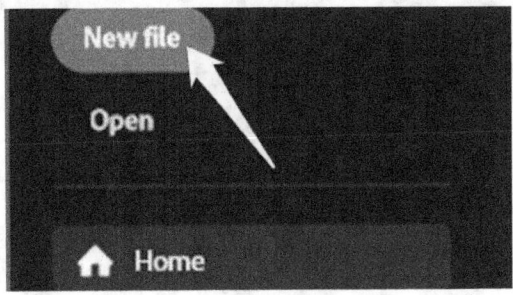

This action causes the opening of the New Document dialog box, as represented below.

3) From the **Header Intent** option, indicate whether you are designing a print, web, or mobile document. For this lesson, the selection is set to "**Print**".
4) Adjust the **Units** to your desired measurement unit. In this case, "**Inches**" have been chosen, and it's worth noting that this configuration can be modified while creating the document.

5) Enter "**Customer Work**" as the document name inside the Name field.
6) In this particular case, verify that the "**Facing Pages**" checkbox is marked to organize the pages as spreads having both left and right pages.

When you choose this option, your document's pages are grouped in pairs, forming spreads where adjacent or facing pages are displayed together in a layout. This is ideal for projects designed to resemble a book or magazine layout. Conversely, deselecting this option arranges pages individually, which is better suited for single-page flyers or documents with only a front and back side.

7) Click on **Blank Document** Preset and specify the number of **pages** (you can modify the number of pages at any time).

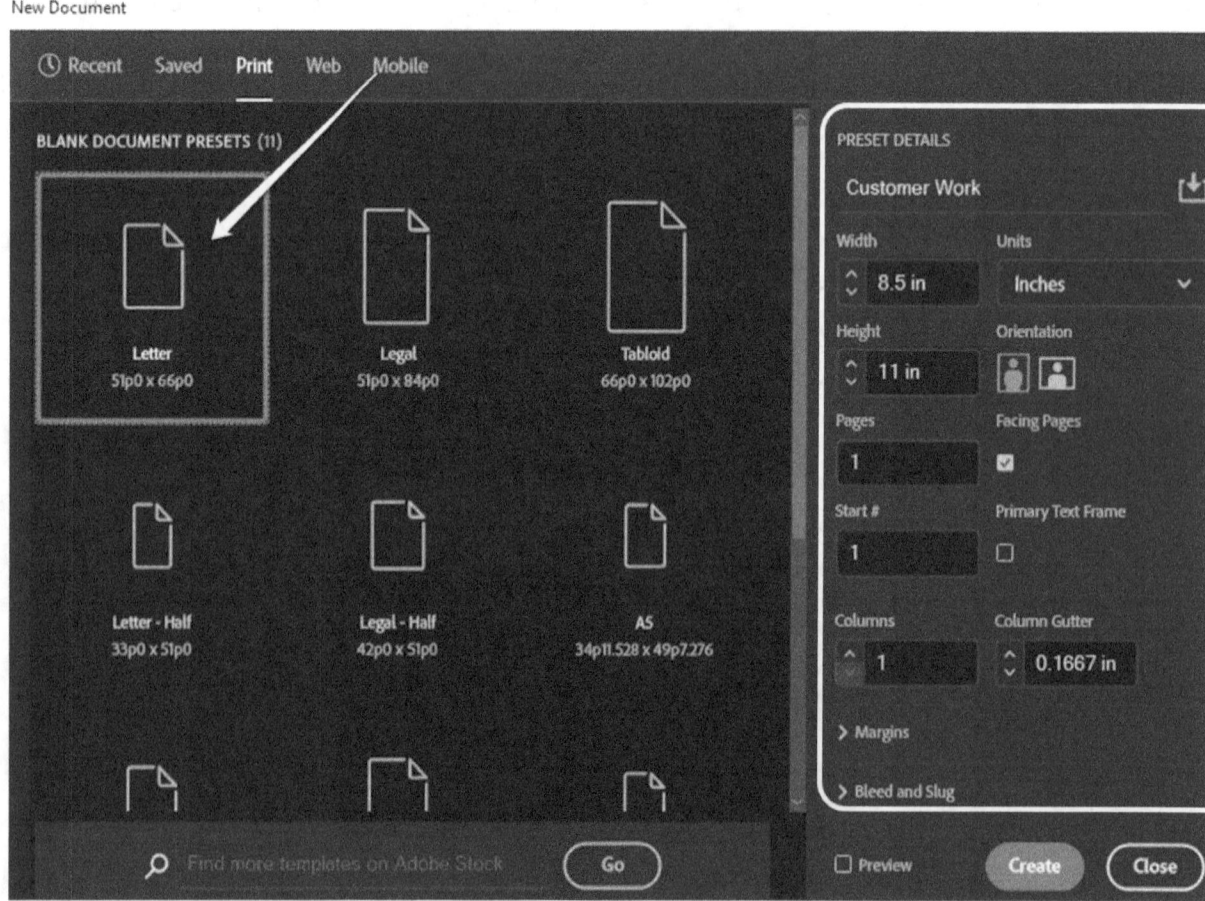

Ensure that the Blank Document Preset matches the paper size for printing or the intended display size. Alternatively, you can customize your document size by inputting values into the Width and Height fields. The Orientation switches between Portrait (tall) and Landscape (wide) based on the dimensions you specify in the Width and Height fields. Your choice of Intent determines the available options in the Blank Document

Presets list. Option for Web allows selection from various screen resolutions, while Mobile offers popular tablet sizes like iPad, Android, or Nook/Kindle Fire. Measurement units can be inputted directly into the size text boxes with the abbreviation accepted (e.g., 8.5 in for 8.5 inches or 11 cm for 11 centimeters). In web or mobile document creation, measurements are converted to pixels.

8) Select a **value** for the number of **columns** on the page.

This step establishes guides for columns that won't appear in the final print or display of your project, aiding in page organization during creation. You can specify the space between columns by entering a value in the Gutter field. More information is coming about columns in one of the subsequent chapters. You can adjust these settings as necessary while working on your document.

9) Specify the **Values** for the page margins.

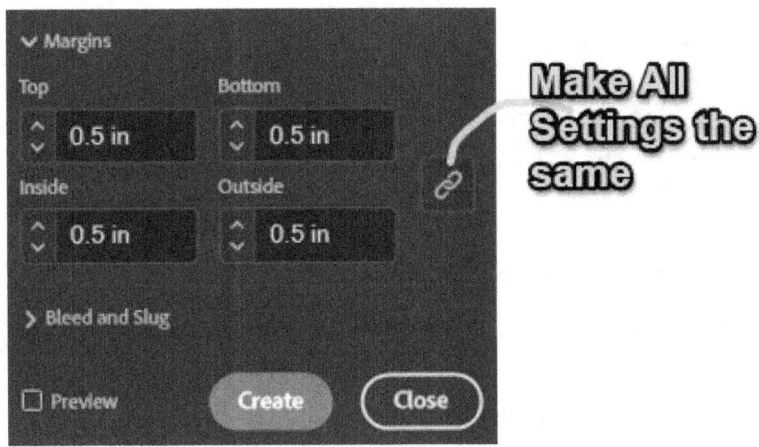

Note : Take note of the "**Make All Settings the Same**" button, represented by a **chain icon**, positioned to the right of the **four** text fields where you input margin values. Click this button to apply the same margin value to all sides, or leave it unclicked to set different values (displaying a broken chain icon).

If you observe options for "**Top,**" "**Bottom,**" "**Inside,**" and "**Outside,**" you're configuring margins for a layout with facing pages, as previously specified. Alternatively, if you see "Top," "Bottom," "Left," and "Right," you're designing a layout without facing pages. The "inside" margins pertain to the middle of the spread, while the "outside" margins refer to the outer left and right edges of a publication like a book or magazine. You can adjust the "Inside" setting to accommodate the binding of a book, which might require more extensive margins than the outside edges.

If you frequently use the same settings, consider saving them as a preset. Configure your settings as desired, then click the "**Save Document Preset**" button located to the right of the document title, under the "Preset Details" header, before clicking "**Create**." Provide a name for the preset, and click "**Save Preset**". Once saved, you can access your preset from the "**Saved**" section in the header menu (whenever you're creating a new document.

10) Once you have completed the configuration, click on the "**Create**" button.

Once you've clicked "**Create**" in the **New Document** dialog box, the new document will be generated with the settings you've just specified.

Note : we shall discuss columns, margins, and page size in detail in **chapter 4** of this user guide.

ACCESSING AN EXISTING WORK

If you have InDesign files stored on your hard drive that you either created or saved from a different source. Follow these steps to open existing InDesign documents:

1) Select **File** > **Open** to display the Open a File dialog box.
2) Navigate through your hard drive and choose the file you want to open.

If you don't have any InDesign files, close the file "**Customer Work**" file that we created in the previous section and reopen it. Click on the document's title to select it. To choose multiple documents, hold down the Command (macOS) or Ctrl (Windows) while clicking on the filenames.

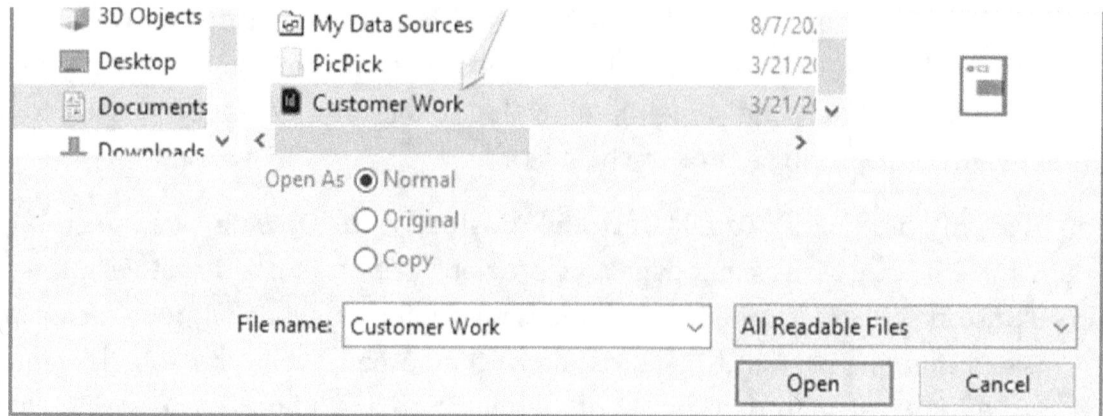

3) Tap the **Open** button to access the file. This opens the file on the workspace.

NAVIGATING THE INTERFACE

InDesign features a standardized layout. Using dock able panels and a single-row Tools panel, you can maximize the available space in your workspace.

Within the InDesign user interface, you'll encounter a plethora of tools and panels, though most users only interact with a handful. You'll find yourself frequently using certain panels, so it's essential to keep them readily accessible. In the default user workspace, many of these panels are already conveniently docked to the right side.

The Windows interface closely resembles the Macintosh edition of InDesign. If your workspace differs, you can restore the default settings by navigating to **Window** > **Workspace** > **Essentials**. Alternatively, if Essentials is already active, select **Reset Essentials** below the **Workspace** menu.

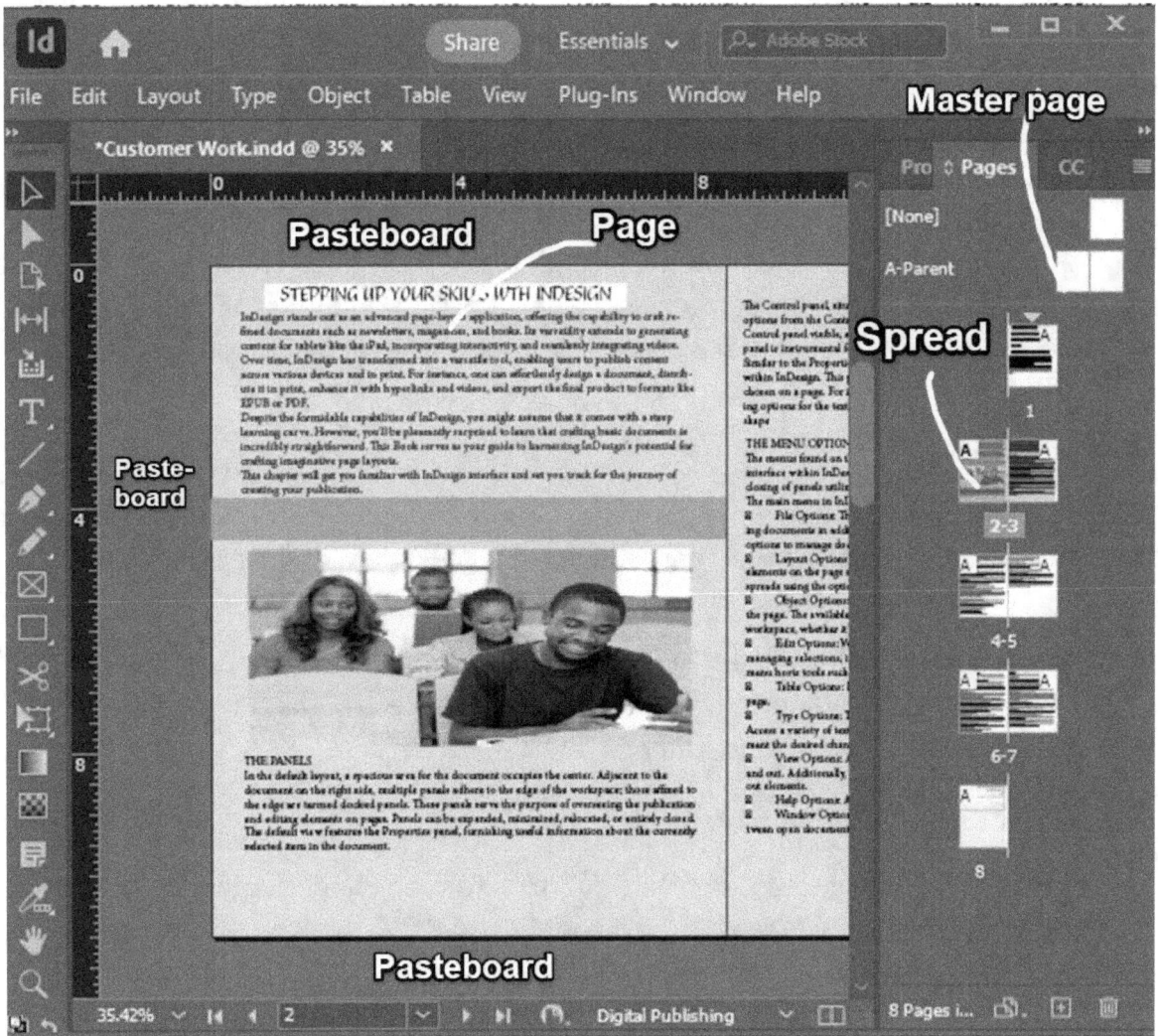

Below are the components of the InDesign workspace:

- ❖ **Page:** The central section of the InDesign workspace is the page, representing the region that will be printed or exported once you complete the layout.
- ❖ **Parent pages:** In InDesign, you can generate the appearance of specific text elements and graphics across an entire document or selected sections using a Parent page. Similar to a document template, it allows for the reuse of elements throughout multiple pages. For instance, if there's a recurring element you want on every page, like page numbering, you can design it on the Parent page for consistent application.

Note :If you need to modify an element on the Parent page, you have the flexibility to do so at any moment, with the changes instantly reflected across all pages where the Parent page is applied. Accessing Parent pages is straightforward through the **Pages** panel, with further insights provided in Chapter 4 of this user guide.

- ❖ **Pasteboard:** The pasteboard refers to the perimeter of a page, serving as a designated area for temporarily storing objects until they are ready to be incorporated into your layout. It's important to note that pasteboards are unique to each page or spread and are not shared across pages. Consequently, any elements placed on the pasteboard for specific pages, such as 2 and 3, cannot be accessed when working on different pages like 7 and 8. In essence, each page or spread maintains its own distinct pasteboard.
- ❖ **Spread:** A spread denotes a grouping of two or more pages intended to be printed adjacent to each other. Spreads are commonly observed in magazines and books, becoming apparent when you unfold or open them, similar to the layout of the book in your hands. In the InDesign document window, if your document consists of only a single page—whether front and back or with content on just one side—a spread will not be visible.

InDesign offers the functionality to display either a single page or, for a double-sided page, both pages simultaneously (provided you reduce the magnification), enhancing the precision of your layout adjustments.

EXPLORING THE TOOLS PANEL

The toolbar is the designated area housing tool for selecting, editing, or manipulating elements within your document. It also contains tools for making alterations to pages. You can easily choose a tool by using the cursor to click on it. the default Tools panel arrangement is shown below.

Note: If a single row of the tools panel doesn't suit your preferences, you have the option to revert to the double row of the tools panel layout (you can click again to switch back to a single row of tools panel. You can achieve this by pressing the **"two arrows"** within the gray bar positioned at the top of the **Tools** panel. Should you wish to reposition the tools, click on the bar located at the top of the tools, beneath the double arrows, and then drag the tools panel to a new place.

The available tools in the Tools panel empower you to perform the following actions:

- Create captivating new content on a page using frame, drawing, and text tools.
- Modify existing objects, such as lines, text, and lines, using the Selection tool to select and make changes to them.
- It enables you to choose existing content on a page for relocation or editing purposes.

- Explore different varieties of views on the page by panning (moving) and zooming (magnifying) in or out.

THE MENU OPTIONS

The menus found on the primary menu bar serve as gateways to key commands, controlling the user interface within InDesign. The menu provides access to essential functions and allows the opening and closing of panels used for configuring, adjusting, and editing settings for the publication.

The main menu in InDesign offers the following choices:

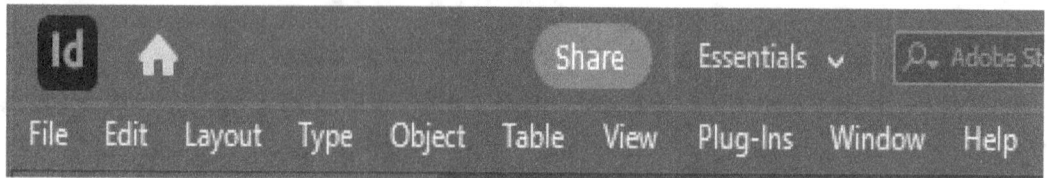

- ❖ **File:** This menu contains fundamental commands for creating, opening, and saving documents in addition to the Place command for importing new content. It provides a range of options to manage document settings, export documents, and initiate printing.
- ❖ **Layout:** Utilize this menu to generate guides, facilitating the precise placement of elements on the page and ensuring proper alignment. Navigate through the document's pages and spreads using the options available in this menu.
- ❖ **Object**: This menu enables you to alter the appearance and positioning of objects on the page. The available options within this menu depend on the type of element you've selected in the workspace, whether it's a text frame or an image.
- ❖ **Edit**: Within this menu, you can access a multitude of commands for editing and managing selections, including functions like copying and keyboard shortcuts. Additionally, the menu hosts tools such as the spell checker and dictionary.
- ❖ **Table:** utilize this menu to create, configure, modify, and manage tables on the page.
- ❖ **Type**: This menu allows you to choose fonts and manage characters within the layout. Access a variety of text-related settings on this menu, this opens the associated panel to implement the desired changes.
- ❖ **View**: Adjust the page view using this menu, which includes options for zooming in and out. Additionally, you can work with guides, rulers, or grids from this menu to assist in placing elements on the page.
- ❖ **Help**: Access the Help documents for InDesign from this menu.
- ❖ **Window**: Utilize this menu to toggle the opening and closing of panels or switch between open documents.

EXPLORING THE PANELS

The document occupies a spacious area in the center of the default layout. Adjacent to the document on the right side, multiple panels stick to the edge of the workspace; those affixed to the edge are termed docked panels. These panels help in managing the publication and editing elements on pages. Panels can be expanded, minimized, relocated, or entirely closed. The default view includes the Properties panel, furnishing useful information about the currently selected item in the document.

If you wish to expand all your panels, simply press the left-facing double arrows located in the gray bar above the panels. To collapse all panels again, press the right-facing double arrows positioned on the gray bar above the expanded panels.

UTILIZING THE CONTROL PANEL

The Control panel situated at the top of the document window, remains hidden by default because numerous options from the Control panel are integrated into the Properties panel on the right. To make the Control panel visible, simply choose the **Window menu** and select **Control**. Similar to the **Properties** panel, the Control panel helps edit the currently selected elements in InDesign.

This panel is context-sensitive, adapting its options based on the specific element chosen on a page. For instance, when text is selected, the Control panel presents editing options for the text. Alternatively, if a shape is chosen, the panel gives options for altering the shape.

USING CONTEXT MENUS

This is also known as contextual menus, which appear upon right-clicking (Windows) or Control-clicking (macOS) with the mouse. These menus dynamically adjust based on the element selected and the active tool on the tools panel. When no elements are selected, the contextual menu displays options for the entire InDesign document, offering options like Zoom, Paste, Rulers, and Guides. On the other hand, if an element is picked, the menu provides choices for transforming, modifying, and editing the specific object.

Ensure that you pick an element on the page before initiating a Control-click (Mac) or right-click (Windows) to access the contextual menu. Failing to pick an object first will result in the displayed menu being for the entire document rather than specific to an object.

THE PAGES PANEL

The Pages panel facilitates the organization, addition, and deletion of pages within your document. For electronic document creation, it serves the additional purpose of generating alternative layouts suitable for both vertical and horizontal displays on tablets. Additionally, you can utilize the Pages panel for seamless navigation among different pages in your document. If the Pages panel is not visible, click the **Window** menu and select **Pages** to make it visible.

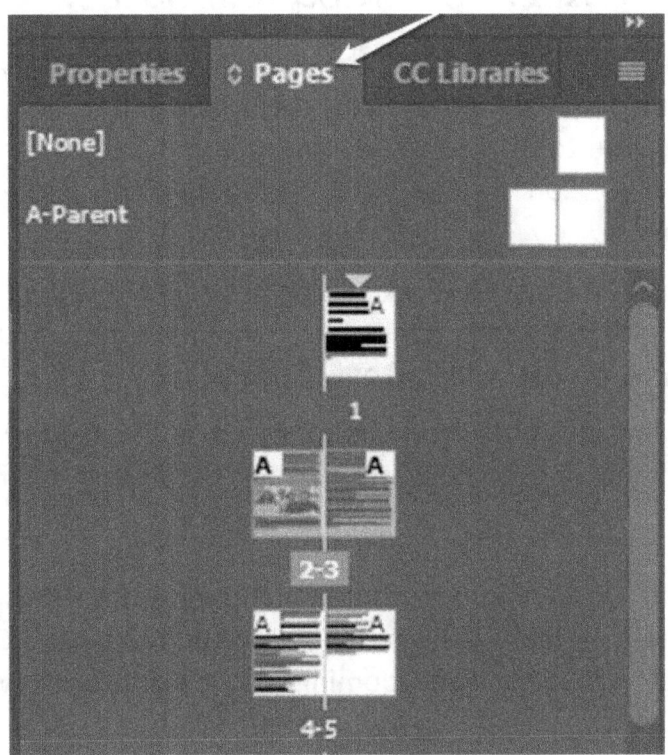

Note: To manage pages in your document, go to the Layout menu and select **Pages**, where you can add or delete pages effortlessly. For a quick page addition, use **Command + Shift + P** (macOS) or **Ctrl + Shift + P** (Windows).

If you need to tidy up your workspace? Simply hit the **Tab** key to hide all open panels, including the **Control** panel. Press the **Tab** again to bring them back into view. InDesign CC provides you the option to keep tools and panels hidden until you need them.

Want to navigate through your document seamlessly? Use the left and right arrow buttons next to the page number in the lower-left corner of the document window.

Alternatively, you can jump to a specific page by entering its number in the **page** field and pressing **Return/Enter** or selecting it from the drop-down menu in the bottom-left side of the **Document** window.

CONFIGURING THE WORKSPACE

Settings of the workspace play a crucial role in expediting the creation of your desired layout. Settings for the overall document control elements like grids or guides, aid in the alignment of elements on the page. Notably, guides and grids do not appear in the printed or published version of your document.

TOGGLE THE VISIBILITY OF GRIDS AND GUIDES

Grids and guides are lines displayed on the screen to assist in layout design but are set not to appear in print by default. The document grid extends to the whole document page area, enabling you to divide the document into different sections for your design needs. Aligning objects on a page with the document grid ensures precision in positioning and spacing.

Another form of grid is the baseline grid, which horizontally passes through the page. utilize the baseline grid to ensure alignment of text in different columns, thereby enhancing the cleanliness of the layout of your page.

The document grid ensures the alignment of objects on the page, while the baseline grid is employed for aligning the bottom of text across several columns.

Follow these steps to display or conceal the document grid/ baseline grid:

- Navigate to **View** > **Grids & Guides** > **Show (or Hide) Document Grid.**
- Go to **View** > **Grids & Guides** > **Show (or Hide) Baseline Grid**. If the baseline grid is not visible, consider zooming in as it may be below the view threshold of **75%.**

Guides are versatile markers that can be positioned anywhere on the page or pasteboard, serving to precisely place objects within a layout. Unlike grids, guides are typically created individually, allowing for precise alignment of specific objects, such as the tops of multiple images displayed through a page. Similar to a grid, objects can also snap to guides.

Observe these steps to create, and show (or hide) guides:

1) Ensure rulers are visible, otherwise, go to **View** > **Show Rulers** or use **Command + R** (macOS) or **Ctrl + R** (Windows) to hide or show rulers.

Rulers will be displayed horizontally and vertically in the workspace. If rulers are already visible, the option to hide them can be found in **View** > **Hide Rulers** on the **View** menu. Avoid hiding the rulers.

2) Position the cursor over a **horizontal** or **vertical** ruler. Ensure that the cursor is placed directly on a ruler.
3) Click the ruler and drag the mouse along the page. A ruler guide will appear on the page as a line.
4) Release the mouse at the exact point where you want the place guide.

Congratulations! You have successfully created a ruler guide.

5) To conceal the guide without deleting it, select **View** > **Grids & Guides** > **Hide Guides**.

This action hides the guide you just created, with the option to easily make it reappear again.

6) To reveal the guide, select **View** > **Grids & Guides** > **Show Guides**.

To modify the color of the ruler guide you generated, place the mouse over it, click once to select it, and then right-click (Windows) or Control-click (Mac). Lastly, choose a new **color** from the **Ruler Guides** option in the **contextual** menu.

Caution: When adjusting the color of guides, make sure no other guides are currently selected. Otherwise, the color change will be applied to all selected guides.

ENABLING THE SNAP FEATURE TO A GUIDE OR GRID

Objects on the page can be set to snap to a guide or grid, providing precise alignment to a guide or grid without the need to watch the alignment of multiple objects to one another. To ensure this setting is activated, go to **View** > **Grids & Guides** > **Snap to Guides** or **View** > **Grids & Guides** > **Snap to Document Grid**. When these options are already enabled, clicking them will deactivate the snapping feature.

EXPLORING SMART GUIDE

The smart guide gives you an added advantage for aligning elements within the InDesign page. You can explore this feature by generating two objects within an InDesign document. just draw or create any two shapes or any other objects for this demonstration.

Using the Selection tool, click and gently drag one object in a circular motion down to the other. Guides will become visible and then disappear, signaling the alignment of the objects at the top, center, or bottom of the remaining object.

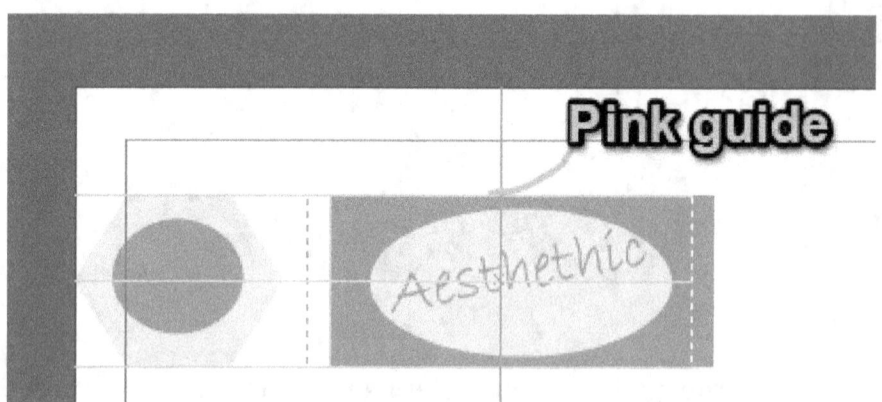

By default, when the object is aligned at the center of the page, pink guides pop up, as shown above.

To view a print preview of your document, simply click the Preview Mode button located at the lower part of the Tools panel. To access Preview Mode, press and hold the Normal button. Upon clicking this button, all object bounding boxes, grid, and the guide will vanish from view.

PERSONALIZING AND ADJUSTING THE MENUS

InDesign includes an extensive array of menus, each offering numerous choices. You may find that you only use a subset of these options. If you realize you're navigating through a surplus of menu items to locate specific functions, InDesign allows you to personalize your experience by hiding menu items that are not frequently used.

Follow these instructions to personalize InDesign menus:

1) Go to **Edit** > **Menus**. This opens the **Menu Customization** pane.

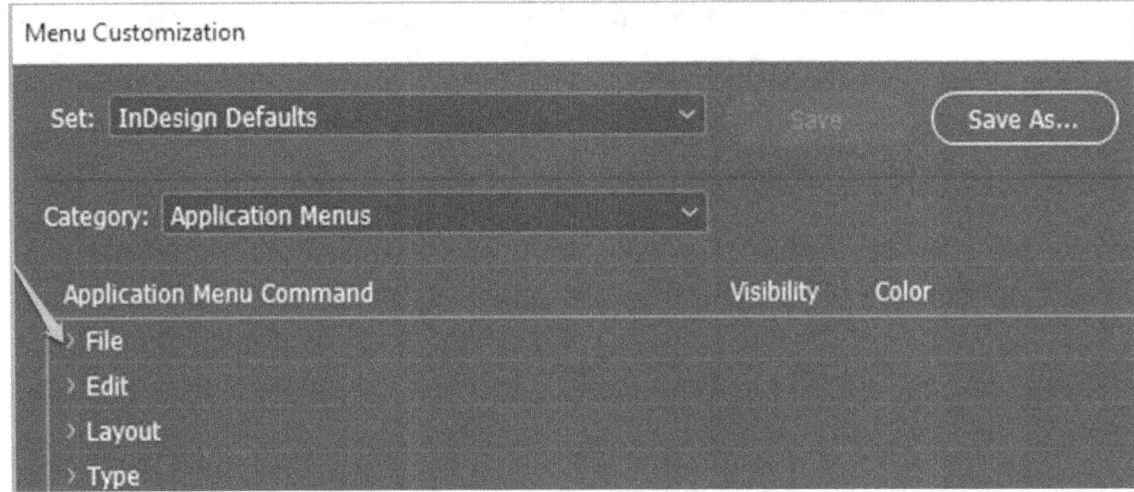

2) Locate the **Application Menu Command** column, and click the **disclosure triangle** next to the menu(s) you intend to customize. For instance, if you seldom use the **Import PDF Comments** feature under the **File** menu, click the **disclosure** triangle to the left of the **File** menu to reveal this option.
3) Tap on the **eye** icon beside the menu item you wish to hide (**Import PDF Comments**) in this case.

Alternatively, if you want to accentuate a menu item, click the color column to the right of the eye icon to assign a color to the menu choice.

4) Hit the **Save As** button located at the window's top to save the menu customization set. Input a name for your personalized menu set, click **OK** to confirm, and then click **OK** once more to close the **Menu** Customization pane. Your customized menus are now saved.

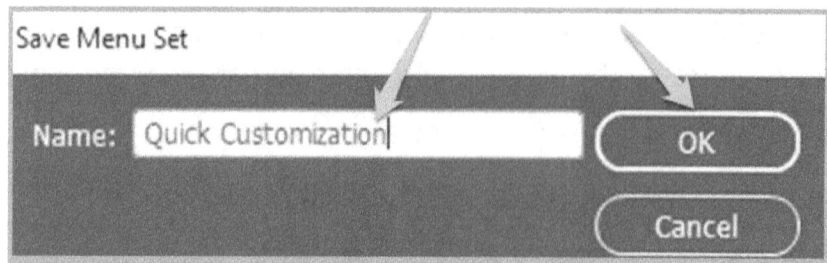

5) To revert to the original default menus or make additional customizations, simply choose **Edit** > **Menus** whenever you are working in InDesign.

PERSONALIZING INDESIGN INTERFACE APPEARANCE

InDesign provides the flexibility to fine-tune the overall appearance of the workspace by customizing the color theme. You have the option to precisely control the darkness or lightness of panels and the pasteboard, or choose from various predefined settings.

To personalize the appearance of the InDesign interface, proceed with the following steps:

1) Go to **InDesign** > **Preferences** > **Interface** (macOS) or **Edit** > **Preferences** > **Interface** (Windows). The Preferences window appears along with the Interface category. The Appearance field at the top allows you to adjust settings that impact the user interface appearance.
2) In the appearance field, modify the color theme for the user interface and pasteboard.

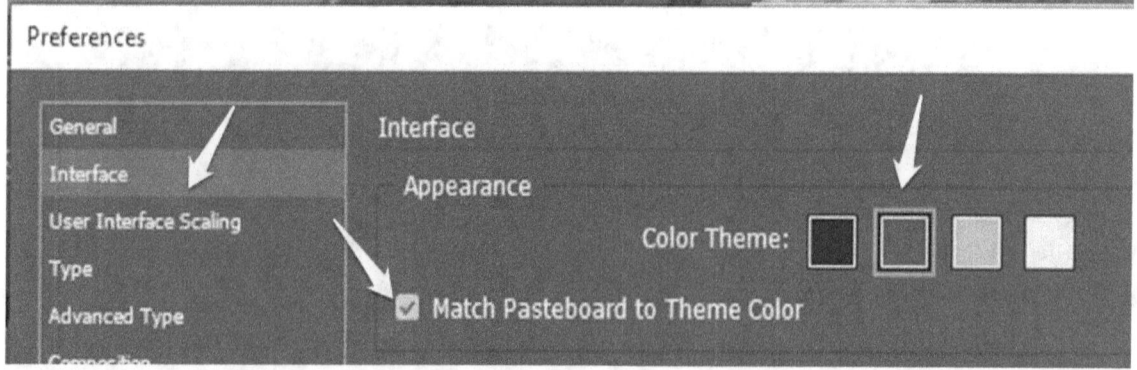

The default setting is Medium Dark, and you can preview each setting as you switch between them. Alternatively, you can input a custom percentage setting for precise brightness adjustments.

3) check or uncheck "**Match Pasteboard to Theme Color**".

By default, this option is selected, resulting in a darker shade for the pasteboard (the area around your document). uncheck this option if you prefer a white pasteboard.

4) Hit on **OK** to confirm your changes. The appearance of the workspace will be updated according to your customization.

SAVING A CUSTOMIZED WORKSPACE

InDesign has several panels within its user interface, and if you discover that you frequently use specific panels over others, you can instruct InDesign to remember the arrangement of these panels. This includes noting the ones that will be visible and the ones that will be hidden. InDesign refers to this configuration as a workspace. When you intend to have a particular set of panels open simultaneously, you can easily revert to the workspace you saved previously.

Follow these instructions to save a customized workspace in InDesign:

1) Set up the **InDesign** workspace with the desired panel configuration, ensuring that any panels you wish to access together are opened.

The currently open panels will be saved as part of the customized workspace.

2) Go to **Window** > **Workspace** > **New Workspace**. This action opens the **New Workspace** dialog box.
3) You can decide whether to save the panel locations or any customized menus alongside. Enter a new name for the workspace in the **Name** text field and Hit **Ok**.

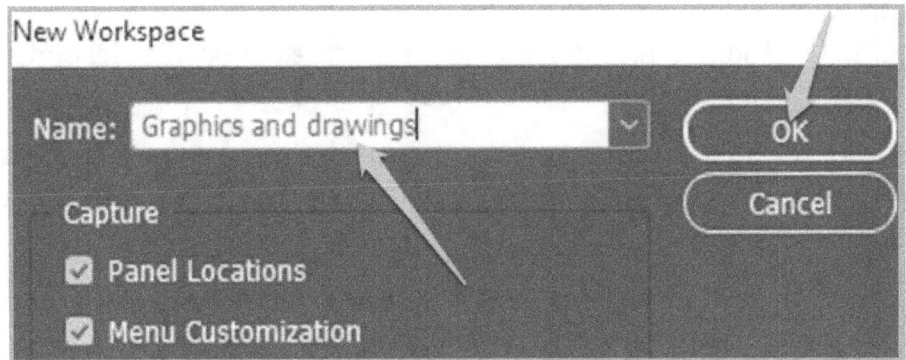

Provide a name that represents the type of work associated with that workspace, such as text editing or graphics and drawing layout.

The custom workspace is now saved, and the name you entered will be displayed on the Workspaces menu for easy access.

GETTING STARTED WITH DOCUMENTS

Once you've become familiar with the InDesign workspace, it's time to start working on a new document. As you progress with your document, it's essential to learn how to import content from other programs and save your work/files on your hard drive. InDesign facilitates the integration of content from various sources, including Creative Cloud applications like Photoshop and Illustrator, as well as non-Creative Cloud applications like Microsoft Word and Excel.

InDesign serves as the platform for organizing, modifying, and seamlessly combining graphics and text into your layouts. In the following sections, we will guide you through the steps required to import content and save new files.

The processes for opening new and existing documents were already covered in this chapter.

IMPORTING CONTENTS TO YOUR DOCUMENT

In an InDesign document, you have the flexibility to incorporate various types of content by importing a wide range of supported file types. This includes importing text, formatted tables, and graphics, allowing you to craft an impactful layout. This versatility facilitates seamless integration with a variety of programs. To import an image file into InDesign, apply these steps (utilizing a bitmap graphic file as an example in this instance).

1) Go to **File** > **New** > **Document**. The New Document dialog box will be displayed.
2) Examine the settings, make adjustments based on the desired size and type of the document, and then hit **Create**.

Do not hesitate to modify the settings to change the **number of pages, page size**, and **intent** before clicking the **Create** button as we did earlier in this chapter. Subsequently, a new document will open.

3) Go to **File** > **Place**. The Place dialog box will be displayed, enabling you to navigate through your hard drive for supported files. If you check the "**Show Import Options**" check box, another dialog box will appear before the file is imported. Keep this option deselected for now.

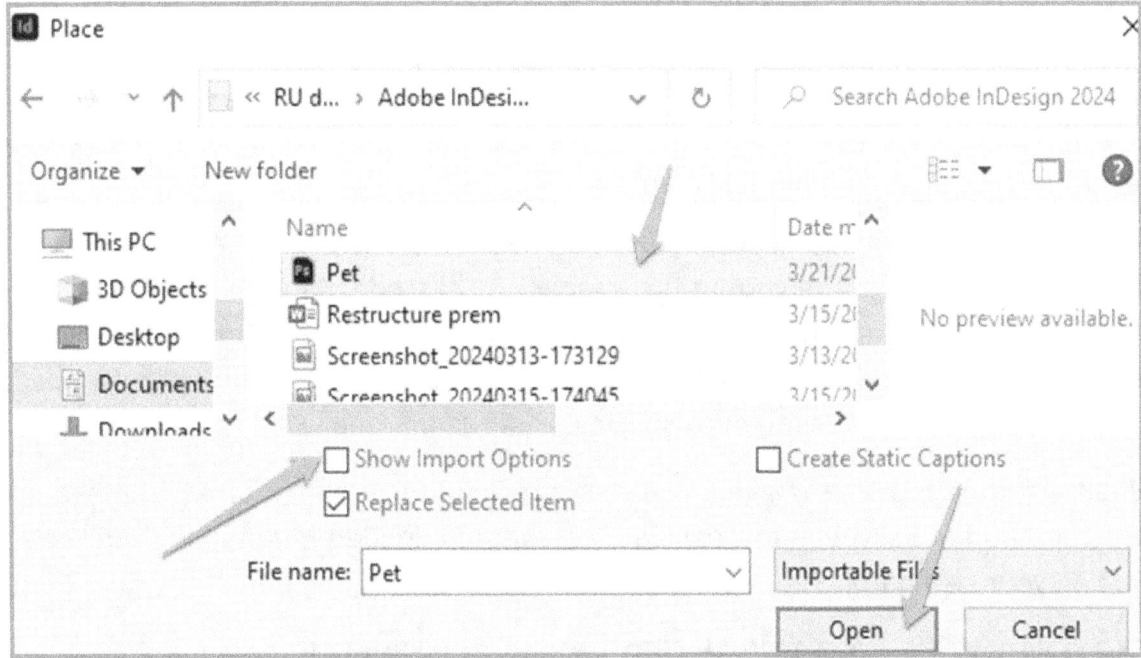

4) Select the file you wish to import (Pet from Photoshop in this case), and then click the **Open** button.

For specific files, such as bitmap (digital) images, graphics, and PDFs, a thumbnail preview will be visible at the bottom or to the right of the dialog box.

Once you click **Open**, the Place dialog box will close, and the cursor transforms into an upside-down **L**, displaying a thumbnail of the image you are about to place.

5) Click on the desired location on the page where you want the top-left corner of the imported file, such as an image, to be positioned. You can also drag across the area of the page where you want to place the object.

The imported file will then be successfully placed on the page.

Note: If you want to position the file within a designated frame size, use the click-and-drag method. Alternatively, if you've established an empty frame on the page, clicking inside the frame will result in the imported object (whether it's text or an image)—being placed within that frame.

You have the option to **Command-click** (macOS) or **Ctrl-click** (Windows) to insert multiple files. Once you've chosen the images and clicked **OK**, each click will position an image on the page. Alternatively, you can maintain the **Shift** + **Command** (macOS) or **Shift** + **Ctrl** (Windows) keys while dragging a rectangle to automatically place all selected images in a grid with even spacing.

When inserting multiple images, you may preview a thumbnail of each image before insertion. Additionally, you can navigate through the loaded images by using the arrow keys on your keyboard.

VARIOUS WAYS TO VIEW INDESIGN CONTENTS

There are various ways to view elements on the pages of your document. For instance, there are occasions when you require a close-up view of objects on a page to make precise edits. InDesign provides several methods for navigating through documents.

- **Keyboard Shortcut:** Press **Ctrl** + **+** (Ctrl and a single plus sign) on Windows or **Command** + **+** (Command and a single plus sign) on macOS to zoom in using the keyboard; substitute the **plus** sign with the **minus** sign to zoom out.
- **Scroll Bars**: To navigate through pages, utilize the scroll bars positioned beneath and to the right of the pasteboard. Click on a **scroll bar handle** and drag it **horizontally** or **vertically** to move pages around.
- **Hand Tool**: Employ the Hand tool to swing the page around. This tool is recognized as one of the most effective and expedient methods for page navigation, this tool allows you to move effortlessly within documents. choose the **Hand** tool by pressing the **spacebar** (when any tool other than the Type tool is in use), and proceed to click and drag for easy movement across the pasteboard.
- **Zoom**: Adjust the display size of your document by zooming in or out. Access the **Zoom** tool (identified by the **magnifying glass** icon) in the Tools panel, then click anywhere on the page to zoom in. To zoom out, hold down the **Alt** key (Windows) or **Option** key (Mac) while clicking.

SAVE YOUR INDESIGN DOCUMENT

Even the most reliable computers and applications can encounter failures, and to avoid the risk of losing your hard work, it's essential to save your publication regularly. Regular saving ensures that you don't lose any progress in the event of a power outage or a computer or software crashes

To so save a file, Go to **File** > **Save** or use the keyboard shortcut **Command + S** (macOS) or **Ctrl + S** (Windows).

Consider saving various versions of your files. This can be particularly useful when exploring different design options and wishing to preserve earlier versions of your work. Utilize the "**Save As**" command to effortlessly create different versions of your documents.

These are the instructions to save a new version of the current document while continuing your work on the new document:

1) Go to **File** > **Save As**. The Save As dialog box will appear.
2) Specify the **directory (folder)** where you want to store the file.
3) Enter a new name for the document in the **File Name** text field.

This action effectively saves a new version of the file. Consider implementing a naming pattern at this stage. For instance, if your file is named **Customer Work.indd**, you could label it as **Customer Work02.indd** to identify it as the second version. Subsequent versions can be named incrementally.

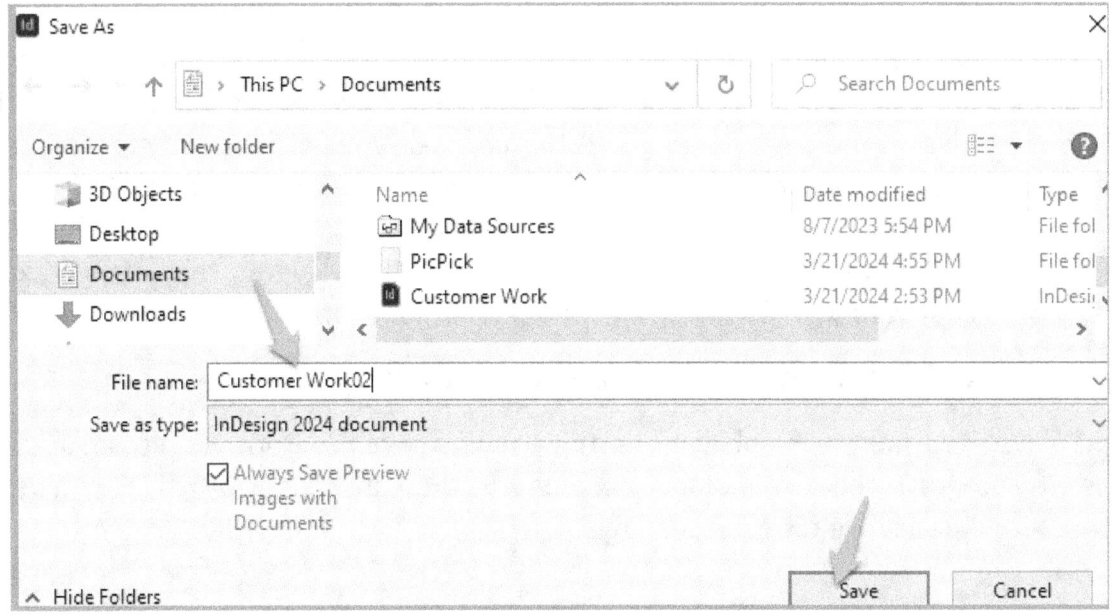

4) Complete the process by pressing the **Save** button.

The document will now be saved in the selected directory under the new name.

Note :The **File** > **Save As** command serves additional purposes, such as saving your design as a template. Once you've crafted the template, go to **File** > Save As, and then pick **InDesign CC Template** from the **Save as Format** (macOS) or **Save as Type** (Windows) from the drop-down list.

Another option is to select **File** > **Save a Copy**. This function allows you to save a duplicate of your current document with a new name, preserving the current state. You can continue editing the original document thereafter. Both commands serve as valuable tools for preserving incremental versions of your ongoing project.

CHAPTER THREE
GETTING STARTED WITH TEXT AND TEXT FRAMES

The majority of the documents you generate include text, emphasizing the need to comprehend text formatting, styling, and control within your layouts. Text consists of characters, and these characters are presented in designated fonts.

Next, you will learn the ins and outs of creating, beautifying, and refining text within InDesign. It all begins with text frames, those handy containers where your written content resides on the page. Throughout this chapter, you will grasp key techniques for seamlessly integrating text into your documents and mastering the art of text manipulation to achieve your desired visual impact. Looking ahead, Chapter 4 of this user guide will unveil strategies for creating compelling layouts that blend text and graphics to captivate your audience and entice them to engage with your creations.

WHAT EXACTLY ARE TEXT, FONTS, AND FRAMES

Text plays a crucial role in publications as it conveys specific information to an audience. It is vital to grasp the terminology presented in the subsequent pages. Text and font, although related, have distinct meanings:

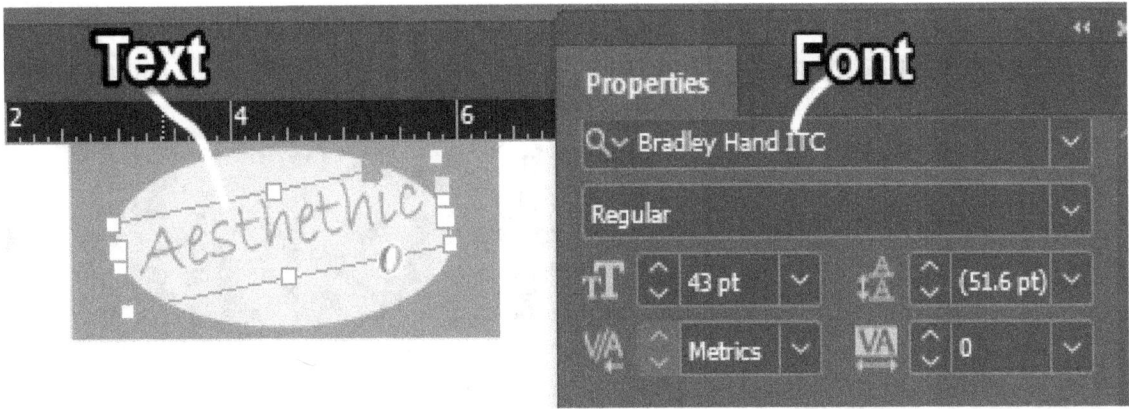

- **Text**: This comprises letters, words, sentences, and paragraphs forming the content within text frames in your publication.
- **Font:** Refers to the unique design that constitutes a set of characters used for text styling. There are numerous font styles available from various manufacturers, many of which come pre-installed in programs on your computer. InDesign's Font menu enables you to preview font faces and designate favorite fonts.

Frames act as containers designed to accommodate content, and in a publication, you can use two types of frames, these are:

- **Text:** it holds textual content on the InDesign document page. You can link text frames, enabling text to flow seamlessly from one frame to another. Additionally, text can be configured to wrap around graphic frames.
- **Graphic:** Functions as a container for images placeholder within your publication.

CREATING AND UTILIZING TEXT FRAMES

Text frames house the textual content incorporated into a publication. There are numerous methods to create a new text frame. In InDesign, you have the flexibility to integrate text into imaginative shapes you draw, transforming them into functional text frames. The process of creating and utilizing text frames within a publication holds significance, especially given the frequent inclusion of substantial text content.

Text frames may be generated automatically upon importing text into a publication.

GENERATING TEXT FRAMES USING THE TYPE TOOL

The Type tool gives you the privilege to craft a text frame. When you utilize the Type tool and click on the page, no action occurs until you've established a frame to contain the text. These are the step-by-step guide on how to create a text frame with the Type tool:

1) Choose the **Type tool** from the **Tools** panel and position it over the page. The Type tool cursor adopts the form of an **I-bar**. Move the cursor to the desired position where you want to place the **top-left corner** of the text frame.

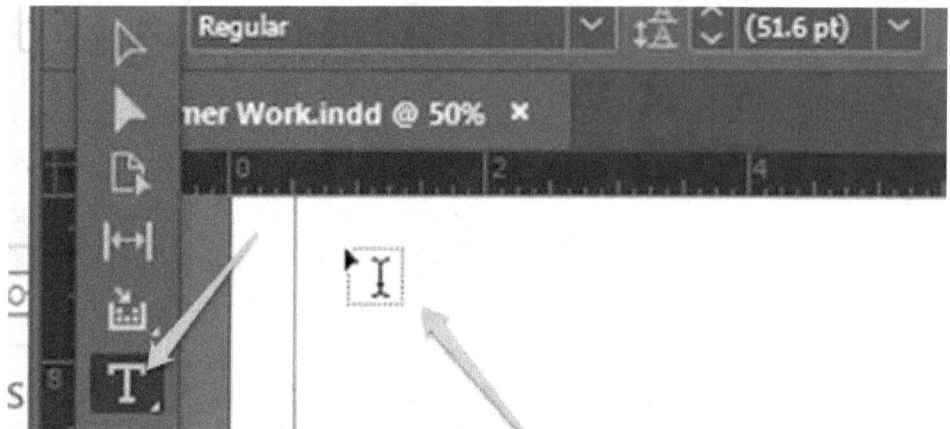

2) Press and drag with your mouse diagonally to generate a text frame. Upon clicking, the mouse exhibits a cross-like appearance. While dragging, an outline of the text frame emerges, offering a visual guide to its dimensions.
3) You can then release the mouse button immediately after the frame attains the desired size. The text frame is now created, and an insertion point is positioned at the top-left corner of the frame. Begin typing on the keyboard to input text, or consider importing text from an alternate source.

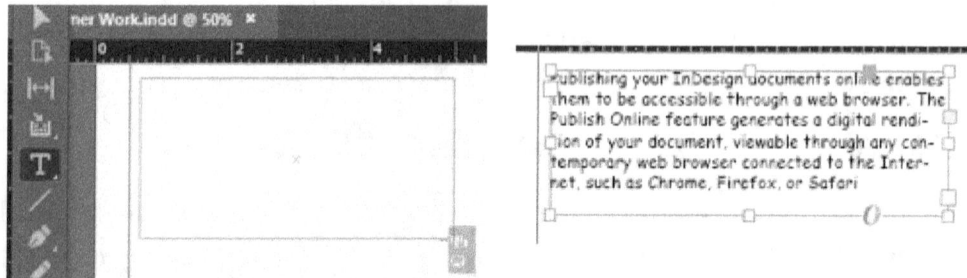

CREATING TEXT FRAMES USING THE FRAME TOOL

The Frame tool can be used to craft frames of various shapes such as rectangular, polygonal, or oval. Subsequently, once the frame is positioned on the page, you have the option to convert it into a text frame, use it as an image frame, or a design element on the page. To begin the creation of a new text frame using the Frame tool, observe these guidelines:

1) Opt for the **Rectangle Frame** tool or any other frame tools in the **Tools** panel and then click and drag diagonally on your InDesign page to generate a new frame. This action results in the creation of a new frame on the page.

2) Switch to the **Type** tool, and click within the frame. This transforms the frame into a text frame rather than a graphic frame.

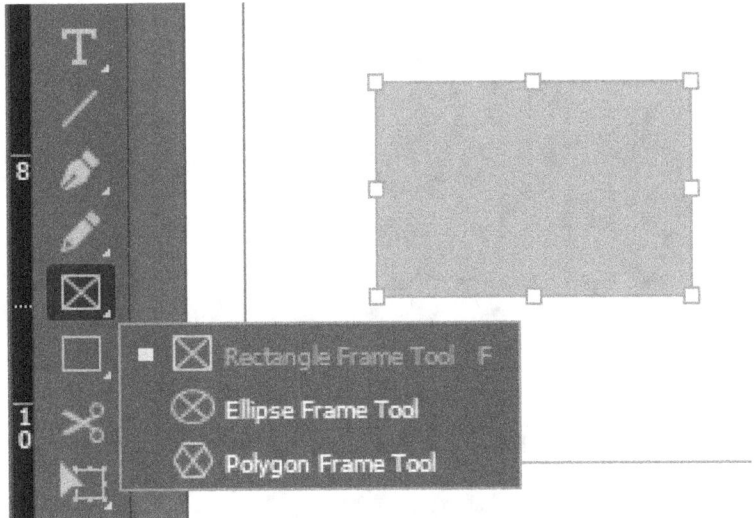

3) Pick the **Selection** tool and utilize it to relocate the text frame. You can move the text frame by clicking within it with the Selection tool and dragging it to a new place.

CRAFTING TEXT FRAMES FROM A SHAPE

If you get a captivating shape crafted using drawing tools or copied from Illustrator, transforming it into a text frame to accommodate text is a straightforward process. Kindly apply these procedures:

1) Use either the **Pencil** tool, **Pen** tool, or **Shape** tool to craft a shape with a stroke color and no fill. Alternatively, you can copy and paste artwork from Illustrator. This action results in the creation of a shape on the page without a solid color for the fill.
2) Choose the **Type tool** from the Tools panel to make it active.
3) Click inside the shape generated in Step **1** and input text or import text.

IMPORTING TEXT TO YOUR PUBLICATION VIA OTHER APPLICATIONS

You can import text that you've crafted or edited using different software like Microsoft Word, Excel, or Adobe InCopy. Importing edited text is a common workflow practice in publication creation, given that specialized text-editing software is frequently used to edit manuscripts before the layout phase.

Follow these instructions to import text into InDesign:

1) Ensure that no other objects are selected and then go to **File** > **Place**. The Place dialog box appears. Choose the **file** you want to import (such as an **InCopy story, Word document, or a plain text file**) by navigating through your hard drive.

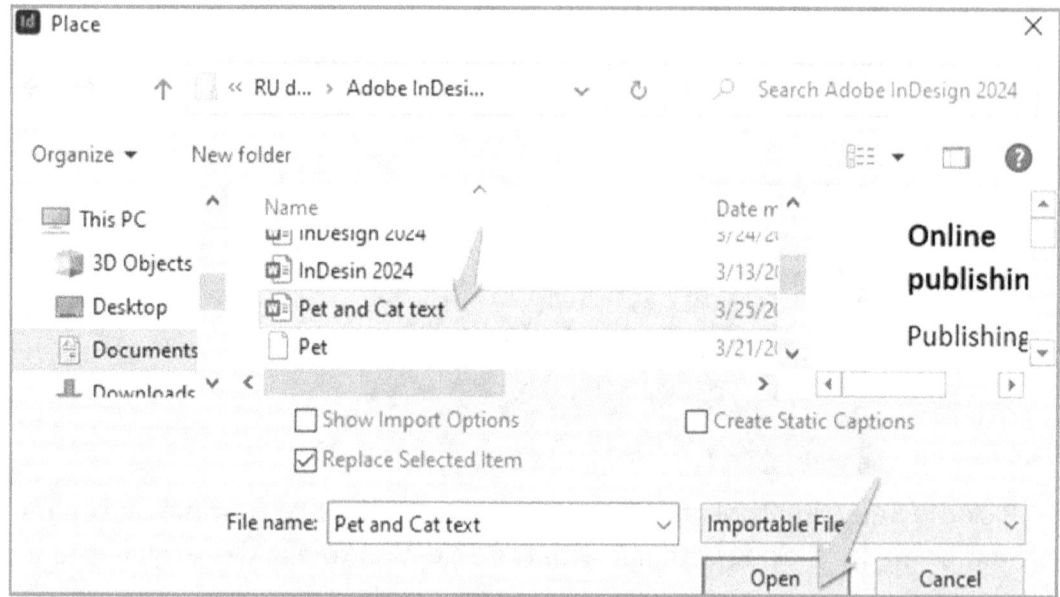

2) When you have selected the file to be imported, then click the **Open** button. The **Place Text** icon, cursor arrow, and a thumbnail image of the text display on the active page. Drag the cursor to the desired location on the page where you want the top-left side of the text frame to be created upon document importation.

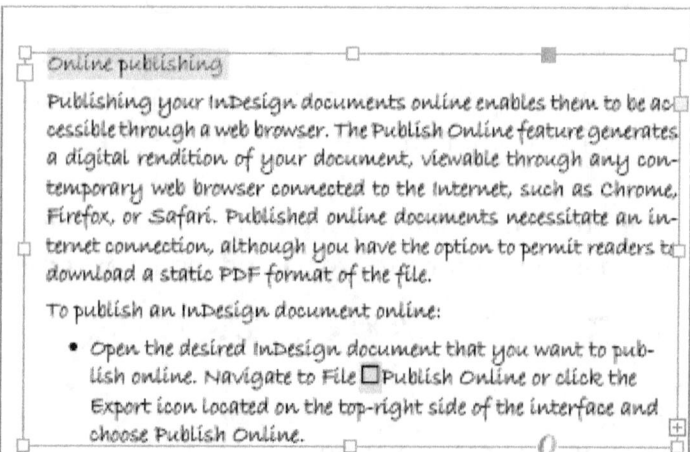

3) Press the mouse to place the imported text. This action generates a text frame and imports the text.

When you select a text frame before importing text, the text will position itself within the frame. Thus, you won't need to manually place the text using the cursor. With the

Selection tool, you're empowered to relocate the text frame anywhere on the page once the text is added. Moreover, you can resize the frame as needed for optimal layout adjustments.

HANDLING TEXT FLOW

Exercise control on how the text flows with these straightforward modifier keys while placing text:

- Go to **File** > **Place**, choose the file you wish to import, and click **Open**. Hold down the **Shift** key, and when the **loaded cursor** transforms into a curvy arrow, click the document. The text will be imported and flows from one column to another or from page to page until exhausted. If necessary, InDesign also generates additional pages.
- Go to **File** > **Place**, pick the file you wish to import, and click **Open**. Hold down the **Option** key (macOS) or **Alt** key (Windows)). Then press and drag a text area. (Ensure not to release the **Option** or **Alt** key!) While continuing to click and drag additional text frames, your text effortlessly flows from one frame to another until the entire text is utilized.

Note: When you check the "**Show Import Options**" box inside the **Place** dialog box, an additional window will pop up. Here, you have the option to disregard formatting and styles from both text and tables, allowing you to import clean, unformatted text for easier editing. If you're using a Mac, simply select the "Options" button to reveal **the "Show Import Options"** checkbox.

INSERTING PLACEHOLDER TEXT

Imagine you are in the process of crafting a publication, but the required text for import into InDesign is not yet available — perhaps it is still in the process of creation or editing. Rather than waiting for the final text, you can utilize placeholder text and continue to develop your publication's layout. The placeholder text is mostly used to temporarily populate a document with text. This text closely resembles normal blocks of text, providing a more natural appearance than repeatedly pasting the same few words to fill a text frame. However, be aware that placeholder text doesn't adhere to any specific language; it serves merely as a temporary filler.

Follow these steps to automatically add placeholder text into a text frame:

1) create a frame on the publication page by selecting the **Type** tool, clicking over the page, and dragging sideways to create a text frame.
2) Go to **Type** > **Fill with Placeholder Text**.

Instantly, the text frame is filled with both characters and words, just as in the screenshot shown below.

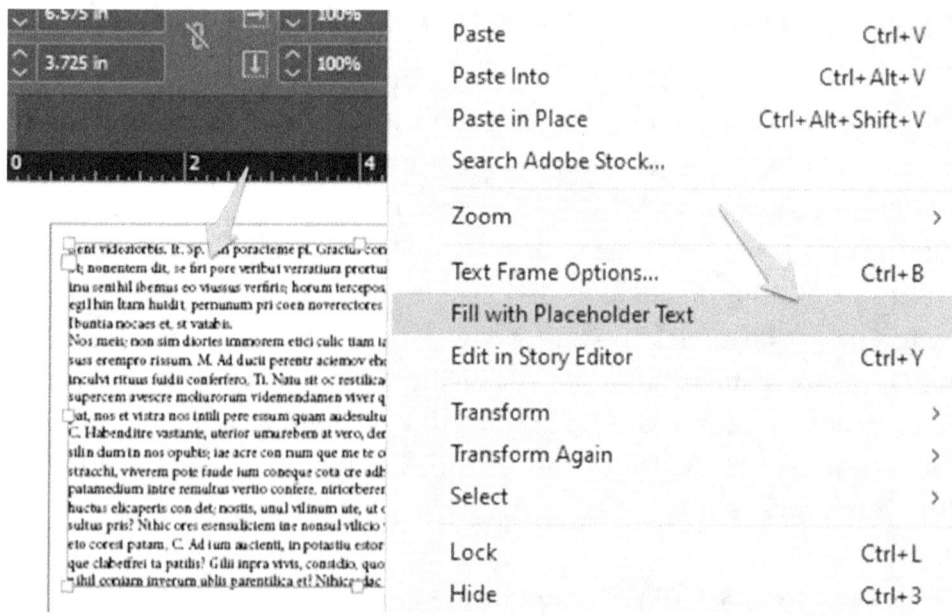

TEXT COPYING AND PASTING

You can send text from another application into an InDesign publication by copying and pasting the text directly. If you've highlighted and copied text in another program, you can paste it directly into InDesign from your computer's Clipboard. Here's the process:

1) Select the text intended for your publication and press **Command + C** (macOS) or **Ctrl + C** (Windows) to copy the text. Copied text resides on the Clipboard until replaced by new content, allowing you to forward this information into InDesign.
2) You can then open **InDesign** and press **Command +V** (macOS) or **Ctrl + V** (Windows) to generate a new text frame and paste the text into it. A new text frame that is centered on the page appears with your selected text within it.

Note : To paste text from the **Clipboard** directly into an existing text frame, simply click within the **frame** and press **Command +V** (macOS) or **Ctrl + V** (Windows). This method works similarly for images. If you wish to access or edit text within a frame, just double-click on the text frame.

To control the formatting of your pasted content, adjust the preferences in InDesign. For macOS, go to **InDesign** > **Preferences** > **Clipboard Handling;** for Windows, go to **Edit** > **Preferences** > **Clipboard Handling**. From there, you can choose between pasting All Information (including swatches, styles, etc.) or Text only.

OBSERVING TEXT FRAME OPTIONS

InDesign provides extensive control over the text in your publications. Adjusting text frame options enables you to modify how text is positioned within a frame. Altering these settings becomes crucial in situations where you are dealing with specific types of fonts.

If you **control-click** (macOS) or **right-click** (Windows) a text frame, there are several available contextual menu options for handling a text frame. This menu provides you options to carry out basic commands like **add or modify strokes**, **cut**, **copy**, **paste**, **fill the text frame with placeholder text**, **make transformations,** and so on. You can access many of these options on the **Object** and **Type** menus.

MODIFYING TEXT FRAME OPTIONS

To adjust the text frame options influencing the appearance of text within a frame, proceed with the following steps:

1) Create a **rectangular text frame** on the page or use an **existing text frame** that already has text, click the frame using the **Selection tool** to select it, and then go to **Object** > **Text Frame Options**. Alternatively, press **Command** +B (macOS) or **Ctrl** + **B** (Windows), or use the **text frame's contextual** menu to access the Text Frame Options dialog box. You can confirm the selection of a text frame by checking the handles around its bounding box.

The **Text Frame Options** dialog box opens, displaying the existing settings for the selected text frame.

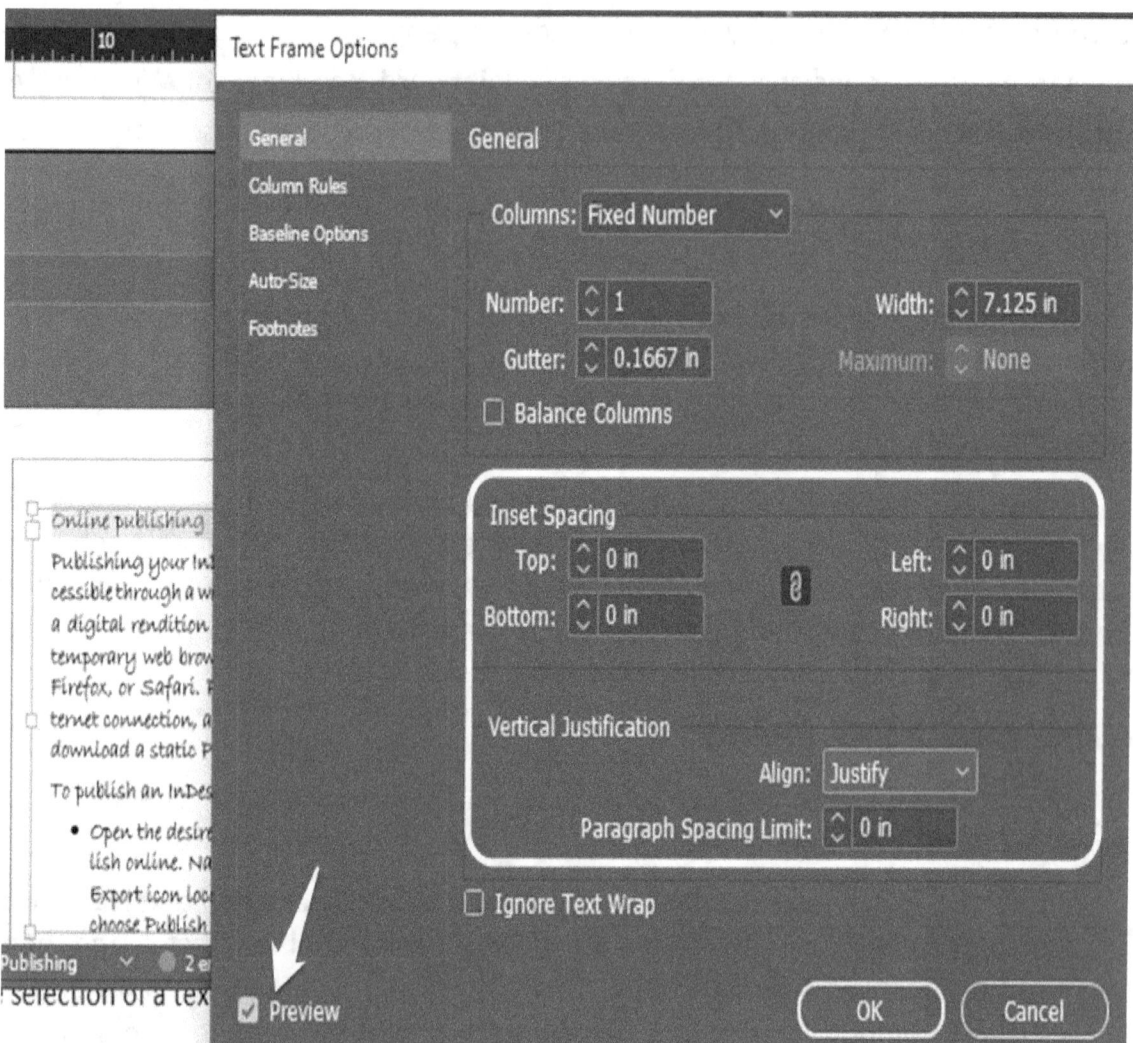

2) Enable the **Preview** checkbox to instantly visualize updates. This allows you to make whatever changes within the dialog box and observe their appearance on the page in real-time, enabling you to preview adjustments before applying them.
3) In the **Inset Spacing** section of the dialog box, modify the **Top**, **Bottom**, **Left**, and **Right** fields. These **values** determine the inset spacing of text from the edges of the text frame, pushing the text inside the frame by the specified value. When the "**Make All Settings Same**" is switched (When the chain symbol is enabled), you only need to input a value into one of the four text boxes.

This dialog box also provides options for indenting text, a topic discussed in the **"Indenting Your Text"** section later in this chapter. Additionally, you can choose the vertical alignment of the text (**Top, Center, Bottom, or Justify**). Options include aligning the text to the top or bottom of the text frame, centering it vertically within the frame, or justifying the lines evenly from top to bottom.

4) Once you've completed the changes in this dialog box, press **Ok** to display the modifications on the text frame.

EXPLORING AND ADJUSTING COLUMNS

When creating a new publication, you have the option to specify a certain number of columns on the page. When you use columns, this ensures that new text frames align correctly and are appropriately spaced. Furthermore, you can customize the gutter, representing the space between columns.

In addition, you can create columns within a single text frame using the Text Frame Options dialog box. This feature enables the addition of up to 40 columns within a single text frame. If there is already text in the frame, it will automatically distribute among the added columns. InDesign provides three types of columns to choose from when designing layouts with text.

- Opt for "**Fixed Number**" when you have a precise count of columns you want in a text frame.
- Select "**Fixed Width**" when you are aware of the exact width of columns within a text frame. If the text frame adjusts in size, the number of columns may expand or contract accordingly.
- Choose "**Flexible Width**" if you prefer the width of columns to adapt based on the text frame's size. With Flexible Width, InDesign dynamically adjusts the number of columns as necessary, depending on the width of the text frame.

The subsequent steps illustrate how to insert columns into a text frame on a page:

1) draw a rectangular text frame on the page using the **Type tool** or **Frame tool**. Columns can be added to any text frames such as rectangular, freehand shapes drawn on the page, or oval shapes.
2) After the creation of the text frame, the cursor is automatically positioned inside the frame, allowing you to input text. You can type text, paste content copied from another document, or insert placeholder text by selecting **Type** > **Fill with Placeholder Text.**

> **Online publishing**
>
> Publishing your InDesign documents online enables them to be accessible through a web browser. The Publish Online feature generates a digital rendition of your document, viewable through any contemporary web browser connected to the Internet, such as Chrome, Firefox, or Safari. Published online documents necessitate an internet connection, although you have the option to permit readers to download a static PDF format of the file.
>
> To publish an InDesign document online:
>
> - Open the desired InDesign document that you want to publish online. Navigate to File ☐ Publish Online or click the Export icon located on the top-right side of the interface and choose Publish Online.

3) While the text frame remains selected, go to **Object** > **Text Frame Options**. In the opened Text Frame Options dialog box, you may choose to enable the Preview checkbox for an instant preview of the changes your settings will apply to the frame on the page.

4) Within the **Columns** heading, modify the value in the **Number** text field. As an illustration, we input "**3**" in the **Number** text field would partition the text in the chosen frame into two columns. If the Preview checkbox is activated, clicking on a different text field within the dialog box prompts the text frame on the page to update and show the new value setting.

5) Adjust the width of the columns by typing a new value in the "**Width**" text field. The column width is automatically determined based on the width of the text frame you created. In this example, we entered **2 inches** into the "**Width**" text field, causing the text frame to resize according to the specified width.

6) Modify the value in the **Gutter** text field. The gutter value dictates the spacing between columns. If the gutter appears too wide, alter the value in the Gutter text field to a lower number. For instance, in this example, we entered **0.2 in** the "**Gutter**" text field.

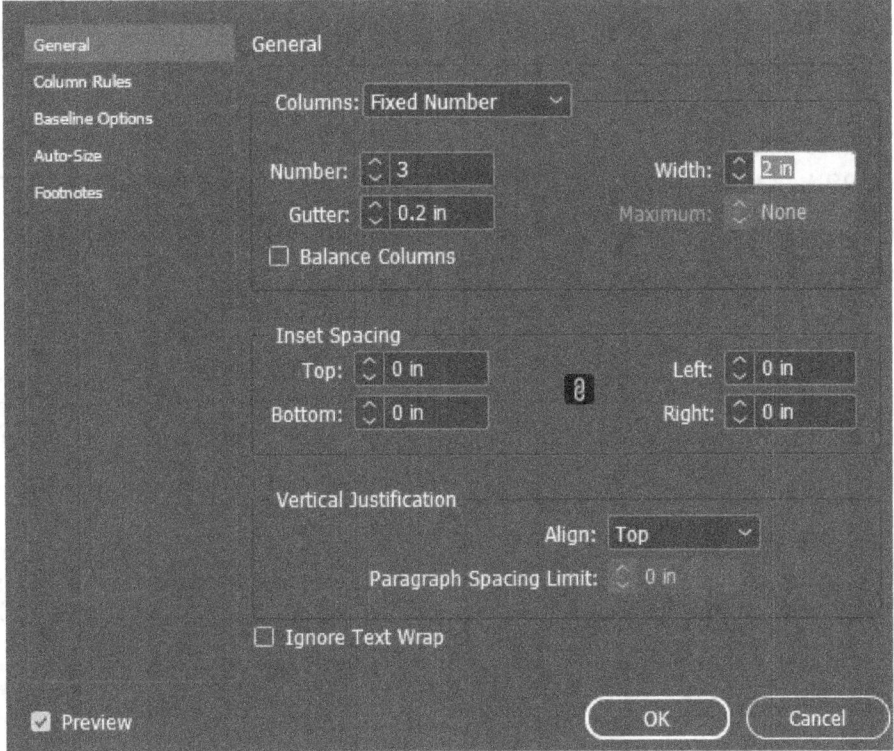

7) Upon completion, press **OK** to implement the changes. The modifications are now applied to the text frame you have edited.

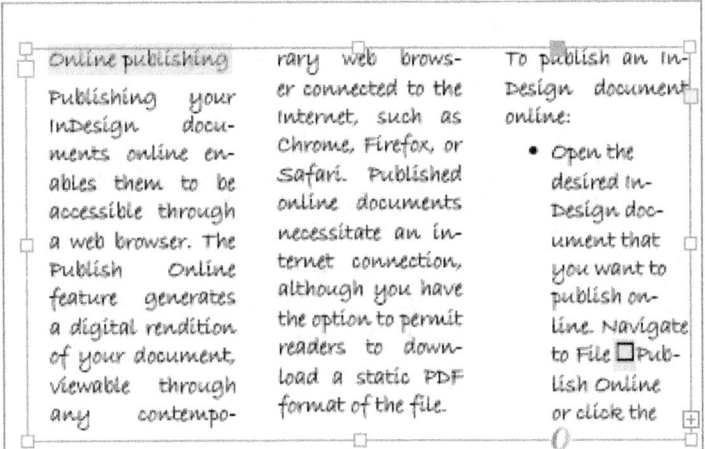

Note : Once you've created columns within a text frame, resizing the frame becomes straightforward using the handles located on its bounding box, we shall be talking more about "**Resizing**" later in this chapter. The columns automatically adjust to maintain the specified number of columns set in the **Text Frame Options** dialog box. Opting for the

"**Fixed Column Width**" choice from the drop-down menu ensures that your text frames maintain a consistent width regardless of resizing actions. Consequently, when adjusting the text frame size, it adheres to the predetermined fixed width.

You have the flexibility to alter the number of columns in the Control panel by selecting the text frame with the Selection tool. Alternatively, you can make adjustments using the paragraph options in the Control panel when the Type tool is active.

ADJUSTING AND LINKING TEXT FRAMES ACROSS PAGES

The ability to modify text frames and establish connections between them in a publication, enabling the continuation of a story on a separate page, is crucial in most publishing scenarios. This is particularly relevant when dealing with extensive stories comprising multiple paragraphs that span across various pages in the document.

When you paste the content that exceeds the visible area of the text frame, the additional text remains present beyond the boundaries of the frame. For example, if you have a text frame that's 15 lines tall and you paste in 60 lines of text, the last 45 lines will be cropped off (this is otherwise known as text overflow). To reveal the entirety of the pasted text, you either need to resize the text frame or enable the text to flow into another frame. An indicator that the frame contains more content is a small **red plus (+) sign** visible in a unique handle at the bottom-right corner of the text frame.

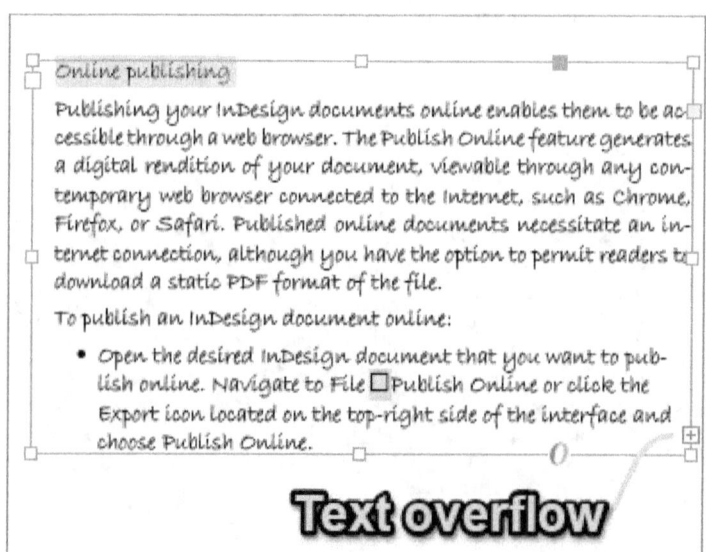

When working with a text frame on the page, it's essential to have the capability to adjust its size, position, and linking. Threading or linking the frame to other frames on the page is necessary to facilitate the flow of text between them. This becomes particularly significant when crafting layouts that incorporate substantial amounts of text.

ADJUSTING THE SIZE AND POSITION OF TEXT FRAMES

In the process of designing layouts, it's common to frequently resize and reposition text frames within the document as you are trying to craft the desired page layout. To resize and move a text frame, apply these procedures:

1) With the **Selection** tool active, select a text frame on the page, this reveals a bounding box with handles. If the text frame contains more text than is currently visible, a small red box with a red plus sign emerges in the lower-right corner of the bounding box.

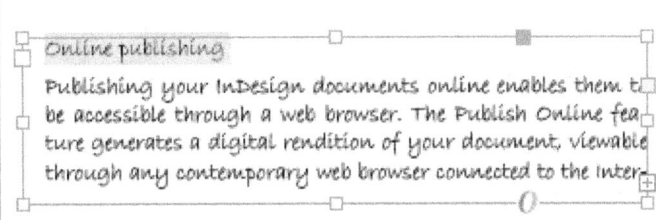

2) Adjust the text frame's size by dragging one of the handles. The frame dynamically updates on the page during the handle manipulation. Modify the width or height by dragging the handles at the center of each side, or simultaneously adjust both dimensions by dragging a corner handle. In this instance, the presence of a red plus sign in the lower-right corner signals that the frame needs to be enlarged to accommodate the current text. For proportional scaling, use the **Shift** key while dragging a corner handle.

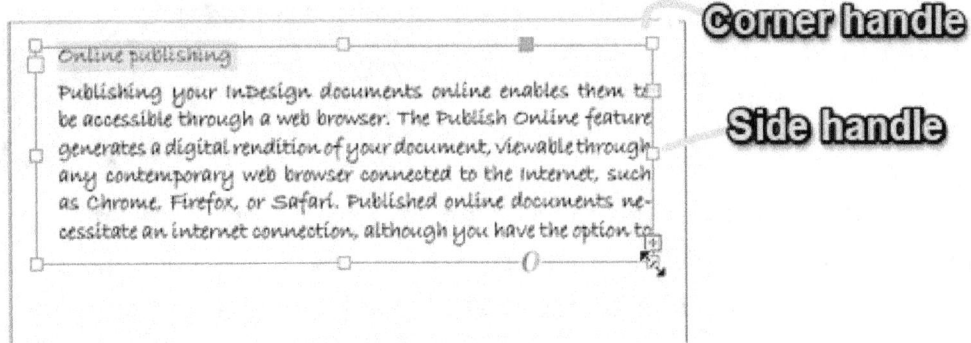

3) Once you've completed resizing the text frame, click the middle of the selected frame and reposition it on the page. A single click within the frame, followed by dragging, allows you to move the frame around the page. An outline of the frame follows the cursor, indicating the position where the frame will be located upon

releasing the mouse button. Simply release the frame to finalize its new placement.

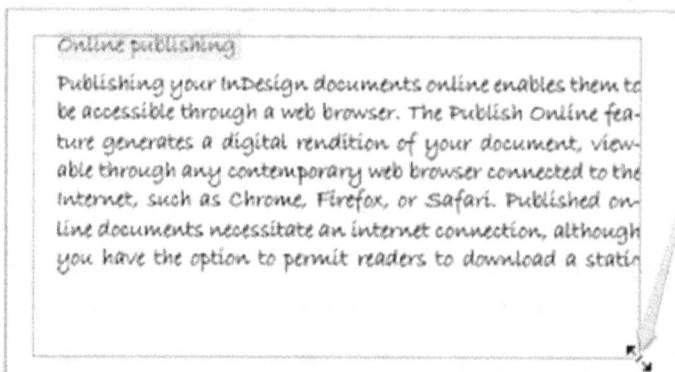

The Transform panel also can be used to alter the dimensions and locations of a text frame. To access the **Transform** panel, go to **Window** > **Object** & Layout > **Transform**. To alter the dimension of the text frame with the Transform panel, type different values to the **W** and **H** fields. This alters the width and frame of the text frame; this is useful for actual text frame measurement. The **X** and **Y** fields allow you to change the location of the text frame on the page.

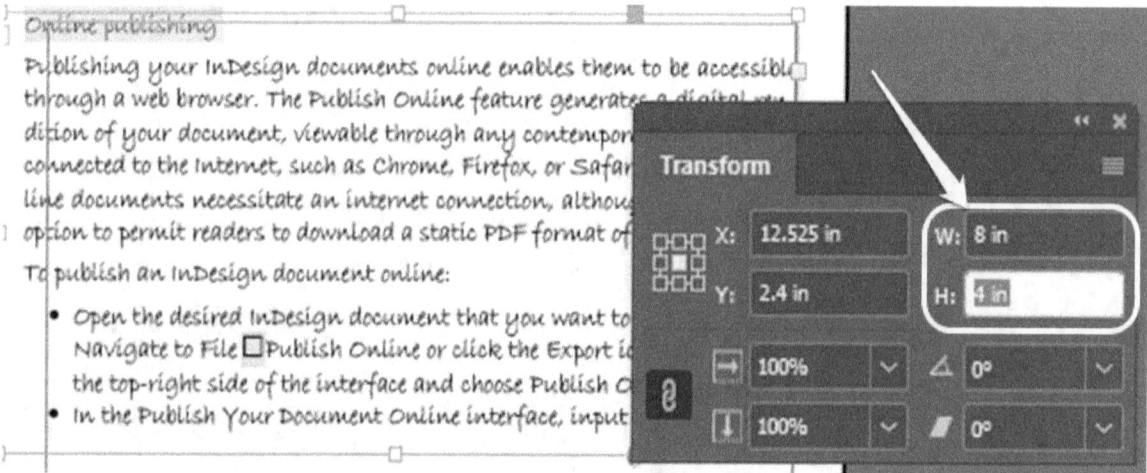

When you're working with guides or grids on your page, the text frame automatically aligns with them. Additionally, when you have a document with columns, the text frame smoothly aligns with the column guides as you move it close to them.

THREADING OR LINKING TEXT FRAMES

Proficiency in threading or linking text frames is essential for creating complex page layouts rich in textual content. Threading includes a strategic arrangement of text frames, where the textual narrative extends from one frame to the next. This technique proves helpful in diverse layouts, recognizing the inherent challenge of accommodating an entire body of text within a single frame.

Let's delve into some of the specialized terms Adobe uses for linked text frames.

- ✓ **Flowing:** This refers to text that begins in one frame and continues into a second frame.
- ✓ **Threading:** This describes the connection between two text frames where text flows from the first frame to the second.
- ✓ **Story:** It's the collective term for a group of sentences and paragraphs within threaded text frames.
- ✓ **In port**: This icon is found on the top-left side of a text frame's bounding box; it shows that the frame either starts a story or receives text from another frame. If there's a small arrow within the icon, it signifies that a story is flowing into it; otherwise, the port icon remains empty.
- ✓ **Out port:** This is positioned on the lower-right side of the text frame's bounding box; this icon shows that text is flowing out of the frame. If the frame is threaded to another, the Out port contains a small arrow; if not, it's empty.

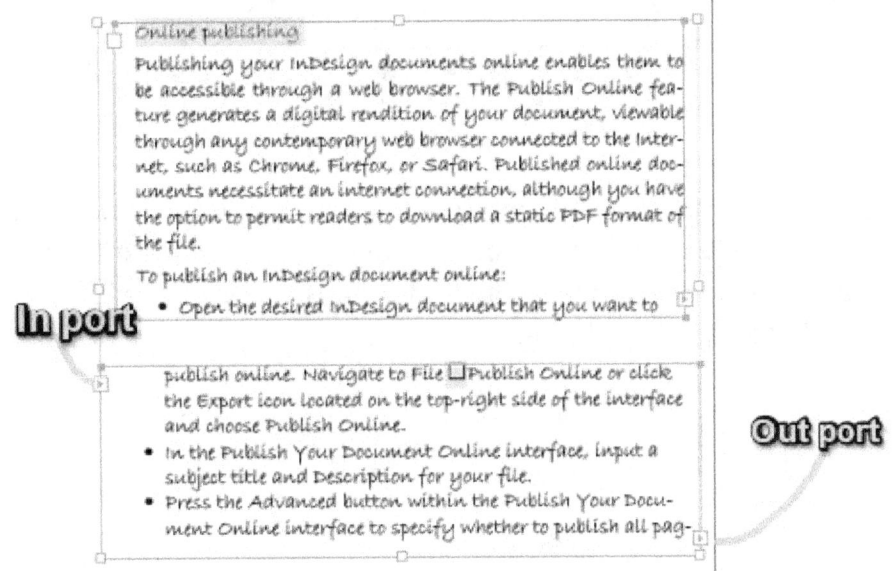

If a text frame isn't linked to another frame and has more text than it can display (overflow text), the Out port displays a small red plus sign (+) icon.

Locate a block of text you wish to thread (for optimal results, choose one with complete sentences rather than placeholder text), and follow these instructions:

1) Copy your text to the clipboard from various sources, such as a document in **Word, Notepad, InDesign Help files, a webpage displayed in a browser**, or a **SimpleText**. The specific content being copied is irrelevant; the key is to ensure that the text comprises a few paragraphs to facilitate seamless flow across frames. A threaded text is signified by a line linking one text frame to another. InDesign displays to you the thread text if you select **View** > **Extras** > **Show Text Threads.**
2) Create two text frames within a page using the **Type tool**, they can stay beside one another or above one another as shown in the screenshot below.
3) With the **Type tool** activated, select the first text frame positioned above the second frame. A flashing insertion point displays in the first frame, this enables you to paste or enter text into the frame.
4) Press **Command** + **V** (macOS) or **Ctrl** + **V** (Windows) to insert the text into the text frame.
5) Use the **Selection tool** to click over the overflow text. The cursor transforms into the **loaded text icon**, allowing you to select or create an additional text frame to continue threading the story.

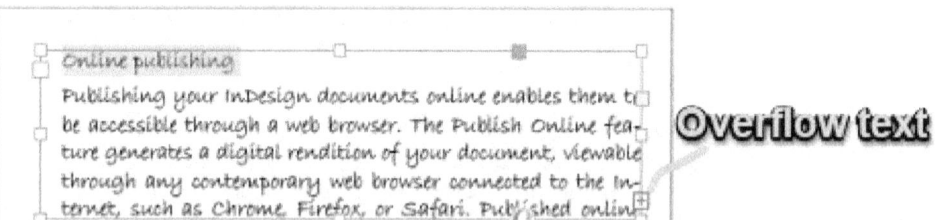

6) Hover the cursor over the **second text frame** and **click**. The cursor transforms into the thread text icon upon hovering over the second text frame. Upon clicking the second text frame, the two frames become threaded, as the text effortlessly continues in the second frame.

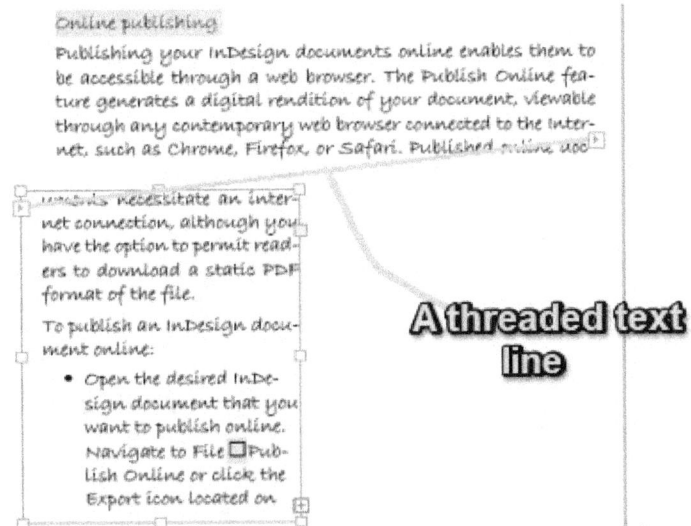

Feel free to keep generating frames and threading them, whether on the same page or across the following pages.

You also have the option to unthread text, essentially cutting the link between two text frames. It's possible to rearrange the frames involved in text threading, like altering the page where the story continues when threaded to a second text frame. To break the connection, simply double-click the "**In port**" icon or the "**Out port**" icon of the text frame you wish to unthread. The frame will then be unthreaded, with no text deletion occurring.

If your document consists of only one page, you can easily add more by selecting **Layout > Pages > Insert Pages**. Simply specify the number of **additional pages** you need, then click **OK** to confirm. Afterward, you can navigate through the pages using the **Page** Field control located at the bottom of the workspace. Finally, you can create a new text frame and link your text within it.

HOW TO ADD A PAGE JUMP NUMBER

For documents with several pages, you can include a page jump number, this reveals the location where the narrative continues when it jumps to a text frame on another page. Ensure that a story is threaded between text frames on two distinct pages before you begin, and then proceed with these instructions:

1) Draw a new "text frame" on the first page and input "**Continued on page**".
2) Select the recently created text frame with the **Selection** tool.

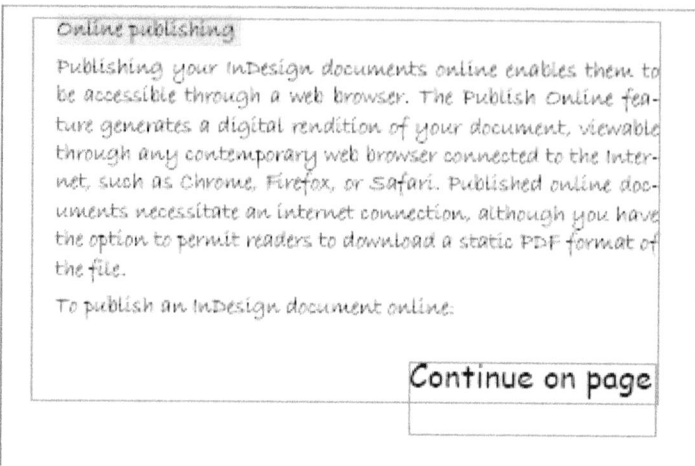

3) Adjust the position of the text frame to let it partly overlap with the frame containing the narrative. If necessary, repeat Steps 1 and 4 from the previous section, "**Threading or Linking Text Frames**" to create a new text frame with overflow text.

4) Allow InDesign to understand the text frame it should track the story from or to. Ensure that the two text frames (the "Continued on page" notice and the story text frame) are overlapped so that InDesign recognizes their association. Subsequently, group these two text frames to move them collectively. To achieve this, select both frames (**Shift-click** using the Selection tool), and then navigate to **Object > Group**.

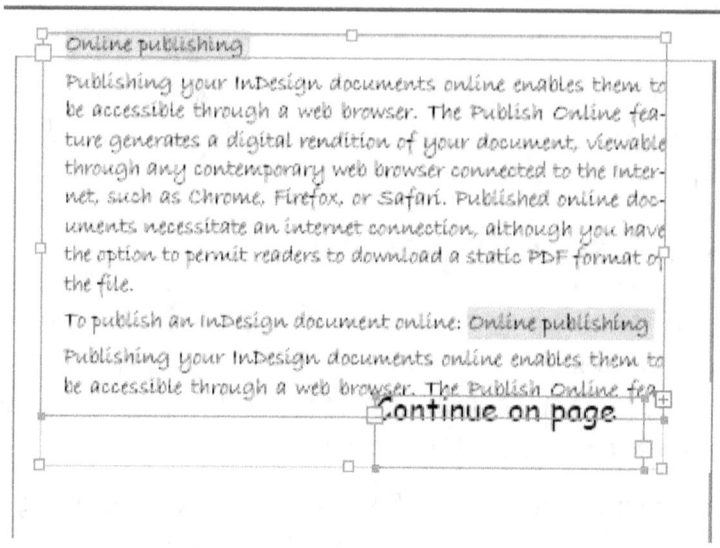

5) Double-click on the newly created text frame containing the text "**Continued on page**". Position the cursor at the desired location where you want to place the page number (known as the insertion point). Ensure there is a space after the

preceding characters to prevent them from running together. In this case, include a space after the word "page".

6) Navigate to **Type > Insert Special Character > Markers > Next Page Number**. A number is inserted into the text frame. This number is responsive to the position of the next threaded text frame, so if you relocate the second text frame, the page number updates automatically.

To repeat these steps at the location where the story is continued from, you will rather select **Type > Insert Special Character > Markers > Previous Page Number** in step (6).

FAMILIARIZING WITH PARAGRAPH CONFIGURATION

Altering paragraph settings of the whole text frame or an individual paragraph within a text frame can be accomplished through various methods. You can adjust the indentation, alignment, and justification of a single paragraph or whole text frame using the Paragraph panel. To access the **Paragraph** panel, go to **Window** >**Type & Tables** > **Paragraph**.

Note: To apply any adjustment made in the **Paragraph** panel uniformly across all text frames you generate, refrain from picking any specific paragraph or text frame before making adjustments. rather, commence by picking the entire text frame or frames present on the page. This ensures that the modifications you make in the **Paragraph** panel will impact all paragraphs within the selected text frames, rather than affecting only one paragraph. Conversely, if you intend for the changes to specifically influence a single paragraph within a text frame, start the process by selecting that paragraph using the Type tool, and subsequently implement your desired modifications.

ADJUSTING TEXT INDENTATION

Paragraph indentation in a story can be accomplished through the use of the Paragraph panel. Indentation involves shifting the paragraph away from the edges of the text frame's bounding box. These are the procedures on how to indent your text:

1) Creating a text frame and populating it with Text:

You can fill the text frame in your own way, such as, Input text directly into it, copy and paste, or opt for placeholder text via **Text** > **Fill with Placeholder Text**.

2) Confirm that the insertion point is actively flashing within the desired paragraph or choose the text frame with the Selection tool.

> Online publishing
>
> Publishing your InDesign documents online enables them to be accessible through a web browser. The Publish Online feature generates a digital rendition of your document, viewable through any contemporary web browser connected to the Internet, such as Chrome, Firefox, or Safari.
>
> Published online documents necessitate an internet connection, although you have the option to permit readers to download a static PDF format of the file.

3) Access the **Paragraph** panel by navigating to **Window>Type & Tables >Paragraph**. This will display the Paragraph panel, displaying the current settings of the text frame.

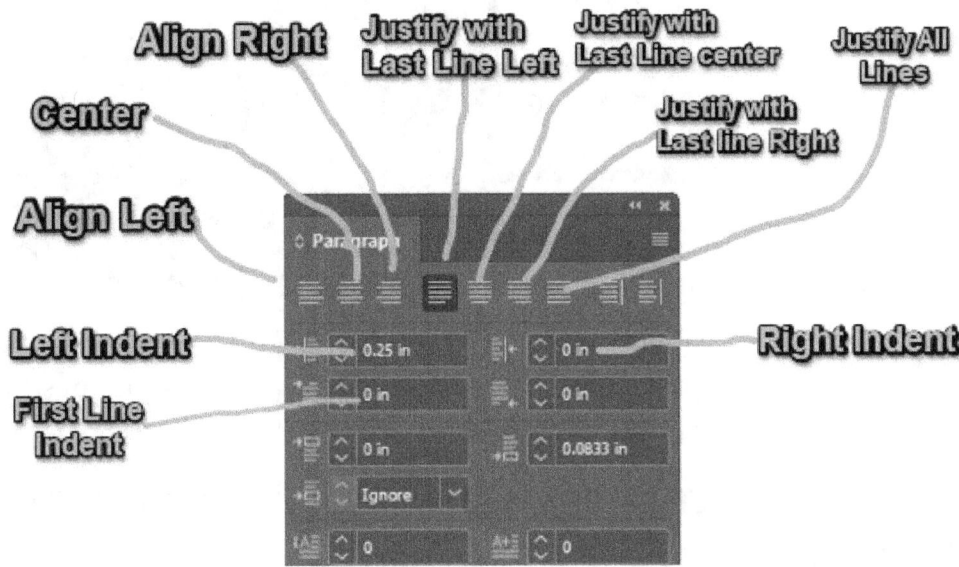

4) Adjust the **Left** Indent by entering a new value in the designated text field and then pressing Enter. A higher numeric input results in a more pronounced indent. Specify the unit of measurement by including "**in**" for inches or "**pt**" for points as you input the value, utilizing any of the measurement formats supported by InDesign.

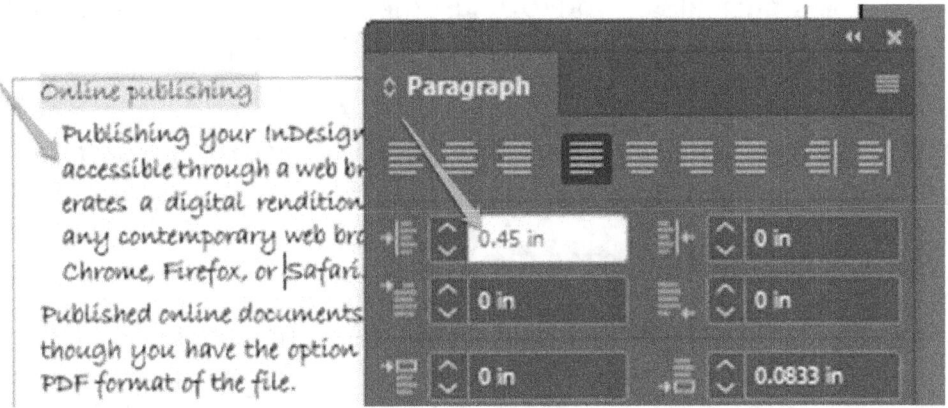

5) Modify the **First Line Left** Indent by entering a new value in its corresponding text field and pressing **Enter**.

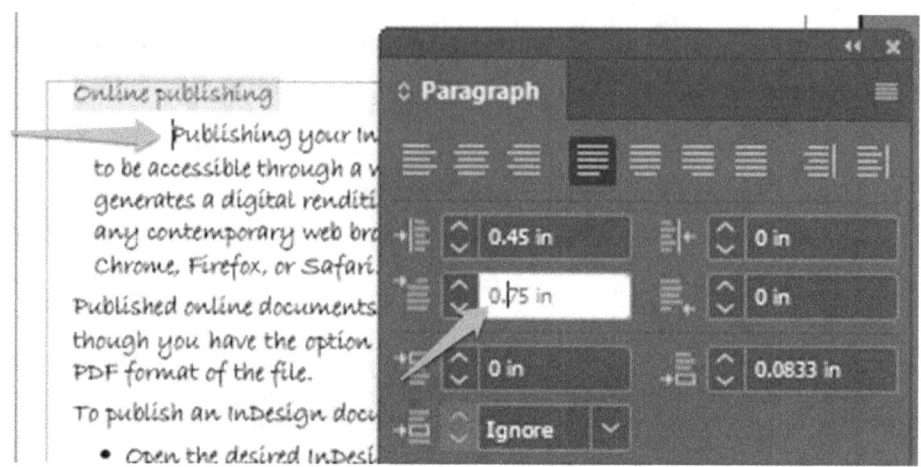

To modify all paragraphs within a story, start by clicking within any paragraph to place the insertion point. Then, go to **Edit** > Select All before adjusting the desired settings. This ensures that all paragraphs within the story are selected for the changes.

FORMATTING TEXT FRAMES WITH ALIGNMENT AND JUSTIFICATION

Utilize the alignment and justification buttons found in the Paragraph panel to format text frames:

- ➢ **Align:** it assists in left, center, or right-aligning text with the edges of the text frames.
- ➢ **Justification:** it allows you to adjust the spacing of text relative to the edges of the text frame and enables you to justify the final line of text within the paragraph.

Aligning or justifying a block of text involves selecting the text or text frame and clicking on either the Align or Justify buttons.

SAVE YOUR PARAGRAPH STYLE

Have you ever invested time in methodically selecting the perfect font, indent, or spacing for your text, only to realize you need to apply those attributes repeatedly throughout your project? Alternatively, perhaps you've determined that a particular indent is too substantial. Imagine the convenience of modifying one indent text box and instantly updating all other occurrences. This efficiency is achievable through the use of paragraph styles in InDesign.

Next, we shall be creating and saving a paragraph style, using these guides:

1) draw a text frame, enter text into it, and apply a first-line indent of your preferred size. It's not necessary to select all the text; just choose a portion.
2) Go to **Window** > **Styles** > **Paragraph Styles**. This action opens the Paragraph Styles panel.
3) In the **Paragraph Styles panel** menu, select the **Create New style** icon at the lower part of the panel – represented as a square with a plus sign inside.

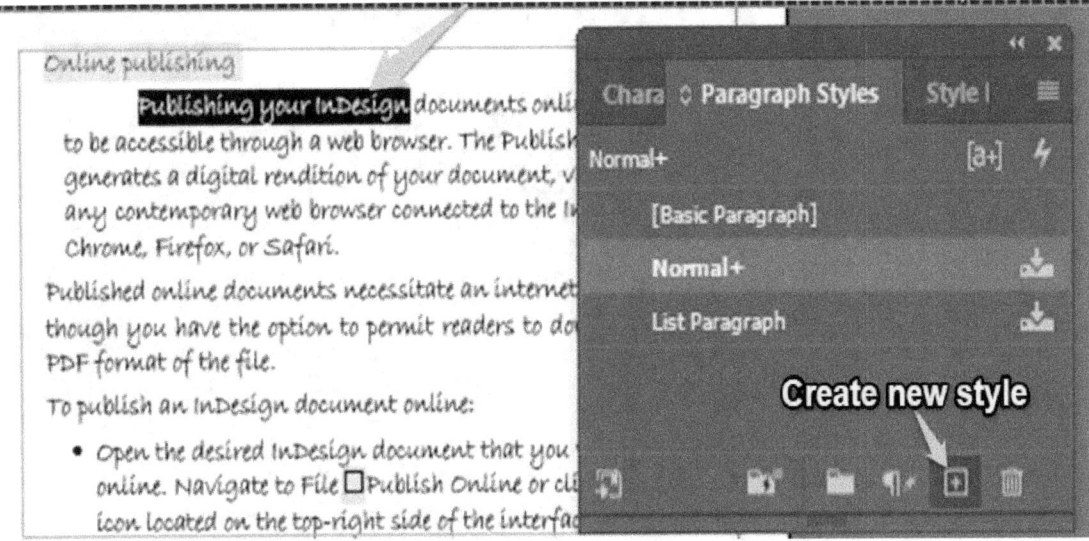

Click once on the newly created style, denoted as **Paragraph Style 1.** Observe that the **Paragraph** panel indicates that all attributes are already recorded within this unnamed style.

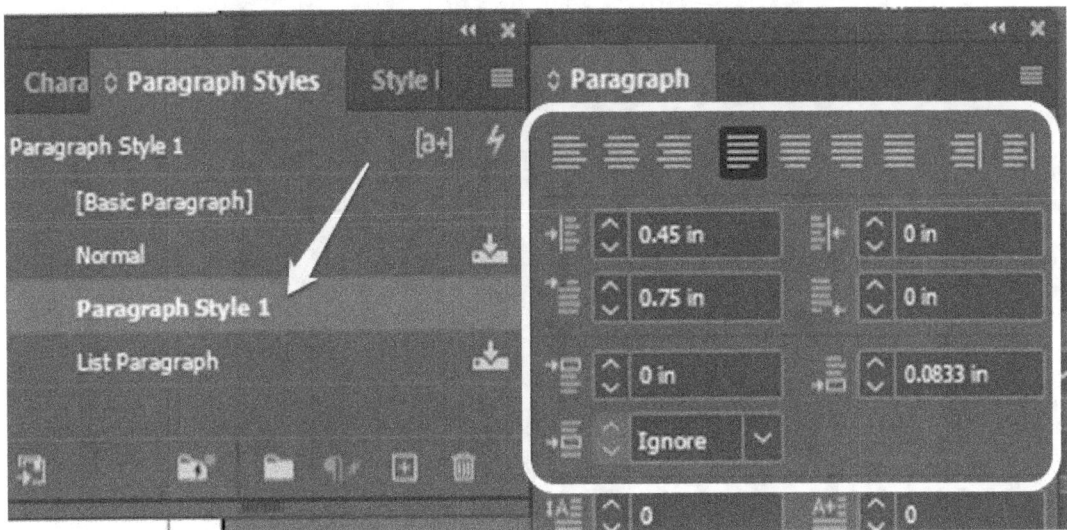

You can then double-click the new style, **Paragraph Style 1,** this opens the **Paragraph Style Options** dialog box. At this stage, simply provide a name for the style; no additional adjustments are necessary.

4) Rename "**Paragraph Style 1**" to a more fitting designation, like "**ParaBody**" and then press **OK**.

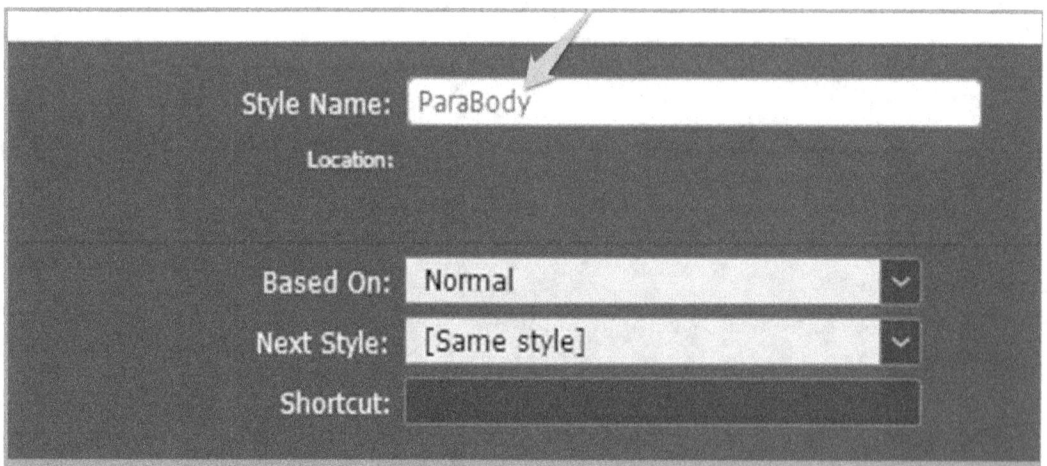

Your new style is now generated! Upon clicking **OK**, the dialog box will close, and the recently created style will be appended to the list in the **Paragraph Styles** panel. If you need to make adjustments, double-click the style name in the **Paragraph Styles** panel. To apply this style to other text frames, select the frame and click on the style within the **Paragraph Styles** panel.

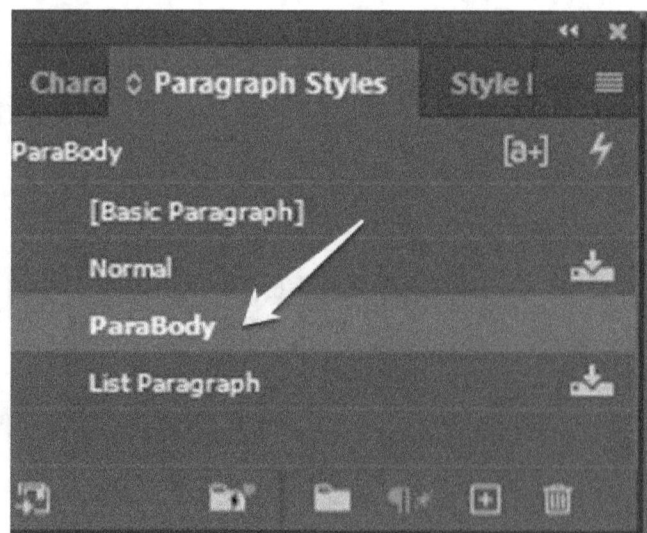

Note: To modify an existing style, go to the **Paragraph Style Options** dialog box, where a comprehensive list of various areas is available on the left side. Select an item from the list to inspect and alter its corresponding paragraph properties on the right side of the dialog box. This action ensures that all instances of that paragraph style are updated accordingly.

If you want to import paragraph styles from other documents or a file saved on your computer. This feature comes in handy, especially when you're working with a specific set of styles for a template. Here's how you can import paragraph styles:

- ✓ Go to the **Paragraph Styles** menu located on the right side of the header and choose "**Load Paragraph Styles**".

An **Open a File** dialog box will appear, prompting you to browse your hard drive for the file containing the styles you want to import.

- ✓ Select the **file**, then click "**Open**". Finally, click "**OK**" to load the selected styles into your document.

EXPLORING THE STORY EDITOR

When it comes to editing text within your documents, InDesign offers a handy built-in tool known as the story editor. This tool proves invaluable when accessing another text editor for making changes is inconvenient or simply not an option.

In addition to its native story editor, InDesign effortlessly integrates with another Adobe product called InCopy. Similar to Microsoft Word, InCopy serves as a text editor but boasts integration capabilities with InDesign, facilitating a smoother workflow for page layout tasks. For teams working in IT or editorial management, where some members focus solely on writing while others handle layout, exploring InCopy as a potential text editor could greatly enhance collaboration and efficiency.

GETTING HAND ON STORY EDITOR

InDesign's story editor provides an alternative view of a story, allowing you to format the text beyond the constraints of narrow columns. To open the story editor and edit a portion of text, check these instructions:

1) Locate the text you wish to edit and select the corresponding text frame using the **Selection** tool. A bounding box with handles will encompass the text frame.
2) Next, go to **Edit > Edit in Story Editor,** or use the keyboard shortcut **Command + Y** (macOS) or **Ctrl + Y** (Windows). This action opens the story editor in a new window directly within the InDesign workspace.

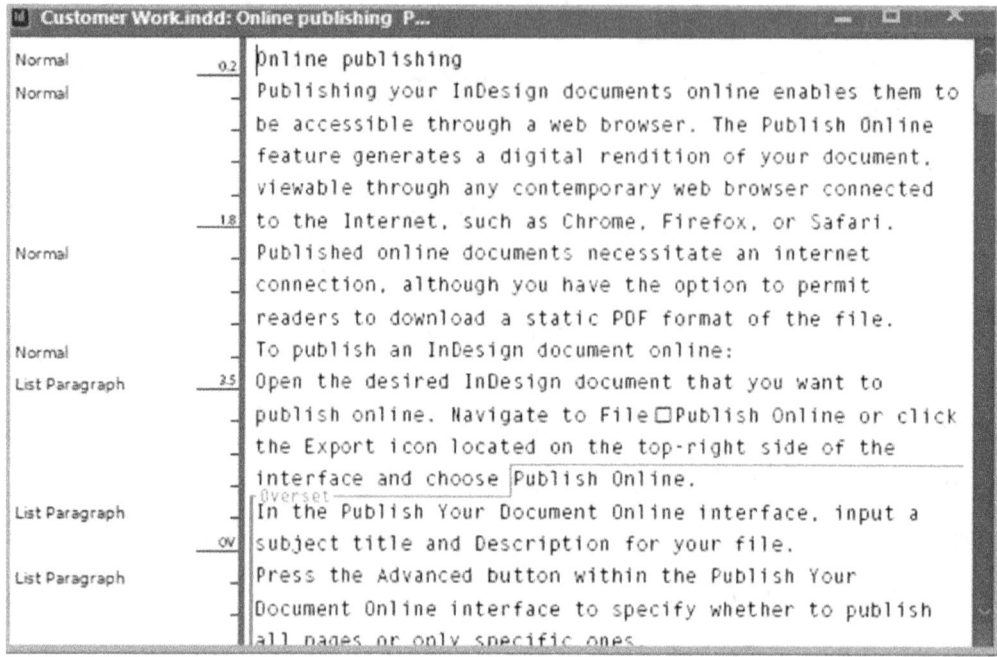

3) Modify the **story** in the window as needed and click the **Exit** button upon completion.

The story will be presented as a single block of text. whichever paragraph styles are applied to the text within the story editor are documented in an Information window located on the left side of the workspace. Take note that if you have tables in your story, they will be visible within the story editor. Simply click on the small table icon to collapse or expand the table directly within the story editor interface.

Note : If you prefer to make text edits while preserving the original text, you can opt for **Type** > **Track Changes** > **Track Changes in Current Story**. This ensures that the original text remains in the story editor alongside your marked changes. In layout mode, only the edited text becomes visible. Subsequently, you or an editor can utilize the Track Changes command in the Story Editor to accept or reject text edits.

VERIFYING ACCURATE SPELLING

Typos and spelling errors are common, making it essential to ensure correct spelling in a document before printing or exporting it to a PDF. Here's how to check for spelling in InDesign:

1) Go to **Edit** > **Spelling** > **Check Spelling**.

2) In the resultant **Check Spelling** dialog box, pick a search scope from the **Search** drop-down list, and then start the process by clicking the **Start** button. The spell check automatically scans the selection, story, or document.
3) Choose from the following options:
   - ✓ Press on the **Skip** button to disregard a misspelled word.
   - ✓ Opt for a suggested spelling correction from the list in the **Suggested Corrections** window and click the **Change** button.
   - ✓ Press **Ignore All** to overlook any additional instances of that word.

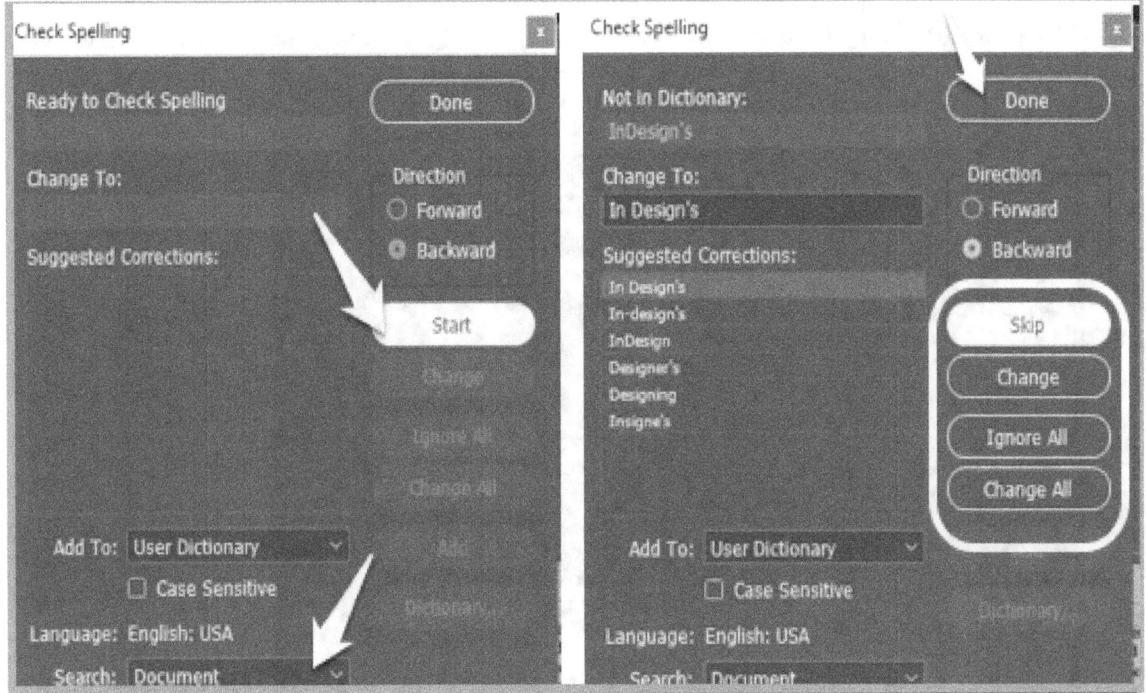

The corrected spelling is applied in the text frame, and the process moves on to the next spelling error.

4) Press the **Done** button to conclude the spell-check process. Alternatively, if InDesign notifies you that the spell check is complete, press **OK**.

Even when using the spell check feature to refine your writing, it's advisable to manually proofread your work. Spell checkers may not catch issues like grammatical errors or improper word usage, making manual proofreading an essential practice for ensuring the quality and accuracy of your writing.

EXPLORING CUSTOM SPELLING DICTIONARIES

When you add words like proper nouns to your dictionary is effortless; simply press the **Add** button.

You have the option to generate a user dictionary or incorporate user dictionaries from prior InDesign versions, files received from others, or a server. The included dictionary is then displayed across all your entire InDesign documents.

Create a personalized dictionary using the following steps:

1) Go to **InDesign** > **Preferences** > **Dictionary** (macOS) or **Edit** > **Preferences** > **Dictionary** (Windows).

The Preferences dialog box will open with the Dictionary area displayed.

2) Choose the **language** for your dictionary from the Language drop-down list.
3) Click the **New User Dictionary** button located below the Language drop-down list.

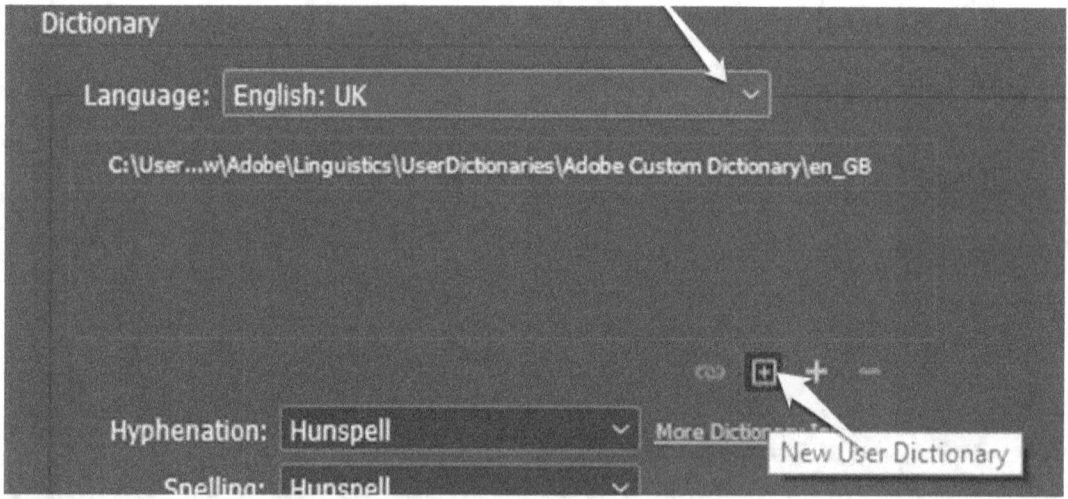

4) Provide a name and designate the location for the user dictionary, then click **OK/Save**.

Note : If you prefer to identify spelling errors without opening the Check Spelling dialog box, you can opt for Dynamic Spelling. This feature is accessible via **Edit** > **Spelling** > **Dynamic Spelling**, it highlights unknown words automatically. To correct spelling, simply **command-click** (macOS) or **right-click** (Windows) on the highlighted word. From the contextual menu that appears, you can choose the correct spelling or add the word to your dictionary.

WORKING WITH TABLES

A table consists of columns and rows that divide it into cells. Tables are a common sight on television, in books, in magazines, and throughout the web. For instance, a calendar can be considered a table, with days arranged in columns, weeks in rows, and each day occupying a cell. It also serves various purposes, such as cataloging products, events, or employees.

Here's an overview of the elements of a table and instructions on how to adjust them in InDesign:

- ❖ **Rows**: These extend horizontally across a table, and you have the flexibility to modify the height of each row.
- ❖ **Cells**: Each cell functions as a text frame where you can input information and format it similarly to any other text frame in InDesign.
- ❖ **Columns**: These are vertical within a table, and you can customize the width of each column.

CRAFTING TABLES:

The most straightforward method to create a table is to have your data readily available. While this isn't the exclusive approach, incorporating existing data is the most dynamic way to explore the capabilities of tables in InDesign.

Use these instructions to explore the table feature:

1) create a text area and input tabbed copy into it.

in this case, the text was entered by simply typing and pressing the Tab key between each new entry and then hitting the **Return** or **Enter** key for each new line. There's no need for the text to be perfectly aligned.

2) Select the text, and then opt for **Table** > **Convert Text to Table**.

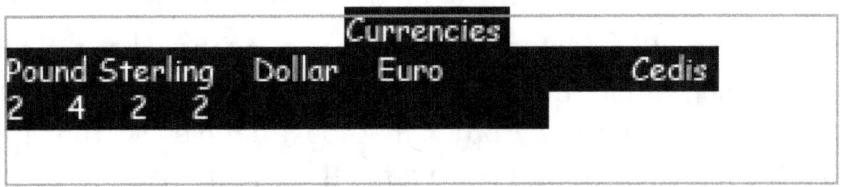

Once you open the **Convert Text to Table** Options dialog box, you'll have the choice to either manually select columns within the window or let the existing tabs in your text define the columns automatically. For further information on table styles, refer to the later section titled "Creating table styles". Furthermore, it's worth noting that you have the option to assign a table style simultaneously while converting text into a table.

3) Click **OK** to use the default settings and select the table.

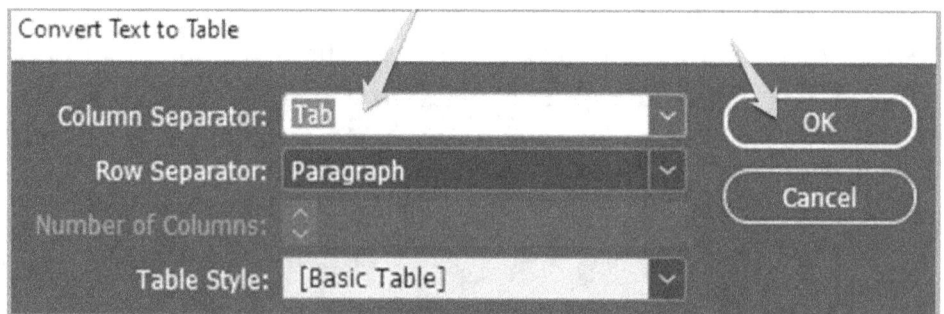

4) Press down the **Shift** key and use your mouse to click and drag the outer right border to expand or contract the table. The cells will adjust proportionally to the new table size.

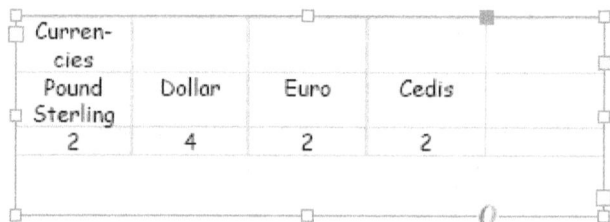

The cells uniformly house the new table size

5) Click twice and drag with the mouse across the top five cells to select them, then opt for **Table > Merge Cells** to combine them.

To craft a new table without existing text, use the following instructions:

1) Use the **Type** tool to draw a new text frame. Ensure that the insertion point is actively flashing within the newly created text frame. If it's not flashing, or if you formed the frame with any other methods, double-click on the text frame to activate the insertion point (I-bar) within the text frame.

Please keep in mind that you're not required to manually create a text frame. Instead, you can opt for **Table > Create Table**, which will automatically generate a text frame for you.

2) Go to **Table > Insert Table**. In the opened **Insert Table** dialog box, input the desired number of rows and columns in the **Rows** and **Columns** text fields. Subsequently, press **OK**.

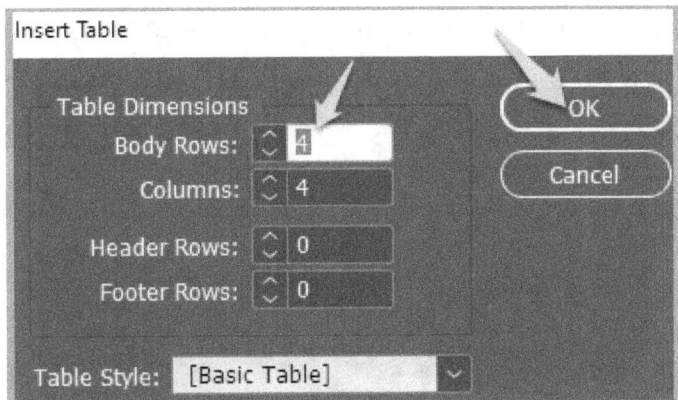

ALTERING TABLE SETTINGS

Various settings for tables can be controlled in InDesign. You have the flexibility to modify the text, fill, and stroke properties either for individual cells or for the entire table. This level of flexibility allows you to craft fully customized tables to present information in a resourceful and intelligent manner. In the following section, we illustrate some fundamental options for adjusting tables.

To get started on the modification of table settings, check the following steps:

1) Click on a cell within the table you wish to modify.
2) Go to **Table > Table Options > Table Setup**.

Upon selecting this option, the Table Options dialog box will appear, with the Table Setup tab activated. Within this dialog box, you'll find various tabs housing settings that can be adjusted for different aspects of the table.

Within the Table Setup tab, you can make modifications to **columns** and **rows**, adjust **borders** and **spacing**, and specify the **rendering of column or row strokes** to one another.

Currencies			
Pound Sterling	Dollar	Euro	Cedis
2	4	2	2

In this particular instance, we have altered the number of columns from five to four. Now, let's adjust the table border weight to a **4-point stroke**.

3) Click the **Preview** option located at the bottom of the dialog box.

Enabling the **Preview** option opens a preview window, allowing you to observe the changes applied to the table directly on the page as you continue to utilize the dialog box.

4) Navigate to the **Row Strokes** tab and adjust the settings.

In this illustration, we opted for an **Alternating Pattern of Every Second Row** from the drop-down list, modified the **Weight** setting to **4**, and altered the **Color** property for every second row to **RGB Magenta.**

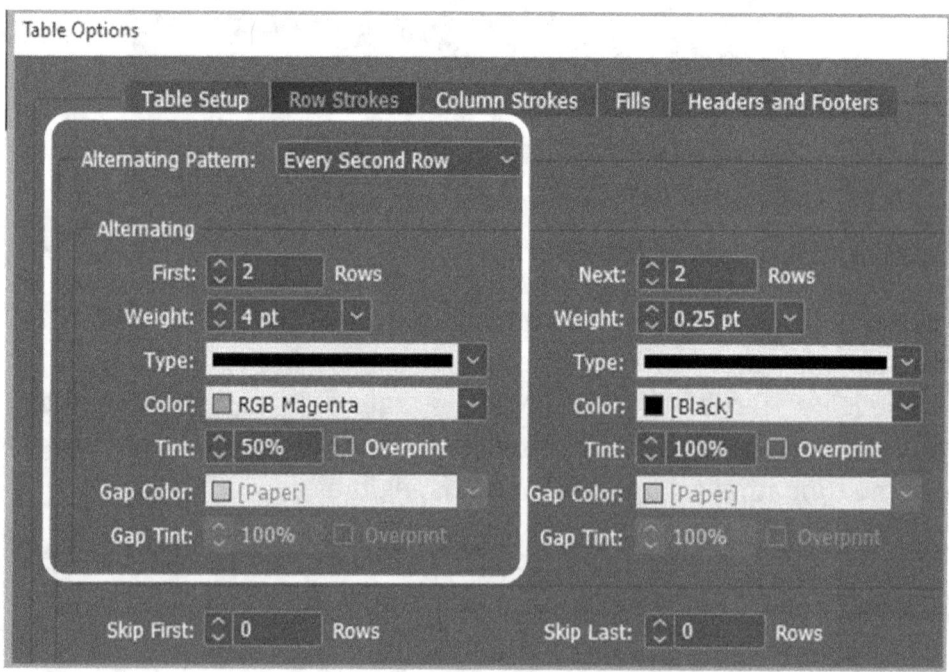

This action results in every second row having a **4-point magenta stroke**. Similarly, you can utilize the **Column Strokes** tab to modify properties for column strokes, as both tabs function similarly.

	Currencies			
	Pound Sterling	Dollar	Euro	Cedis
	2	4	2	2
	4	5	1	1
	2	4	4	6

5) Proceed to the **Fills** tab and make the necessary adjustments.

In this scenario, we chose **Every Other Row** from the **Alternating Pattern** drop-down list, changed the **Color** property to the same magenta, and set the **Tint** at the same default value of **20** percent. This step transforms the first row and every alternate row into a magenta-tinted appearance.

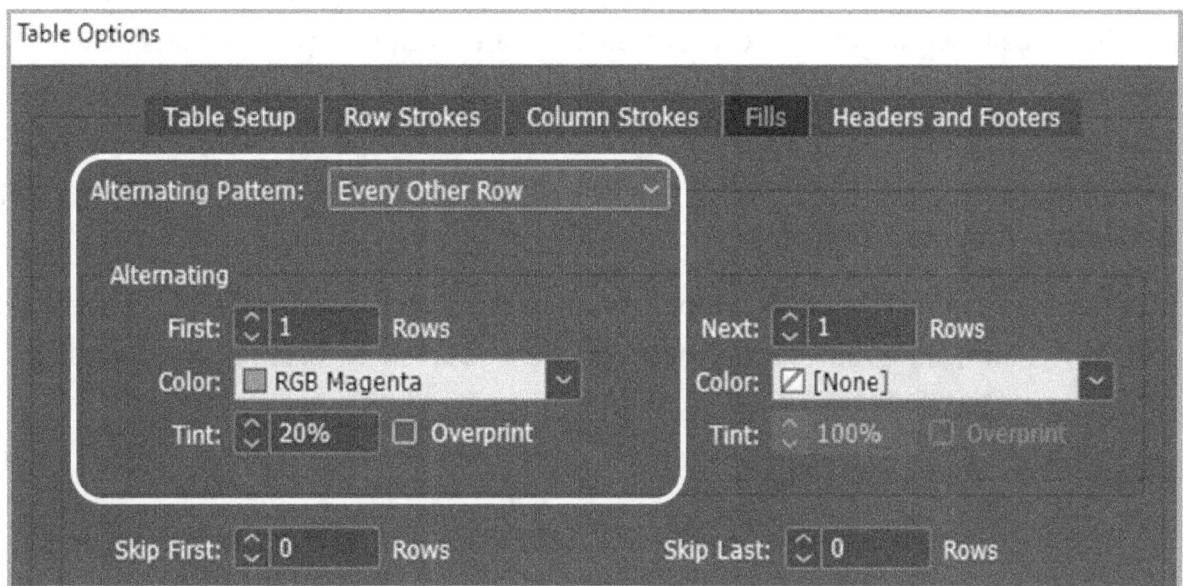

6) Press **Ok.** (The modifications made in the **Table Options** dialog box will be implemented on the table).

	Currencies		
Pound Sterling	Dollar	Euro	Cedis
2	4	2	2
4	5	1	1
2	4	4	6

7) Select a table cell to activate the insertion point. When the selected cell is highlighted, locate an image that you can copy to the Clipboard and press **Command + C** (macOS) or **Ctrl + C** (Windows) to copy the image.
8) Go back to **InDesign** and insert the image into the table cell by using the keyboard shortcut **Command + V** (Mac) or **Ctrl + V** (Windows).

Note : The image will be placed in the table cell and the width and height of the cell altered based on the size of the image. confirm that the insertion point is active in the cell before pasting to the cell.

Just bear in mind that inserting a large image into a table cell might cause it to overflow, hiding the image from view. To resolve this, you can resize the image using Photoshop before insertion or simply create a frame for the image by clicking and dragging when the cursor indicates it's loaded.

You have flexibility not only in adjusting the table itself but also in customizing individual cells within it. You can access the **Cell Option**s by selecting **Table > Cell Options > Text**, or fine-tune each cell's properties via the **Paragraph** panel. Additionally, you can modify the table's structure, including row and column count as well as their dimensions, through the **Tables** panel. Simply navigate to **Window > Type & Tables > Table** to access it.

InDesign also supports importing tables from external programs like Excel. To do this, go to **File > Place**, and your spreadsheet will be imported as a table into InDesign for further editing as needed.

CREATING TABLE STYLES

When you invest time in adjusting fills, strokes, and spacing within your table, preserving those settings as a style becomes essential. The process of creating a table style enables you to efficiently apply your customized table setup to future tables. To begin the creation of a table style, check these instructions:

1) Customize the appearance of the table to your preferences.

The straightforward method for crafting a table style is to finalize the table setup and set up a table appearance the way you desire.

2) Highlight the table. Use the text tool to press and drag, selecting the entire table.

Currencies			
Pound Sterling	Dollar	Euro	Cedis
2	4	2	2
4	5	1	1
2	4	4	6

3) Go to **Window > Styles > Table Styles**. This action opens the **Table Styles** panel.
4) While holding down the **Option** key (macOS), or **Alt** key (Windows) press the **Create New Style** button located at the bottom of the **Table Styles** panel. The **New Table Style** dialog box will be displayed.

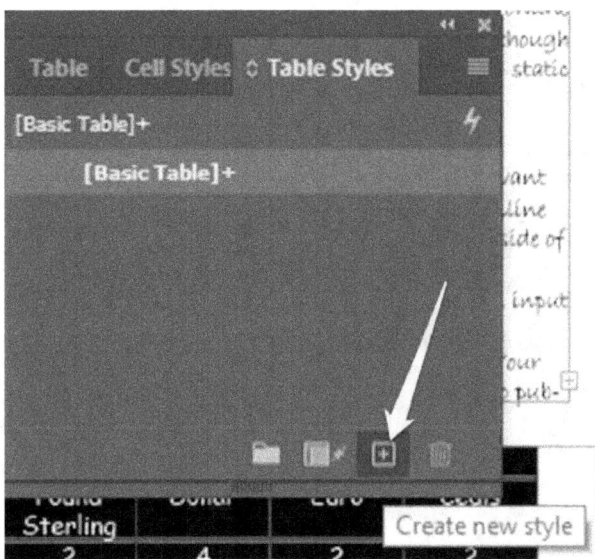

5) Provide a name for the style and press **OK**.

Your table's customized attributes are now saved as a style for future use.

Note: To modify the attributes of a table style, ensure that no elements are currently picked, then double-click the designated style in the Table Styles panel to adjust it.

EXPLORING TEXT ON A PATH

Text on a path offers the opportunity to produce captivating effects. The **Type On a Path** tool allows you to have text follow the curvature of a line or shape. This functionality proves especially valuable when aiming to craft engaging title effects on a page.

Use the following instructions to create text on a path:

- Draw any **shape** of your choice on the page with the Pen tool. At least you should create one curve on the path with the Pen tool. We shall discuss the Pen tool at full length in **Chapter 5** of this user guide.
- Click and hold the **Type tool** to see the full menu and select the **Type On a Path** tool.

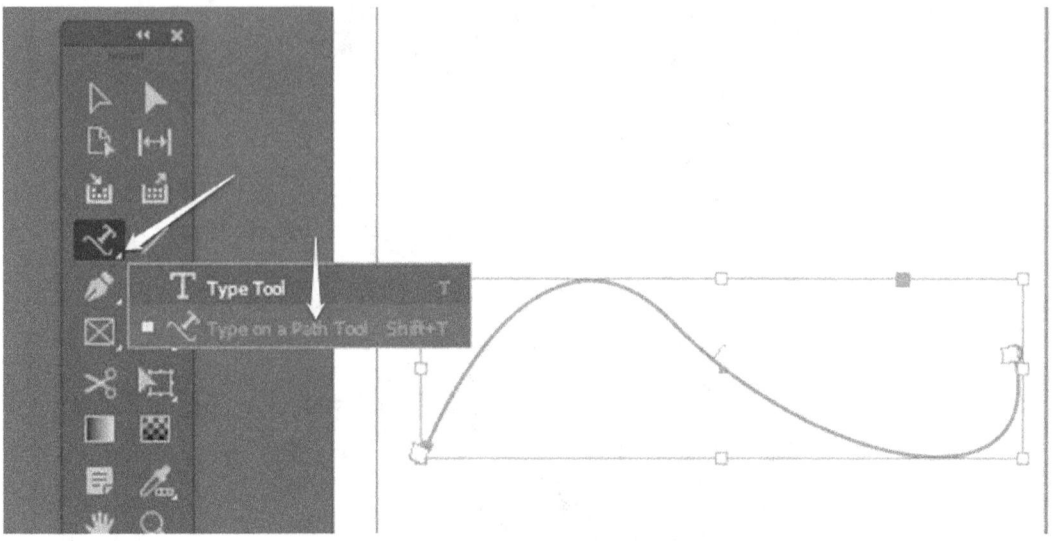

- Position the cursor close to the created path.

When you place the curse close to the path, a plus **(+)** sign displays beside the cursor, click when this plus **(+)** sign shows enabling you to type along the path.

- Click when the + icon appears, and enter the text along the path.

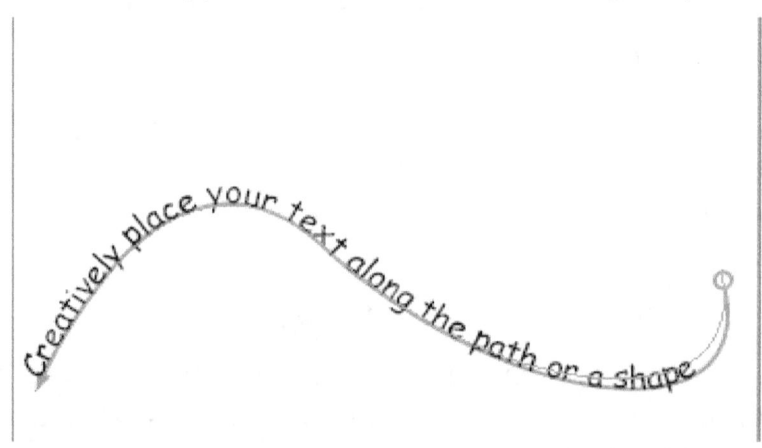

when you click on the path, an insertion point pops up at its starting point, allowing you to begin adding text along the path. Selecting text on a path is similar to selecting regular text: just drag over it to highlight.

To alter the properties of text on a path, simply select the text and access the **Type On a Path Options** dialog box. You can find this by going to **Type > Type on a Path > Options**. Inside this dialog, you have the freedom to apply various effects to alter how each character interacts with the path. try to experiment with options like flipping the text, adjusting character spacing, and aligning characters to either the path or to stroke of the path via the "**Align**" and "**To Path**" drop-down menus respectively. Feel free to play around with these settings to see their impact on your text. Once satisfied, click **OK** to apply changes. Should you wish to revert any undesired alterations, simply press **Command + Z** (macOS) or **Ctrl + Z** (Windows) to undo.

To maintain text visibility while hiding the path, simply set the stroke weight of the path to **0** pt.

CHAPTER FOUR
GETTING FAMILIARIZED WITH PAGE LAYOUT

This section will guide you through the process of combining graphics and text to begin the creation of page layouts. Engaging and imaginative page layouts serve to captivate attention, enhancing the impact of both images and words within a publication. A compelling layout encourages a broader audience to engage with the text presented on a page.

IMPORTING PICTURES

Several types of image files, including PSD, PDF, AI, PNG, JPG, and TIF, can be inserted into an InDesign document. Images are brought into graphic frames, which can be created in advance or automatically generated by InDesign if a frame is not already present when the image is inserted into the page.

Importing an image into your InDesign document creates a link to the original image file, which remains necessary for printing or exporting the final document. By utilizing the Link features, you can conveniently monitor the image's status and receive notifications if any changes occur to the original, prompting you to update it accordingly. Furthermore, when importing an image, you have access to additional settings through the Image Import Options dialog box.

Consider these instructions to import an image into your InDesign layout:

1) Ensure that nothing on the page is currently selected. If there's a selected object, press on an empty area to deselect everything before proceeding.
2) Go to **File** > **Place** to insert locally accessible images. The Place dialog box will appear, giving you the privilege to browse your hard drive for image files to import. This dialog box facilitates the import of various file types, not limited to images.
3) Choose the **image** you wish to import and press Open. The Place dialog box will close, and the cursor will now display a thumbnail of the selected image.

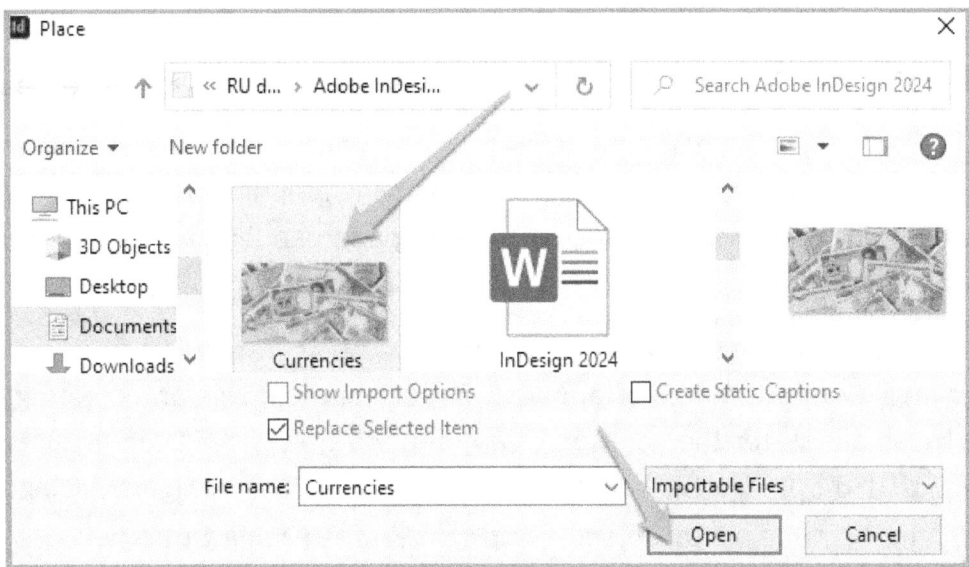

if you want to import several images at one time, kindly hold-down the **Command** (macOS) or **Ctrl** (Windows) and click all the files to select multiple images or files

4) Position the cursor at the desired location for the top-left corner of the first image on the page, and then click the **mouse**. If you've chosen multiple images, utilize the left and right arrow keys to navigate through the thumbnail images within your loaded cursor before clicking on the page. Each click made on the page places the next image until all selected images have been placed.

Note : In your publication, images are brought in and positioned within a graphic frame. Using either the **Selection** or **Direct Selection** tool, you can resize, relocate, and adjust the image as needed. Alternatively, you can manipulate both the frame and the image simultaneously by using the **Selection** tool.

When adding multiple images, streamline the process by placing them all at once. Simply select the desired images and press the **Shift + Command** keys on Mac or **Shift +**

Ctrl keys on Windows while dragging a rectangle with your mouse. This action evenly spaces the images in a grid layout, enhancing efficiency and precision.

If the imported image appears too large for your layout or requires cropping, there's no need to fret. For guidance on selecting and modifying graphic frames, refer to **Chapter 5** of this user guide. Likewise, to explore importing and handling text and stories, consult **Chapter 3**.

Occasionally, it's simpler to begin with an empty graphic frame and subsequently insert an image into it rather than simultaneously importing the image and creating the frame. This approach allows for the creation of an empty frame with fitting properties preset, to ensure that the image fits seamlessly upon import. To configure fitting properties within an empty frame, go to **Object** > **Fitting** > **Frame Fitting Options**.

IMPORTING YOUR PDF FILES

You can import PDF files and use them as images within InDesign layouts. During the import process, you can preview and crop pages with the **Place PDF** dialog box. (To access this dialog box, choose **File** > **Place**, pick the **Show Import Options** checkbox, and click **Open**.

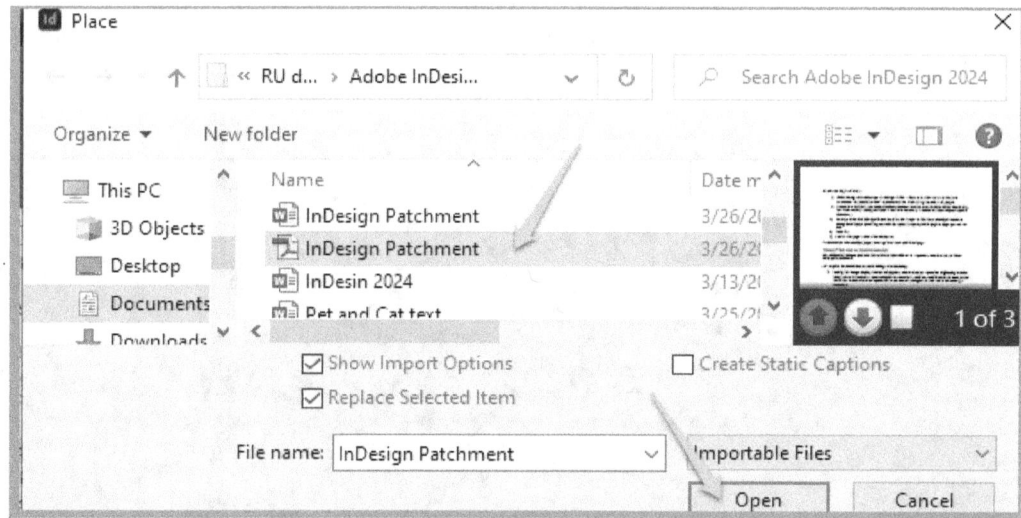

On a Mac Operating System, you need to press the **Options** button to reveal the **Show Import Options** checkbox.) It's important to note that you import one page at a time, using the **Forward** and **Back** buttons beneath the preview to select the page for placement. Additionally, it's not possible to import video, sound, or buttons, and once imported, the PDF cannot be edited within InDesign—it functions more like importing a static image, such as a JPEG file.

The options available in the Place PDF dialog box include:

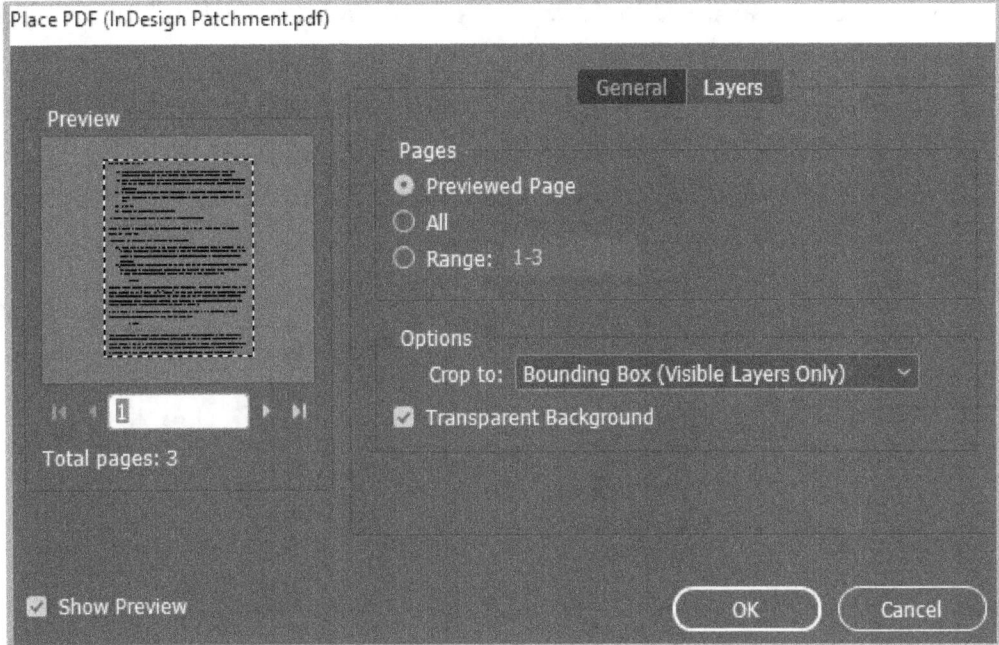

- ➢ **Crop To**: This drop-down list allows you to crop the page being imported. The available options may vary depending on the content of the PDF. The hatched outline in the preview provides a visual representation of the crop marks.
- ➢ **Transparent Background**: Enabling this checkbox results in a transparent background for the PDF, allowing elements on the InDesign page to show through. If this option is not selected, the PDF background is imported as a solid white.

If your monitor provides sufficient space to simultaneously display your document window and computer folders, you have the convenience of dragging and dropping image files directly into your layout. This bypasses the need to use the Place command altogether to streamline your workflow.

IMPORTING INDESIGN DOCUMENTS INSIDE ANOTHER

It is possible to embed one InDesign document within another, allowing for seamless integration. This functionality may seem unconventional at first, but it offers numerous benefits. For instance, you can effortlessly include a page from a book in a catalog without the need to convert the book page into an image format. This approach not only streamlines the process by eliminating an extra step but also results in a higher-quality representation of the image within InDesign.

Explore the benefit of this feature using the following instructions:

1) While having a document open, either go to **File** > **Place** or use the keyboard shortcut **Command + D** (macOS) or **Ctrl + D** (Windows) The Place dialog box will be displayed.
2) Ensure to select the **Show Import Options** checkbox located at the bottom of the Place dialog box. On a macOS, clicking the **Options** button is necessary to reveal the Show Import Options checkbox.).

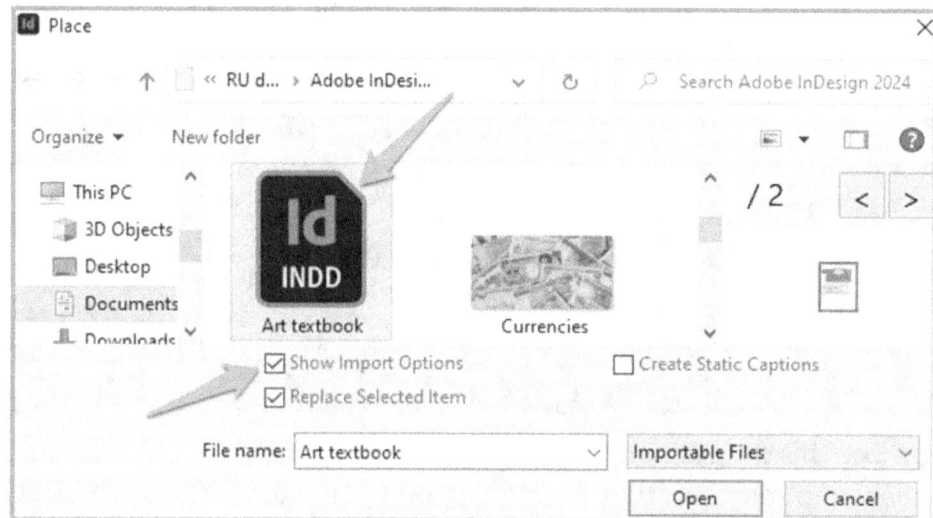

3) Go to your desired InDesign file and double-click to open it. The Place InDesign Document dialog box displays, providing you with the option to specify which page or pages you wish to add.

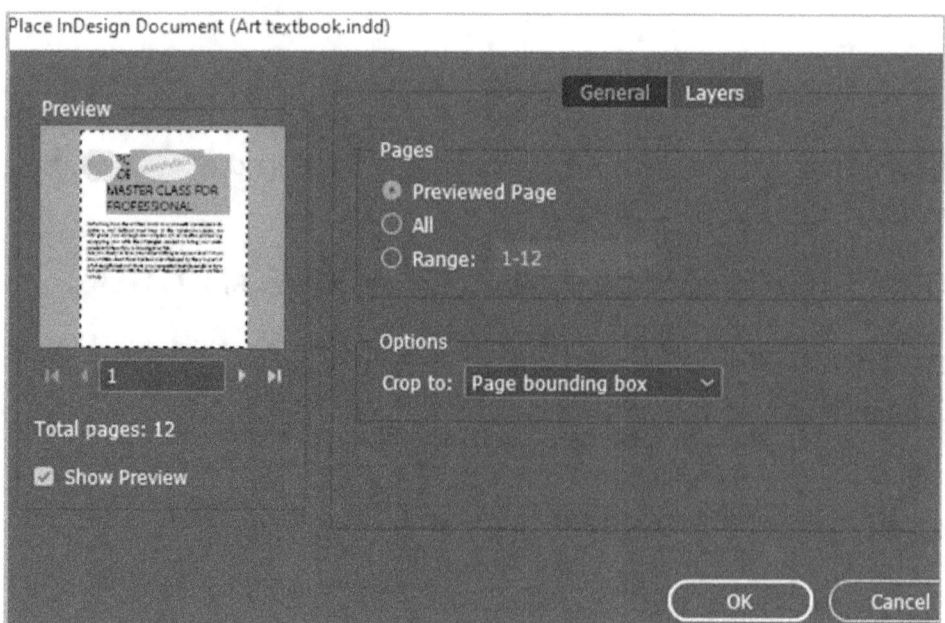

4) Press **OK** and click on the page to insert the document.

For documents with multiple pages, Press again for each additional page.

CONNECTING AND EMBEDDING IMAGES

When importing images, you have the option to either link them to your document or embed them inside your document.

Let's explore the distinction between linking and embedding.

- ➤ **Linking:** The image displayed in the InDesign document serves as a preview, originating from an image stored elsewhere on your computer or network. Should any modifications be made to the linked file, it necessitates an update to ensure that the changes are reflected in the InDesign document.
- ➤ **Embedding:** The image is duplicated and stored within the InDesign document itself. The original file's location or any subsequent alterations to the file become irrelevant, as the embedded image is independently copied and saved directly inside the InDesign document.

When printing or exporting a document, InDesign relies on the linked images to gather the essential data required for producing high-quality printed documents, PDF files, or images suitable for web posting. InDesign monitors linked files and notifies you of any relocations or modifications. To update links for an image, you can choose "**Update Link**" or "**Relink**" from the **Links** panel menu after selecting the image in the Links panel. This prompts you to locate the file on your hard drive, establishing a new link to the updated location. When sharing your InDesign file with others, it's essential to include the linked files along with the document. We shall discuss further on this in Chapter 8

Note: Opting for image embedding over linking results in an increase in your publication's file size, attributable to the additional data stored within the document.

To determine whether files are embedded or linked, go to the **Links** panel. Simply access it by going to **Window** > **Links**. Once open, you can easily identify any linked or embedded images listed within the panel.

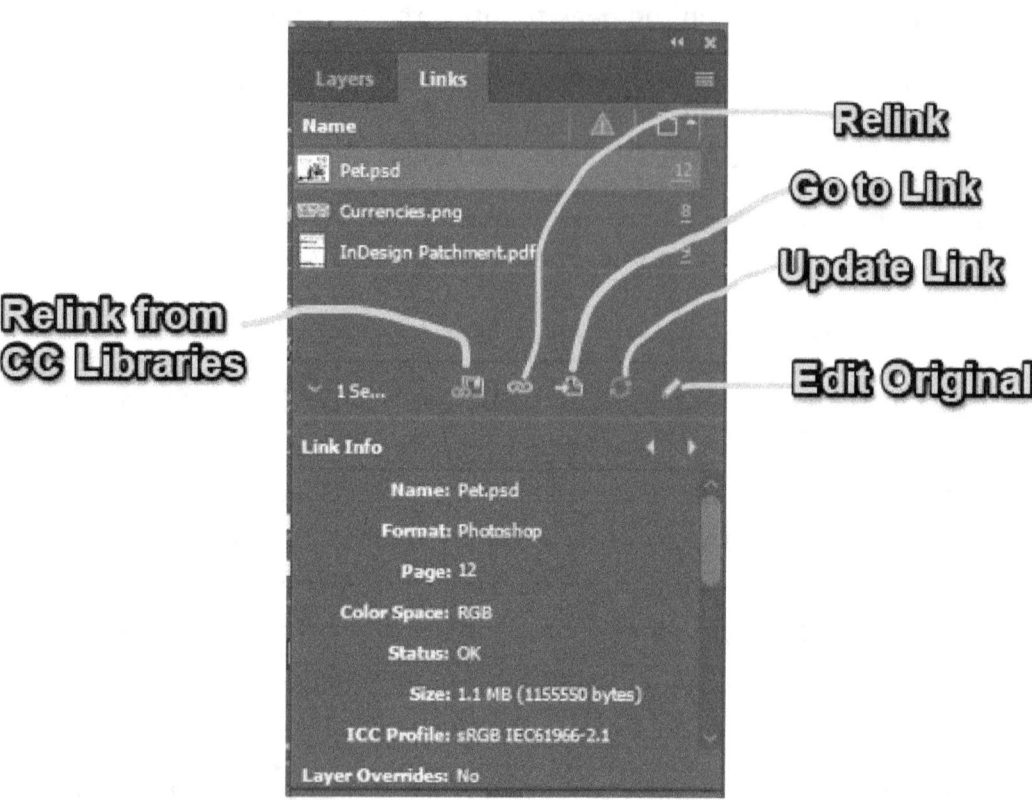

To embed a file with the **Links** panel menu. From the list of linked files, select the desired one, then click on the Link panel menu located in the top-right corner. Choose "**Embed Link**" if you prefer the linked file to be embedded within the document. Conversely, opt for "**Unembed Link**" from the Links panel menu to maintain the file as a linked asset rather than embedding it. It's advisable to link all images to prevent excessive file sizes and to retain the flexibility of altering the image files independently.

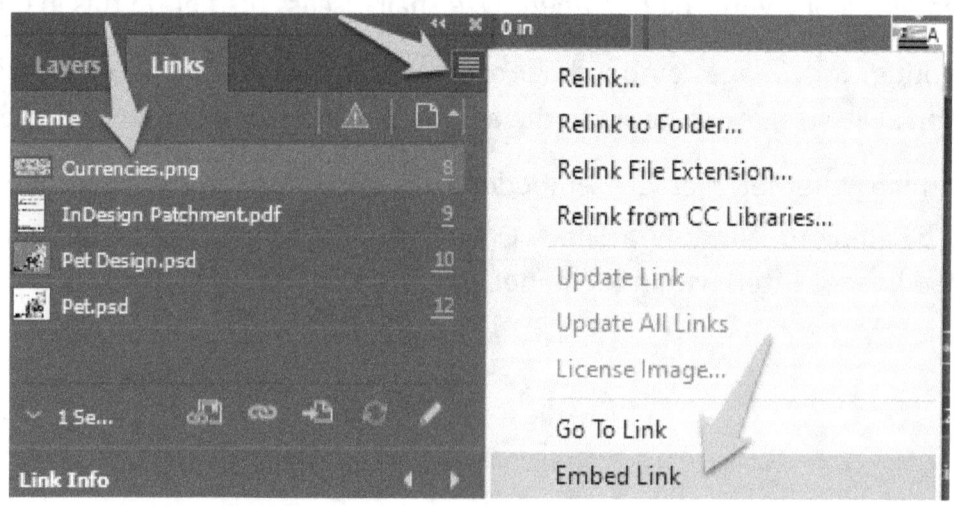

CONFIGURING IMAGE QUALITY AND DISPLAY

You have the option to choose quality settings that influence how images appear within an InDesign layout. These settings can be advantageous in enhancing workflow efficiency, particularly on older or slower computers or when dealing with numerous images. Opting for higher resolution when displaying images provides a more accurate preview of the final print project, potentially minimizing the need for multiple proof prints. It's important to note that these settings solely affect the way images are visualized during the document creation process in InDesign and do not have any impact on the quality of the final printed or exported work.

To modify the image display quality, locate **InDesign** > **Preferences** > **Display Performance** (macOS) or **Edit** > **Preferences** > **Display Performance** (Windows)). From there, you can pick one of the available settings from the **Default View** drop-down list.

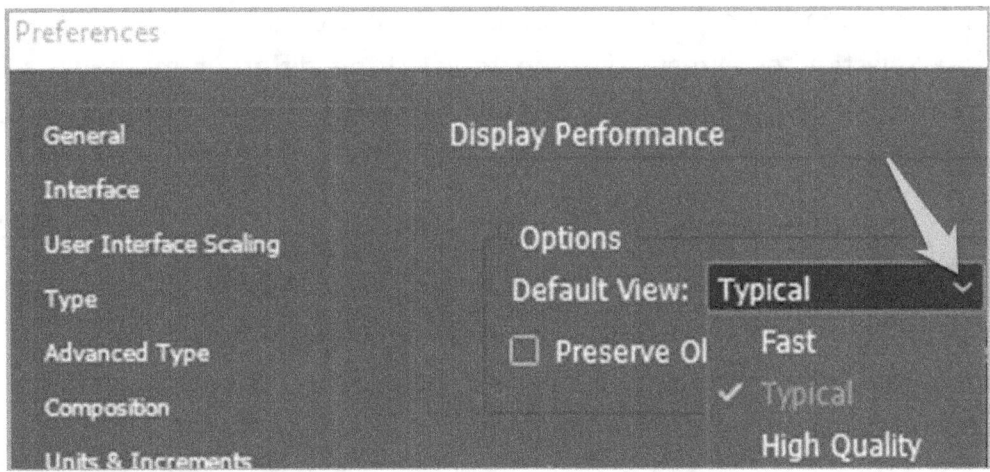

- **Typical (default)**: This option may result in slightly blocky appearances for bitmaps, especially when zoomed in. Choosing this setting enhances the speed of zooming in and out. InDesign utilizes a preview it generated (or one already imported with the file) to show the image on the screen.
- **Fast**: To optimize performance, the whole image or graphic is displayed in a grayscale format.
- **High Quality**: the original image is displayed on the screen, allowing for a precise preview of the final layout. However, it's worth noting that selecting this option may lead to slower performance in InDesign.

Take note of the distinctions among these settings illustrated below:

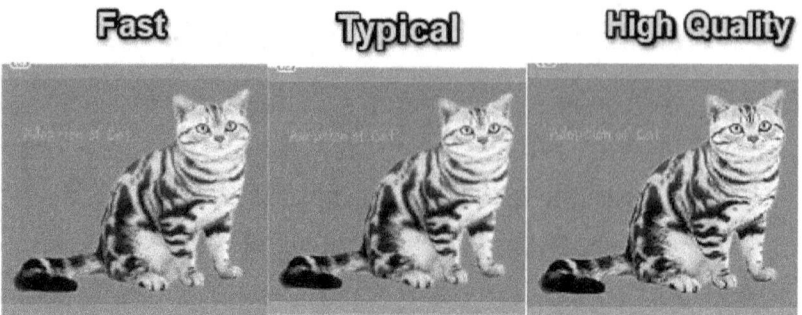

To adjust the display settings for a specific image, first, select the graphic frame containing the image. Then, navigate to Object ⇨ Display Performance. From the submenu that appears, select one of the three available options to modify the display performance according to your preference.

SELECTING IMAGES

Once an image is imported into a document, there are various ways to select it using either the Selection or Direct Selection tools. Using different methods is beneficial based on whether you intend to pick and edit solely the graphic frame or exclusively the image within it.

To choose and subsequently modify an image on the page, check the following instructions:

1) Import an image into InDesign, placing it within a graphic frame.
2) Using the **Selection tool**, drag one of the corner handles on the graphic frame inward toward the center of the frame.

When you resize the graphic frame, only the frame itself adjusts, not the image within it. Consequently, the image may seem cropped because the frame's dimensions have changed, while the image retains its original size within the frame. This effect is illustrated below.

3) Go to **Edit** > **Undo** or use the shortcut **Command +Z** (macOS) or **Ctrl + Z** (Windows) to reverse any alterations made to the image. This action restores the image to its original appearance on the page.
4) Keep on using the **Selection tool** to click on the center of the picture, where a circle appears, and move the image inside the frame. Although the frame retains its original size, the content within is repositioned.

5) Toggle to the **Direct Selection** tool, and subsequently, click within the image. Drag to relocate the image within the bounding box of the graphic frame.

As you hover the cursor over the graphic, a hand icon appears. When you drag the image slightly beyond the boundaries of the graphic frame, that portion of the image becomes hidden—it won't appear in printouts or exports.

Note: You have the option to configure the frame or image for resizing by navigating to **Object** > **Fitting** and choosing an appropriate option. It is also possible to specify this fitting preference before placing an image, particularly useful when crafting templates. To resize before placing an image, go to **Object** > **Fitting** > **Frame Fitting Options.**

The Links panel serves as a valuable tool for locating images within documents, facilitating their opening for editing purposes, and providing essential information about selected images.

ALTERING TEXT AND GRAPHICS WITHIN A LAYOUT

InDesign provides a rich array of tools designed to facilitate the seamless integration of text and graphics within a layout. Whether through the Tools panel, various commands, or panel options, InDesign empowers users with extensive control over the manipulation of graphics and text across a spread.

PAGE ORIENTATION AND DIMENSIONS

In the process of creating a new document, users have the flexibility to define its page orientation and size. Should the need arise to modify these settings post-document creation, simply navigate to **File** > **Document Setup** and adjust the following options, which apply to all pages within the document

- ✓ **Page Orientation:** Opt for either Landscape or Portrait. When initiating a new document, one of the primary decisions involves page orientation. Landscape entails a wider layout, while Portrait offers a taller one.
- ✓ **Page Size:** Select from a variety of standardized preset sizes including Letter, Legal, and Tabloid. Alternatively, customize the page size according to your requirements. Ensure the page size aligns accurately with the type of paper intended for printing or screen size if you want to publish your work digitally.

You can utilize the **Pages** panel to customize the dimensions of individual pages, this allows for variations in size across different pages if needed. Further details on this topic are discussed later in this chapter, specifically in the section titled **"Managing Pages and the Pages Panel"**.

MARGINS, COLUMNS, AND GUTTERS

For an accurate page layout, margins, columns, and gutters play pivotal roles in dividing a page and defining its dimensions:

- ✓ **Margin:** This space exists between the page's edge and the primary printed content. Collectively, the four margins **(top, bottom, left, and right)** form a rectangular frame around the page. Margins remain invisible in printed or exported publications.
- ✓ **Column:** The column splits a page into a section dedicated to arranging text and graphics. Initially, a page features at least one column situated between the margins. Users can introduce additional column guides, represented by paired

lines with a gutter area in between. Column guides do not appear in printed or exported publications.
- ✓ **Gutter:** this is the gap between two columns on a page, serving to prevent them from merging. The width of the gutter can be specified by accessing **Layout** > **Margins** and **Columns**.

In Chapter 2 of this user guide, we delve into setting margins and columns when initially creating a new document. However, it's important to note that you can also adjust these settings after the document's creation, this allows you to customize values on individual pages.

You also have the flexibility to modify the gutter, which determines the width of the space between each column. To make these adjustments, navigate to the Margins and Columns dialog box by selecting **Layout** > **Margins** and **Columns**. From there, you can tailor the settings for each page according to your preferences.

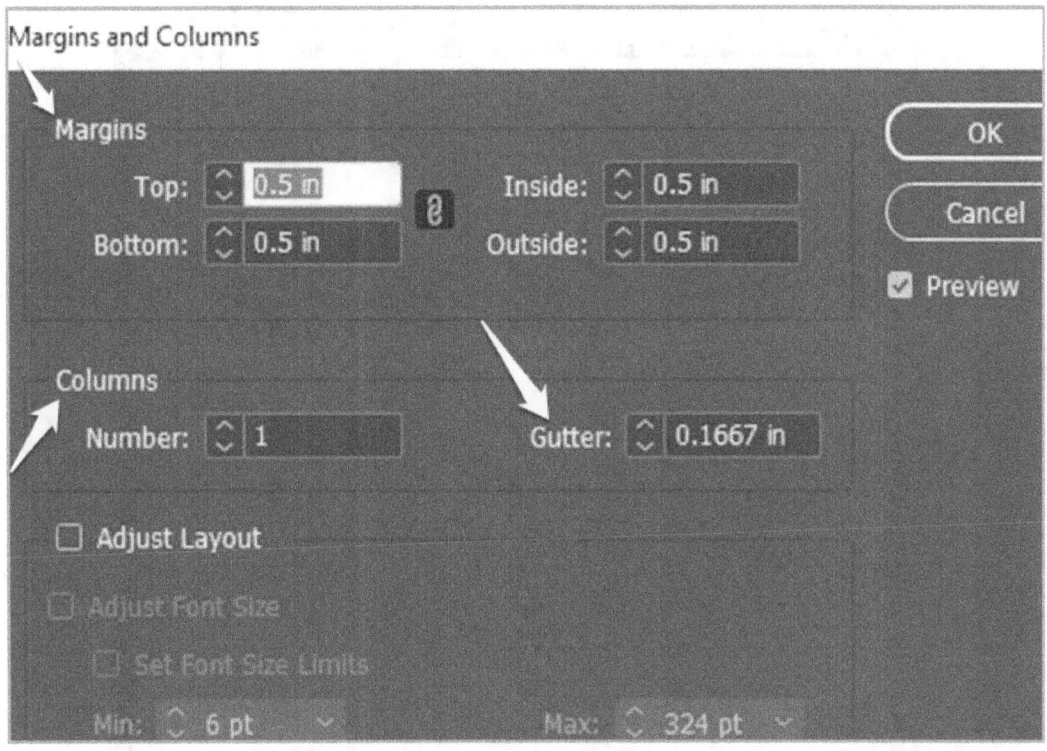

Margins and columns serve as helpful guides for positioning and aligning objects on a page. They enable objects to snap into place accurately, facilitating precise alignment of multiple elements.

UTILIZING GUIDES AND SNAPPING

Incorporating guides during the creation of page layouts is highly beneficial as they assist in accurately aligning elements and positioning objects within the layout. Aligning objects by visual estimation can be challenging, as it's often difficult to discern slight misalignments without zooming in to a significant degree.

Ensure snapping is activated by navigating to **View** > **Grids and Guides** > **Snap to Guides**. Snapping enhances the usefulness of guides and grids. When dragging an object close to the grid, it automatically attaches to the guideline, as if magnetized. Aligning objects to guides becomes effortless once created, and InDesign conveniently displays temporary guides when objects are moved near each other or close to a guide.

Guides play a crucial role in crafting a layout. The following are the various types of guides you can explore in InDesign:

- ✓ **Column Guides**: These guides evenly divide a page into columns and are useful for aligning text frames within a document. Within InDesign, column guides can be generated when creating a new document with multiple columns. Additionally, they can be adjusted post-document creation by accessing **Layout** > **Margins** and **Columns**.
- ✓ **Margin Guides:** These guides demarcate the space between the page edge and the main printable area. We have discussed this in the earlier section.
- ✓ **Ruler Guides**: this is manually set and can be utilized for aligning graphics, measuring objects, or specifying asset placement within a layout.
- ✓ **Smart Guides**: As previously discussed, smart guides enable precise alignment of objects on an InDesign page, whether to other objects or to the page itself. Smart Object alignment facilitates effortless snapping to page item centers or edges or page center itself, with visual feedback indicating the object being snapped to.
- ✓ **Liquid Guides**: Particularly handy when designing layouts intended for various tablet displays.

For instructions on displaying and concealing grids and guides, go to Chapter 2 of this user guide.

InDesign provides you with the capability to remove all guides simultaneously. Simply **Control-click** on the ruler (on macOS) or **right-click** on the ruler (on Windows), then select "**Delete All Guides on Spread**" from the contextual menu.

LOCKING OBJECTS AND GUIDES

You can fasten elements such as objects and guides in place, which proves particularly beneficial after meticulously aligning elements on a page. Locking objects or guides avoids unintentional movement from their designated positions.

To lock an object, check the following guides:

1) grab a drawing tool to generate an object on a page, then use the Selection tool to select the object. A bounding box with handles will appear upon selection.
2) Go to **Object** > **Lock**.

The object is now fixed in place. Attempting to move the object using the Selection or Direct Selection tools will not alter its current position.

To lock guides in position, check these instructions:

1) Drag a pair of ruler guides onto the page by clicking within a ruler and dragging towards the page. A line will appear on the page. (If rulers are not visible around the pasteboard, Go to **View** > **Rulers**.

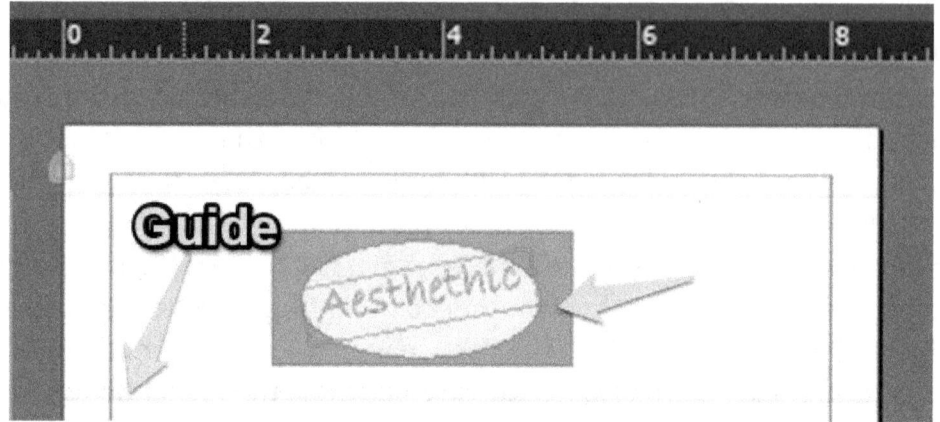

2) You may adjust the position of a ruler guide, if necessary, and once satisfied with their placements, select **View** > **Grids & Guides** > **Lock Guides**.

Note : All guides within the workspace will be locked. Attempting to select and move a guide will keep it in its current position, rendering it immovable. If there are any column guides on the page, they will also be locked.

In your publications, you can use layers as a means of organizing diverse content types, including guides. Think of layers as transparent sheets overlaid on one another, allowing for the stacking of elements on a page. For instance, you might stack graphics or group similar items like images or text onto the same layer. Each layer is assigned a distinct bounding box color, aiding in identifying which item corresponds to which layer. if you are familiar with Photoshop, you will have a deeper understanding of layers.

UNITING TEXT AND GRAPHICS ON A PAGE

Text and graphics on a page should seamlessly complement each other to craft an appealing layout. Fortunately, using text wrap enables you to achieve a harmonious visual balance between text and graphics. In this section, you'll discover how to wrap text around images and graphics in your publications.

WRAPPING TEXT AROUND OBJECTS

Text wrapping around images is a common practice in both print and web page layouts. To modify text wrap settings, open the Text Wrap panel via **Window** > **Text Wrap**. At the top of the panel, you'll find five buttons enabling you to choose different text wrap styles for the selected object. Below these buttons are text fields where you can input offset values for the text wrap. These fields are grayed out if the option is unavailable.

Furthermore, the Text Wrap panel contains a dropdown menu at the bottom, offering various contour options. Here's what happens when you select one of these buttons to put text around a shape:

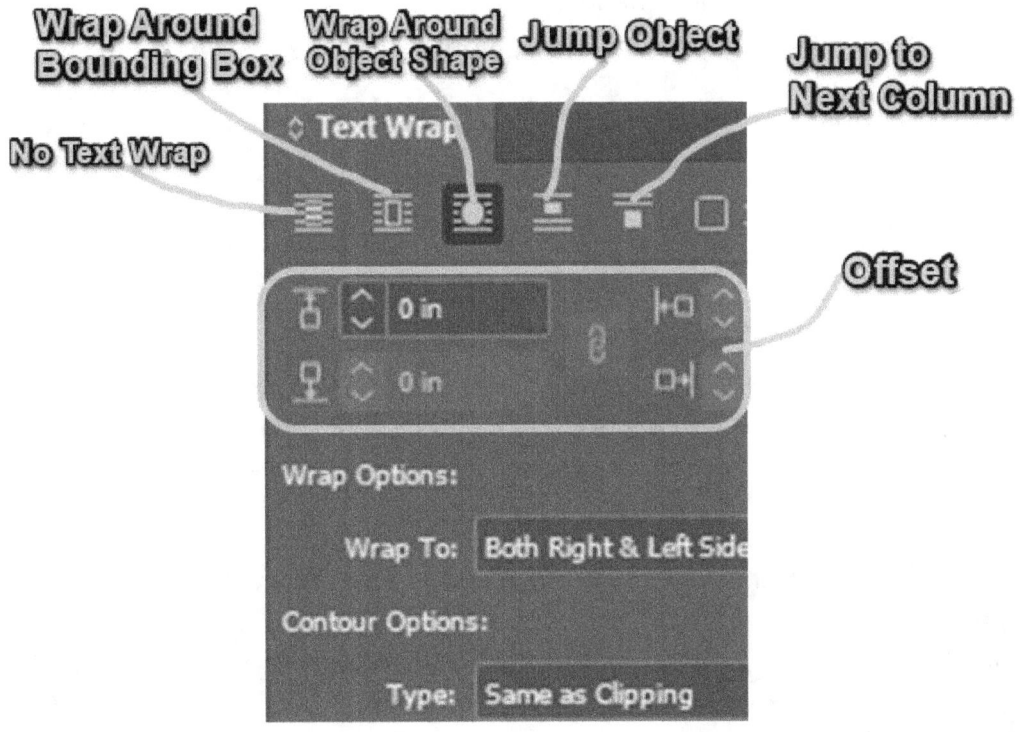

- ❖ **No Text Wrap**: Opt for the default setting to eliminate any text wrapping from the selected object.
- ❖ **Wrap around Bounding Box:** it wraps text around all sides of the object's bounding box.
- ❖ **Wrap around Object Shape**: Text conforms to the edges of the object's shape.
- ❖ **Jump Object**: Text surrounding the image shifts vertically, from above to below, without wrapping horizontally within the column.
- ❖ **Jump to Next Column**: Text ends above the image and continues in the next column without wrapping around the sides of the image.
- ❖ **Offset**: Input offset values to fine-tune text wrapping on all sides of the object.
- ❖ **Wrap Options**: Specify which sides of the object text should wrap around.
- ❖ **Contour Options:** From the dropdown list, choose a contour to determine how InDesign identifies the edges of the image. Options include **various vector paths** or **the detection of edges around an object** or **image with transparency.**

To apply text wrapping to an object, whether it's an image or a drawing, study these guides:

1) Create a **text frame** on a page containing a graphic. Populate the text frame by typing text, pasting text from another source, or using placeholder text. Ensure that the text frame is slightly larger than the graphic frame you intend to use, as the text will wrap around the image.
2) Go to **File** > **Place** and insert an image onto the page.

3) With the image chosen, go to **Window** > **Text Wrap** to open the **Text Wrap** panel.
4) While keeping the image selected, click the "**Wrap around Object Shape**" button in the **Text Wrap** panel. This action causes the text to wrap around the image rather than hiding behind it.

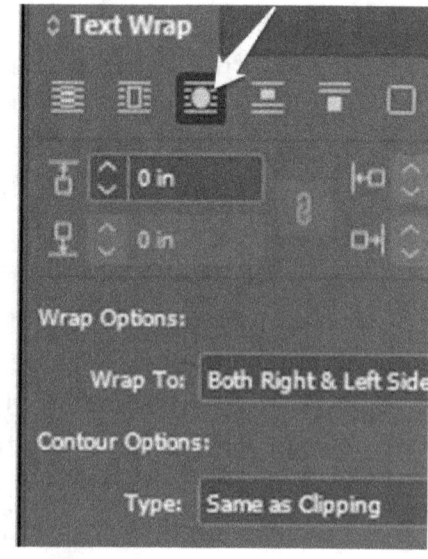

5) When dealing with an image that contains a transparent background, opt for the "**Wrap around Object Shape**" button to allow InDesign to detect the edges automatically. Consequently, the text will wrap around the image's edges.

To create distance between the text and the image, adjust the Offset by increasing it.

ADJUSTING TEXT WRAPS

Once you've applied a text wrap around an object, as illustrated in the preceding section, you can adjust it to suit your needs. In the case of an image with a transparent background, InDesign generates a path along its edges for text wrapping. Alternatively, if you've drawn a shape using InDesign's tools, the software automatically utilizes those paths for text wrapping.

As you are about to go ahead with the steps outlined below, confirm that the object is configured with the "Wrap around Object Shape" text wrap. If not, access the Text Wrap panel and activate the "Wrap around Object Shape" button to use this text wrapping. Remember to opt for "Detect Edges" if you're dealing with an image that has a transparent background.

To adjust the path around an image with text wrapping using the **Direct Selection** tool, consider these instructions:

1) Use the **Direct Selection** tool to select the object. This action highlights the image, revealing the path around it.
2) Click on one of the anchor points along the text wrap path using the **Direct Selection** tool. Then, click and drag the point to relocate it. As you move the point, the path adjusts accordingly. The text wrapping immediately adapts based on the modifications made to the path around the object. We shall treat more on path manipulation in **chapter 5**.

3) Choose the **Delete Anchor Point** tool from the **Tools** panel.

Note: This tool is nested within the **Pen** tool. Use it to remove an anchor point. As you delete anchor points, the path adjusts again, and the text wrapping around the object alters accordingly.

You can adjust the **Offset** values within the **Text Wrap** panel to control the distance between the surrounding text and the object's edge. Just increase the values to create more space between the text and the object's boundary.

MANAGING PAGES WITH THE PAGES PANEL

Pages serve as the central canvas for any publication, forming the visible foundation of your work. Effectively navigating and controlling pages is essential within InDesign. The Pages panel facilitates the selection, adjustment, movement, and navigation of pages within a publication. By default, pages are organized as facing pages, presenting as two-page pairs or spreads. Alternatively, pages can be laid out individually. The layout configuration, whether as part of a spread or as a single page, is reflected in the Pages panel and can be specified during document creation or adjusted within the Document Setup window.

You can access the **Pages** panel by navigating to **Window** > **Pages**. Within this panel, you can perform various tasks such as adding new pages, duplicating existing ones, deleting pages, or adjusting page sizes. The Pages panel shown below comprises two primary sections: the upper portion displays parent pages, while the lower section contains the document's pages.

Note: the term **master page** and **parent page** mean the same thing, we will be using them interchangeably in this user guide.

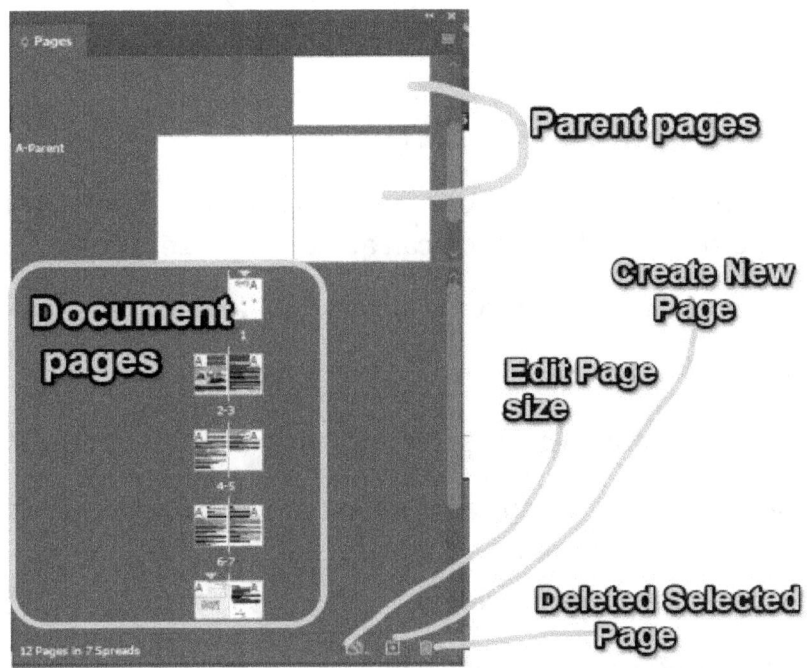

Note: It's worth noting that the image of the **Pages** panel shown was generated by switching the panel view to **Jumbo** size. To enlarge your panel view, simply go to the **Panel** menu located in the top-right corner of the **Pages** panel, choose **Panel Options,** and choose **Jumbo** from the **Page Size** drop-down menu inside the **Panel Options** dialog box.

You will learn about Parent pages in detail and how they affect regular pages of your document in the section titled **"Applying Master Spreads in Page Layout"** section, later in this chapter.

SELECTION AND RELOCATING PAGES WITHIN YOUR PUBLICATION

To choose and relocate page(s) within your publication, utilize the Pages panel. You can single out a page or a spread for manipulation. Simply click on a page to select it as a single page, furthermore, you have the option to select multiple pages simultaneously, to select multiple pages **Command-click** (macOS) or **Ctrl-click** (Windows) **pages**. The Pages panel facilitates the movement of pages to different positions within the document. First, identify the desired page within the document pages area of the panel. Then, simply drag the page to the desired location. As you drag, a **small line** and a modified cursor will indicate the projected placement of the page. You can position a page between two pages within a spread; an outlined line will signify this transition. Alternatively, if you relocate a page before or after a spread, a **solid line** will manifest.

Upon releasing the mouse button, the page will be successfully relocated to its new position.

INSERTING AND DELETING PAGES

To add or remove pages from your publication, the Pages panel provides a straightforward method. Here's how you can add a new page:

1) Navigate to **Window** > **Pages** to unveil the Pages panel.

The Pages panel will become visible.

2) Click on the "**Create New Page**" button at the bottom of the **Pages** panel.

This action will insert a new page to your document. If you **Option-click** (macOS) or **Alt-click** (Windows) the "**Create New Page**" button, you can specify the precise number of pages to add and their designated location.

3) Choose a **page** from the **Pages** panel.

The chosen page will be visibly highlighted within the Pages panel.

4) Press the "**Create New Page**" button once more.

This will insert a new page immediately following the selected page.

To remove a page, first, choose it in the Pages panel, then click on the "**Delete Selected Pages**" button. This action will delete the chosen page from your document.

Furthermore, you have the option to perform tasks like adding, deleting, or rearranging pages directly from the **Layout** > **Pages** submenu, without relying on the Pages panel.

PAGE NUMBERING

When handling longer documents, it's advisable to include page numbers before printing or exporting the publication. Rather than manually inserting page numbers, InDesign offers a dedicated tool for automatic numbering. This feature proves especially handy when rearranging pages within the document. You're relieved of the task of manually updating page numbers each time you make such edits, thanks to this convenient tool.

To include page numbers, check these instructions:

- Use the **Type** tool to generate a text frame on the desired page where you intend to place the page number.
- Go to **Type** > **Insert Special Character** > **Markers** > **Current Page Number**.

the current page number will fill the text frame you designated. If you've inserted the page number on a Parent page, the letter of the Parent page will display in the field instead.

If you aim to display page numbers on every page throughout the document, include the text frame within a Parent page. It's important to note that page numbers will only be applied to the pages associated with that specific Parent page. For instance, if you wish to add page numbers on both the left and right sides of a book or magazine, you'll need to replicate this procedure on the respective left and right sides of the Parent pages. Remember, if you solely add a page number to a document page without including it on a Parent page, the page number will only appear on that individual page.

To adjust automatic numbering settings, go to **Layout** > **Numbering and Section** Options. From there, you can specify whether numbering should commence from a particular number or adopt an alternative style, like Roman numerals.

APPLYING PARENT SPREADS FOR PAGE LAYOUTS

Parent pages act as templates to format page layouts uniformly, ensuring consistent application of settings like margins and columns across each layout. For example, if you add a page number to a Parent page, it automatically reflects on every page using that layout. Publications have the flexibility to incorporate multiple Parent pages, this enables you to assign specific masters to designated pages as needed.

A Parent page usually contains layout elements that are shared across multiple pages, including page numbering, text frames, standard headings, or background images. By default, elements positioned on a Parent page cannot be edited directly on the pages where that master is applied. Nevertheless, you have the option to override or detach these Parent page elements for direct modification on a document page. To accomplish this, simply press Command + Shift (macOS) or Ctrl + Shift (Windows) while clicking on the Parent page element. This functionality proves valuable for unique situations, such as adjusting the background of a single page or eliminating a specific page number.

Parent pages are labeled alphabetically, with the default first Parent page being named **A-Parent**. If you generate a second Parent page, it will automatically be named **B-Parent**. Upon creating a new publication, all initially opened pages in the document are assigned the A-Parent by default. However, you have the flexibility to insert pages at the end without a parent page applied to them.

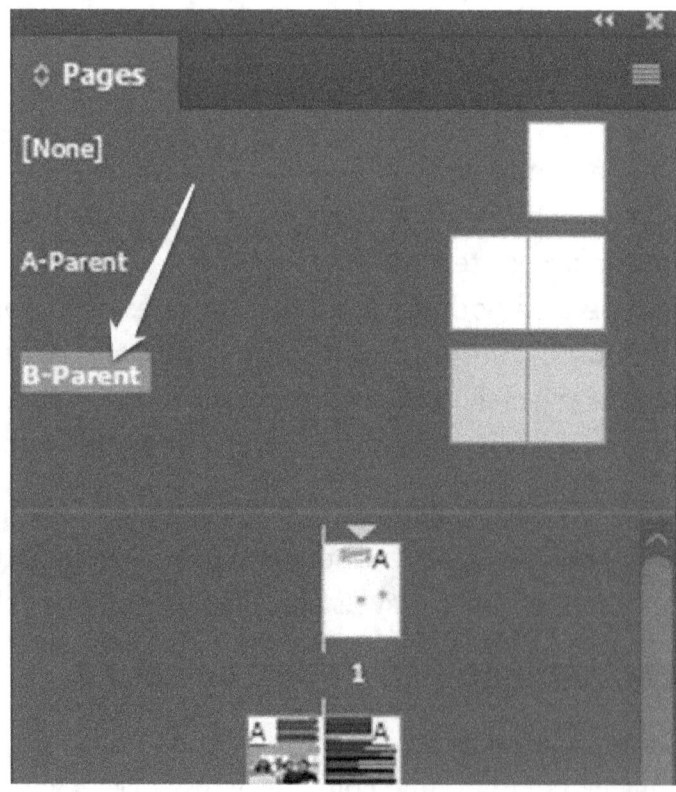

By creating and implementing parent pages in your publication, you launch a reusable format that significantly enhances your workflow efficiency when compiling documents in InDesign.

HOW TO CREATE A PARENT PAGE

There may arise instances where you require more than one master page or spread for a document, especially when certain series of pages necessitate a unique format. In such cases, you'll need to create a second parent page. You have the option to generate a master page or spread from any existing page within the publication or create a new one using the Pages panel.

Follow one of these methods, to create a Parent page:

- ✓ Select "**New Parent**" from the **Page panel's** menu and confirm by clicking **OK**. This action generates a blank parent page.
- ✓ Alternatively, drag a page from the pages section of the panel into the Parent page section of the Pages panel. Consequently, the document page transforms into a Parent page.

When attempting to move a page to the Parent pages section, if it's part of a spread, ensure to select both pages within the spread before dragging them into the Parent pages section. For individual pages not belonging to a spread, you can drag them into the parent page section independently.

APPLYING, DELETING, AND REMOVING PARENT PAGES

Once you've created a Parent page, you have the option to apply it to a page within your document. Additionally, you can remove a page from a Parent page layout or choose to delete a Parent page entirely.

To apply Parent page formatting into a page or spread within a publication:

1. Go to the **Pages** panel. Locate the Parent page you wish to apply from the Parent page section.
2. Drag the selected **Parent page** over the page you intend to format in the document pages section.

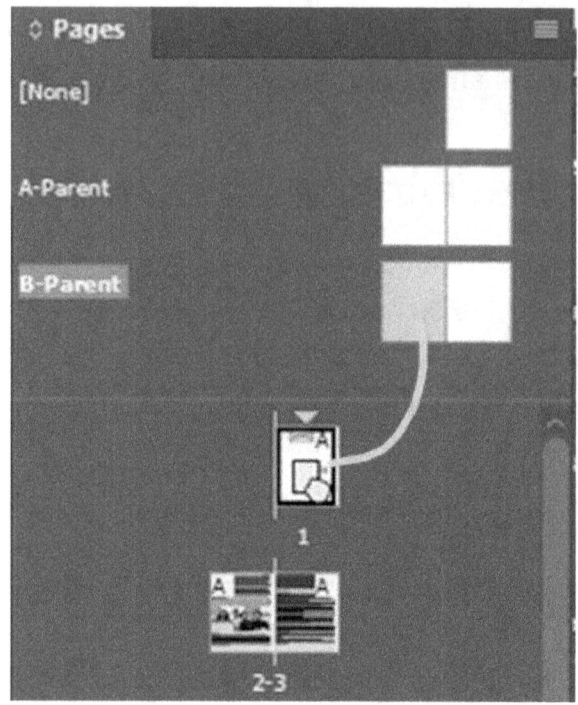

As you drag the Parent page over the target page, a thick outline appears around it.

3. Release the mouse button once you observe this outline, signifying that the formatting is applied to the page.

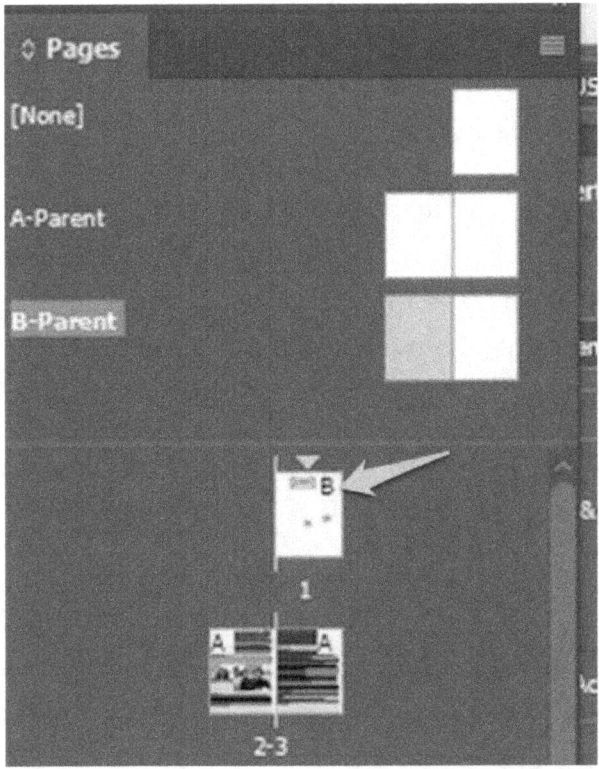

To remove any Parent page applied to a document page, follow these steps:

1. Summon the Pages panel. From the parent area within the **Pages** panel, locate the **"None"** page. Drag the "**None**" page from the parent area onto the target document page.
2. If necessary, use the scroll bar within the Parent pages area of the Pages panel to locate the "**None**" page.

To delete a Parent page, apply these steps:

1. Open the Pages panel. Select the **Parent page** you wish to delete.
2. From the panel menu, choose "**Delete Parent page**"

Keep in mind that this action permanently deletes the Parent page, and it cannot be recovered. Therefore, exercise caution before deleting a Parent page.

ALTERING PAGE SIZES INDIVIDUALLY

Within the Pages panel, you can customize the dimensions of individual pages in a document. This feature becomes particularly valuable when managing pages that fold out and are larger than others. Moreover, it streamlines the process of crafting a cohesive document that contains various elements like a business card, letter head, and an envelope.

To resize individual pages with the Pages panel, observe these instructions:

1) Navigate to the **Pages** panel and select the **page** whose size you want to adjust by clicking on it.
2) Press the "**Edit Page Size**" button situated at the bottom of the **Pages** panel, and then choose the **desired new size.** Keep in mind that the visual illustration of a page in the Pages panel might not precisely represent its actual dimensions.

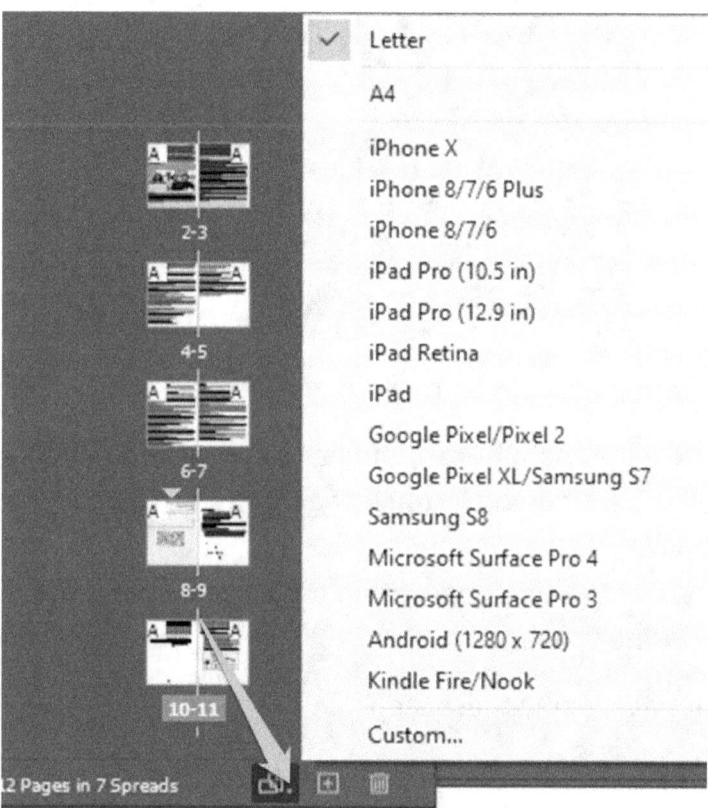

3) Keep doing these procedures as required to modify the size of any other pages.

Once you've finished adjusting the page sizes, proceed to refine their design and layout as you would with any other pages. The primary distinction is that certain pages within your document may vary in size.

CHAPTER FIVE
CREATING ARTWORK IN INDESIGN

Several tools available in the InDesign Tools panel facilitate the creation of lines and shapes directly on a page. Inside InDesign, you can produce a wide range of designs, from simple shapes to detailed drawings without the need for a dedicated drawing program like Illustrator. While InDesign doesn't replace Illustrator's extensive array of drawing tools and options, it proves sufficient for many drawing tasks. In this chapter, you'll explore the most commonly used drawing tools in InDesign and learn how to enhance illustrations with vibrant fills.

Even if drawing isn't your primary focus in InDesign, it's worthwhile to review the sections on "Altering Frame Corners" and "Exploring Fills" later in this chapter before moving forward.

GETTING HANDS-ON DRAWING

In the process of creating a new document, you can decide to include drawn shapes and paths into the layout. For instance, you might desire a star shape for a famous person's page displaying a talent show, or perhaps you need to arrange text along a path. Whatever your specific requirements may be, drawing shapes and paths enables you to accomplish various tasks effectively.

PATHS AND SHAPES

Paths come in several formats, varying between open or closed, and can also come with a stoke or not.

- ✓ **Path:** this is the outline of a shape or an object. Paths may be closed, forming no gaps, or open paths, resembling lines on the page. Freeform paths, like hand-drawn squiggles, can be created freely by hand.
- ✓ **Stroke**: A-line style and thickness applied to a path, which can resemble either a solid line or the shape outline.

Paths consist of points where the path's direction can alter, as explained further in the subsequent section titled "Points and segments". These paths can be crafted using either freeform drawing tools such as a Pen or Pencil tools or through the use of basic shape tools like Rectangle, Ellipse, Polygon, or Line.

The basic shape tools generate paths in predefined configurations, facilitating the creation of fundamental geometric shapes like stars or ellipses. Simply select the desired shape tool, drag the cursor onto the page, and the shape appears automatically. This method significantly simplifies shape creation compared to manual drawing with the Pen or Pencil tool. Shapes drawn using the shape tools from the Tools panel are shown below.

Shapes can be converted into freeform paths similar to those crafted with the Pen or Pencil tools, and vice versa. Therefore, the initial choice of tool should not be a cause of concern.

The star and starburst shown below were produced by double-clicking the Polygon tool and modifying its settings. Further details about the Polygon tool are elaborated upon in the later section "**EXPLORING THE POLYGON TOOL**" in this chapter.

It's important to note that you can also draft a rough shape, such as a triangle, and subsequently refine it by selecting **Object** > **Convert Shape** and opting for **Triangle** to rectify the shape.

POINTS AND SEGMENTS

Paths consist of points and segments:

- ✓ **Point:** This indicates where the path changes, such as a change in direction. Multiple points along a path can be connected by segments. Points are also known as **anchor points**. Two types of points can be created:

- **Corner points**: it is connected by straight lines between them. Shapes like stars and squares typically contain corner points.
- **Curve points**: Found along curved paths. Paths with circular or serpentine shapes contain numerous curve points.

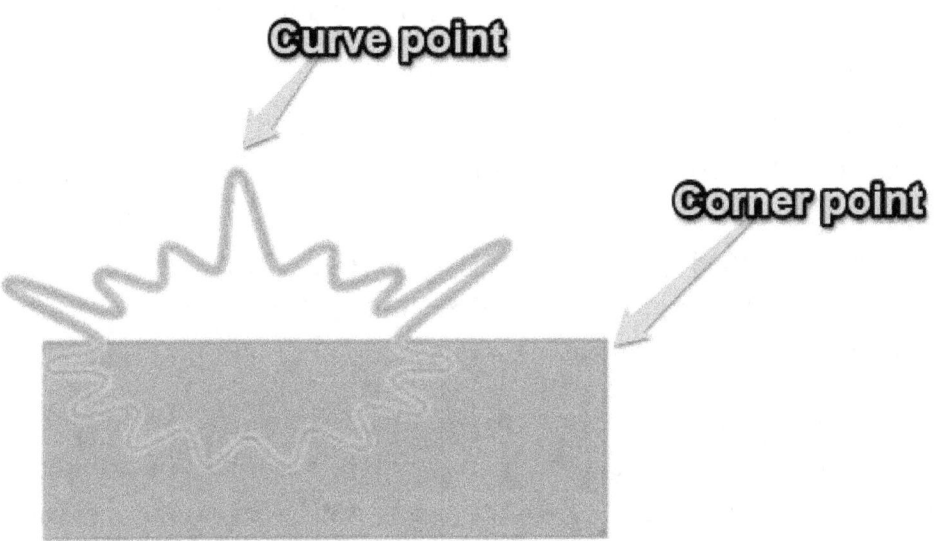

✓ **Segment**: A line or curve that joins two points, much like connecting the dots.

GETTING ACQUAINTED WITH ESSENTIAL TOOLS

The forthcoming sections acquaint you with the tools you'll likely use frequently while crafting drawings in your publications. As you draw with these tools, you manipulate strokes and fills to fashion designs. These sections outline the capabilities of these common tools, aiding you in crafting both simple and intricate illustrations within InDesign.

The Pencil tool enables users to sketch both simple and intricate shapes directly onto a page. Unlike basic shape tools that automatically generate shapes, the Pencil tool offers freeform flexibility, allowing users to freely move it across the page to create lines or shapes as desired. It's an excellent and user-friendly tool, with further guidance on its usage available in the later section titled "Drawing Freeform Paths."

The Pen tool can be used to craft intricate shapes within a document. It collaborates seamlessly with complementary tools like Add, Remove, and Convert Point tools. By strategically adding and adjusting points along a path, the Pen tool enables users to manipulate the segments connecting these points, facilitating the creation and refinement of complex shapes.

Using the Pen tool can be challenging initially, often requiring considerable time to master. Don't get discouraged if you don't grasp it immediately; practice is key to achieving desired results with the Pen tool. You will learn its usage in the later section titled "Drawing Freeform Paths"

Basic shapes and frame shapes, such as lines, rectangles, ellipses, and polygons are readily available in the Tools panel. These shapes can be drawn directly or converted into frames, which serve as containers for content within a document. Frames can used for text or graphics, allowing flexibility in layout design. To convert a basic shape into a frame, go to **Object** > **Content** > **Text, or Object** > **Content** > **Graphic**. Further details on graphic and text frames are covered in Chapter 3.

Although both frames and shape tools may appear similar and serve similar function s, it's crucial to note their differences. Shapes created with shape tools typically come with a default 1-point black stroke, which might not be immediately visible on screen but could be noticed when printed. To avoid unexpected outcomes, it's advisable to use frame tools instead.

HOW TO DRAW SHAPE IN INDESIGN

Creating shapes in InDesign is a straightforward process. Follow these instructions to generate a basic shape:

1) create a new document by going to **File** > **New** > **Document**.
2) In the New Document dialog box, opt for the **Print** option, select a suitable blank document preset size, and proceed by clicking **Create**.

This action will open a new document.

3) Locate and select the **Rectangle tool** from the Tools panel.
4) Click on any area of the page and drag the mouse diagonally to define the dimensions of the rectangle.

Once the rectangle reaches the desired size, release the mouse button to finalize the shape.

That's all it takes to craft a basic shape. Similarly, you can use these steps with other basic shape tools like the Ellipse, Line, and Polygon tools to generate various shapes. To access these additional shapes from the Tools panel, check these instructions:

1) Begin by clicking on the **Rectangle tool** and holding down the mouse button. This action opens a menu containing all the basic shapes.

2) Release the mouse button to keep the menu open. Hover over the menu items, and each item will be highlighted when the mouse pointer is placed over it.
3) Select a desired **basic shape** tool by clicking on the highlighted menu item. This activates the chosen tool, allowing you to create shapes following the same order of steps.

To draw a square shape, utilize the Rectangle tool and press the **Shift** key while dragging the mouse on the page. This ensures that all sides of the shape are of equal length, resulting in a perfect square. Similarly, you can maintain perfect proportions with the Ellipse tool by holding down the **Shift** key while using it, ensuring a perfect circle. Remember to release the mouse before releasing the **Shift** key to ensure this constraint shape technique functions as intended!

DRAWING A SHAPE WITH PRECISE DIMENSIONS

This entails a few additional steps beyond simply dragging on the page. If you aim to create a shape with specific measurements, check the following instructions:

1) Choose either the **Rectangle** tool or the **Ellipse** tool from the Tools panel. The selected tool will be highlighted within the panel.

2) Click once **anywhere on the page**, but refrain from dragging the cursor.

Upon clicking, this point is made as the top-left corner of the bounding box for the **Rectangle** or **Ellipse**, defining the object's **vertical** and **horizontal dimensions**. Subsequently, upon placement of a corner, the Rectangle or Ellipse dialog box emerges.

3) Input the desired dimensions for the shape into the **Width** and **Height** text fields and then Proceed by clicking **OK**.

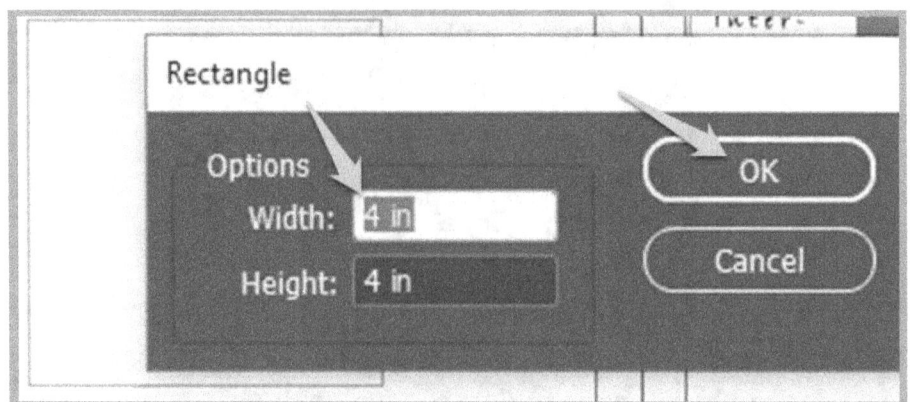

The shape will be generated on the page, positioned in its top-left corner at the location where you initially press on the page.

EXPLORING THE POLYGON TOOL

This allows you to create shapes with multiple sides. While a square constitutes a four-sided polygon, the Polygon tool grants you the flexibility to determine the precise number of sides for the shape you intend to create. Before starting the drawing process with the Polygon tool, you have the option to adjust the default number of sides to suit your preferences.

To tailor the shape of a polygon, check these instructions:

1) Ensure that no other shapes are currently selected. pick the **Polygon** tool from the Tools panel by selecting the **Rectangle** tool and holding down the mouse button until the menu appears.
2) Double-press on the **Polygon** tool within the Tools panel. This opens up the Polygon dialog box.
3) In the "**Number of Sides**" text field, enter the preferred number of sides for the new polygon, then click **Ok/Enter** for confirmation and drag across the page to draw your desire shape.

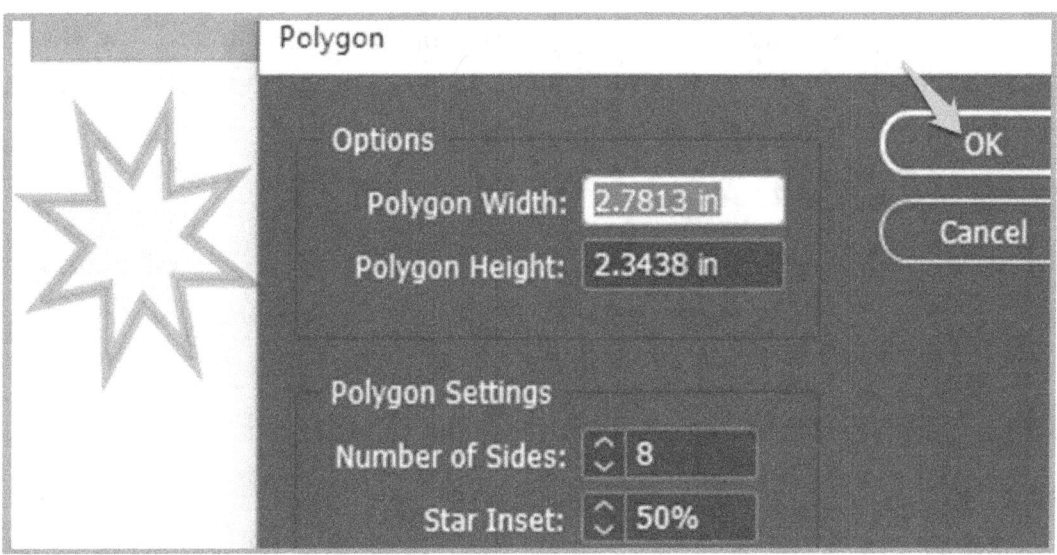

To create a star instead of a polygon, specify a value in the **Star Inset** text field to determine the percentage of inset for the new shape. A greater percentage results in deeper inset sides towards the center of the polygon, thereby forming a star. Opt for a value of **0%** if you prefer a regular polygon over a star. For a star shape, input **50%**; whereas for a starburst appearance, input **25%**.

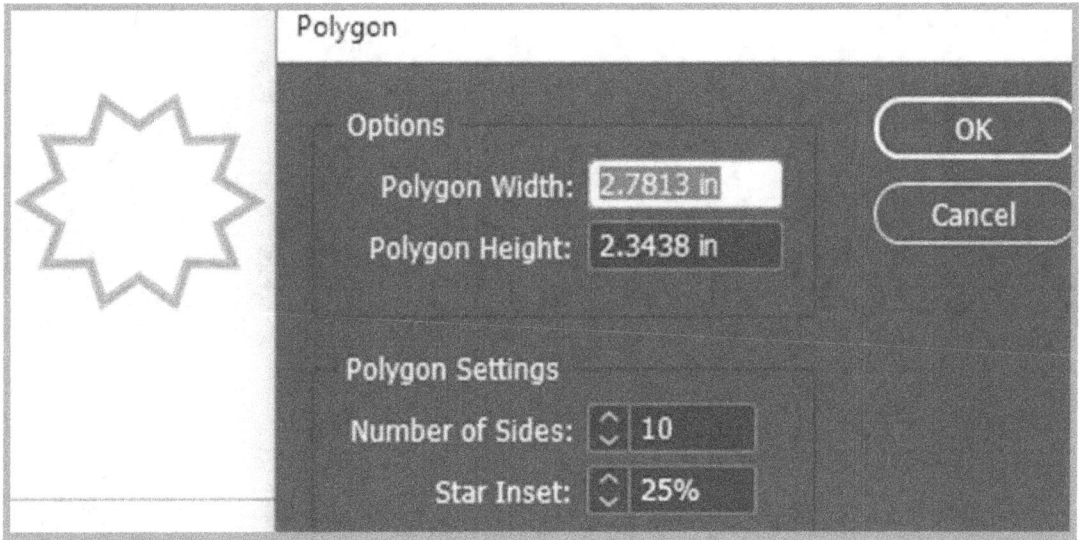

4) Click **Ok** and position the cursor on the page, then click and drag to generate a new polygon or star.

various polygons and stars with diverse configurations are displayed above, indicating their distinct appearances based on different settings.

After creating a polygon, you can refine its attributes by selecting it and then double-clicking on the Polygon shape tool. This action allows you to adjust the number of sides, the inset of the polygon, and the polygon width and height.

MODIFYING BASIC SHAPES

Altering basic shapes empowers you to craft original designs precisely tailored to your preferences. You're not limited to predefined shapes like squares or ovals; instead, you can manipulate these forms to adopt highly customized shapes.

USING THE TRANSFORM PANEL TO ALTER SHAPE SIZE

To adjust the size of a shape, use the **Transform** panel. While comprehensive coverage of the Transform panel is provided in Chapter 7, this section introduces its fundamental functionalities. Below are the steps to effortlessly resize shapes within InDesign:

1) Use the **Selection** tool (the solid black arrow tool used for object selection) to choose the shape you intend to resize. The bounding box displays around the selected shape as shown below in step 2.
2) Summon the **Transform** panel by navigating to **Window** > **Object and Layout** > **Transform.**

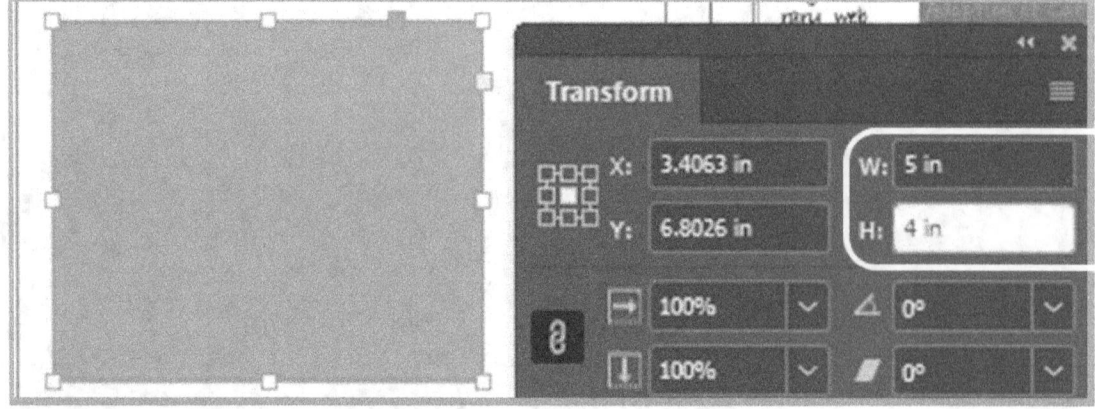

3) Within the Transform panel, input varied numerical values into the **W (width)** and **H (height)** fields to adjust the size of the shape. The shape is instantly updated to reflect the new dimension you entered.

USING THE FREE TRANSFORM PANEL TO ALTER SHAPE SIZE

Adjusting object sizes in InDesign is simple with the Free Transform tool. To resize a selected object using this tool, follow these steps:

1) Ensure that only the object you wish to resize is picked.

If you need to resize multiple objects simultaneously, consider grouping them. To group objects, start by selecting **one object**, then hold down the **Shift** key and click on the **other objects** you wish to include in the selection. Finally, press **Command + G** (macOS) or **Ctrl + G** (Windows) to group them.

2) Choose the **Free Transform** tool in the Tools panel.
3) Press on any corner point and drag to resize the object. While resizing, hold down the **Shift** key to maintain proportional constraints on the object.

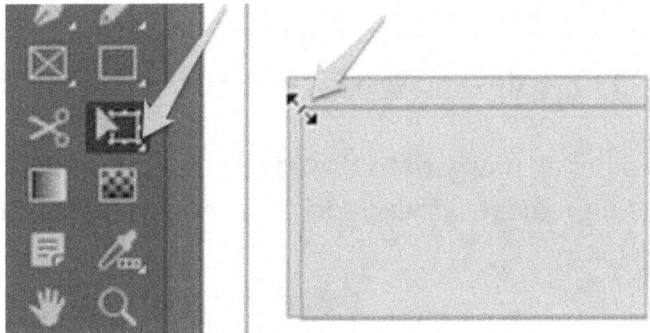

CRAFTING OWN CUSTOM SHAPES

This can be challenging, even for skilled freehand artists. InDesign offers the Pathfinder panel to assist in crafting custom shapes. Next, we shall use the Pathfinder panel to experiment few Pathfinder features using the following exercise.

1) Ensure you have an existing document open, and switch to a new page or create a new page.
2) Select the **Ellipse** tool and click-drag to create an Ellipse. To draw a circle, hold down the **Shift** key while dragging. Note that the Ellipse tool might be hidden within the **Rectangle** or **Polygon** tool, depending on the last tool used.
3) Select the **Rectangle** tool and click-drag to generate a rectangle. Hold down the **Shift** key while dragging to create a square if desired.

Next, we will use the Selection tool to intersect the shapes as step (4).

4) With the Selection tool place a circle on top of the rectangle to overlap one another. Then Ensure both **shapes** are selected by clicking on one and then holding the **Shift** key while clicking on the other with the Selection tool.

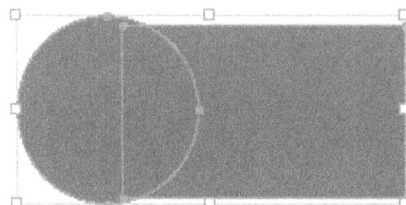

5) Go to **Window** > **Properties** and click on **Fill** to modify both shapes to your desired color.
6) In the **Properties** panel, navigate to the **Pathfinder** section and choose **Exclude Overlap**; this action removes or excludes the point of intersection between the concerned objects.

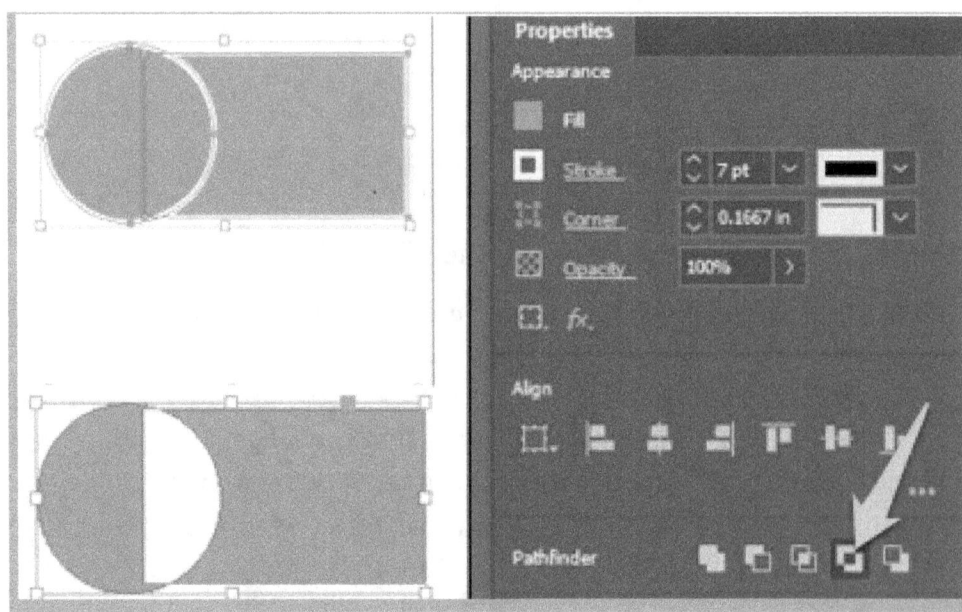

Note: you can experiment with other Pathfinder features to see their effects. You can try this with two or more shapes as you desire.

ALTERING THE (STROKE) OUTLINE OF A SHAPE

One can modify the outline, also known as the stroke, of shapes that have been crafted. The stroke outlines the edge of the shape. Its thickness can vary from no stroke at all to a considerably thick outline, measured in point sizes. Notably, even if a shape's stroke is set to 0 points, it still possesses a stroke; however, it remains invisible.

To adjust the stroke of your shapes, adhere to the following procedure:

1) Select any **shape** on the page. Upon selection, a bounding box will encircle the chosen shape.
2) Opt for a different width for the stroke by accessing the **Stroke Weight** drop-down list found in the **Control** panel or **Properties** panel.

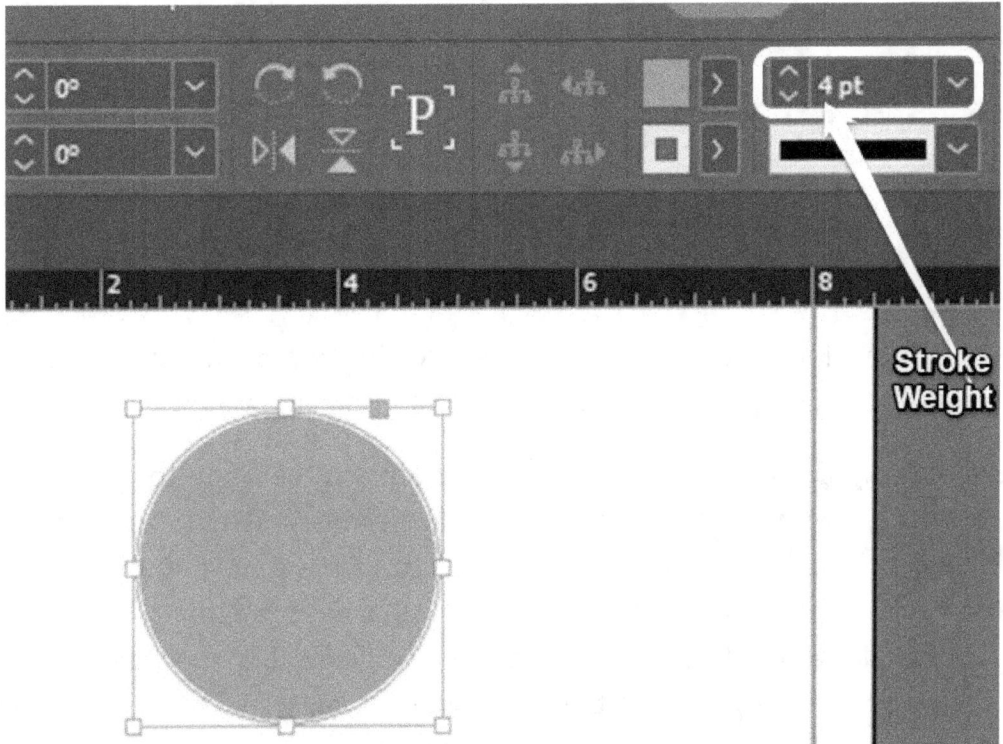

Once a value is selected, the stroke on the page immediately adjusts accordingly. This value is calculated in points. Further options are available in the subsequent steps of the process.

To manually set the **stroke width**, click on the **Stroke Weight** text field and input a numerical value. Increasing this number results in a thicker stroke appearance.

You can also modify the stroke style from the **Control** panel by observing these instructions:

1) After selecting a **basic shape**, choose the **stroke type** from the drop-down list in the **Control** panel and select a **new line**. Once a new line is chosen, the stroke adjusts automatically.

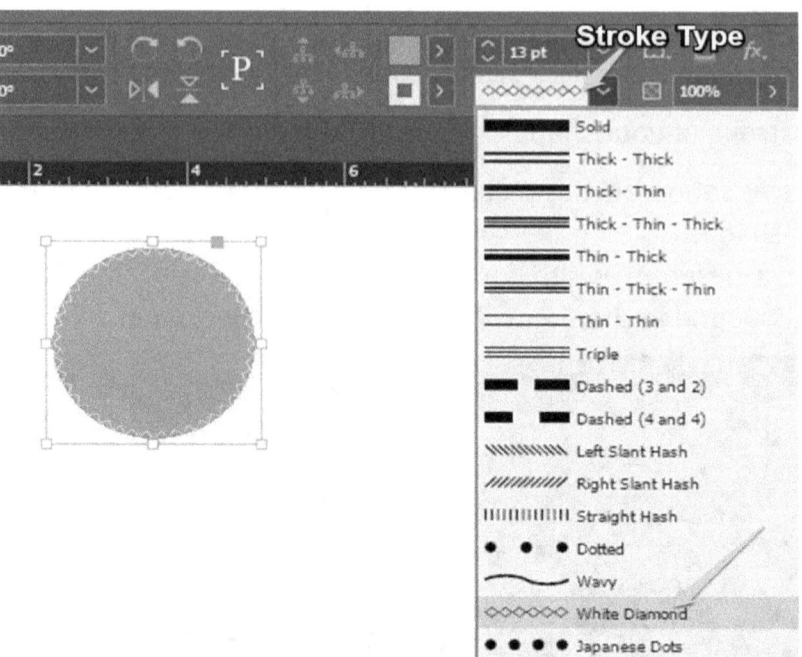

2) Pick a new line weight from the **Stroke Weight** drop-down list. For instance, if you select **13** points, the shape will automatically update on the page.

To create custom dashes and access additional options, navigate to **Window > Stroke**. Select **Stroke Styles** from the **panel** menu located in the upper-right corner. Then, choose **New** to define the **dash** and **gap size**. You can customize **dashes** by clicking on the ruler and dragging the triangles to specify the dash length. You can add further dashes by clicking on the ruler, entering a single value for even dashes or multiple values for customized dashes suitable for diagrams, maps, fold marks, and so on. Once created, your custom stroke will appear in the Stroke panel.

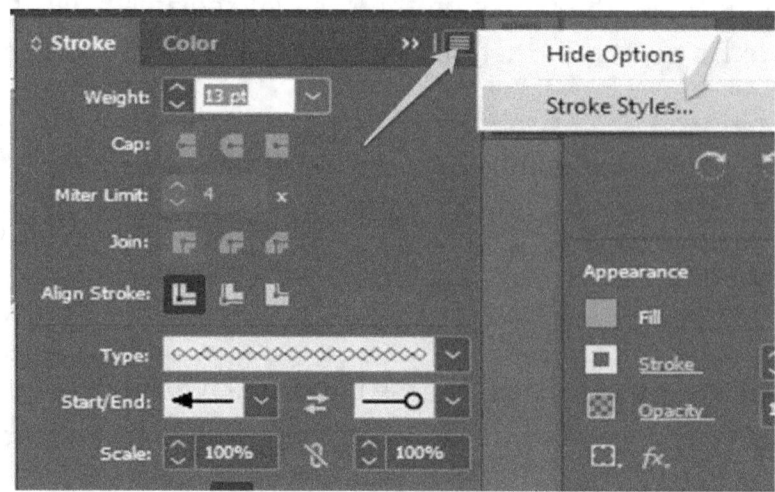

Enhance lines with special ends using the **Start** and **End** drop-down lists. Options include adding **arrowheads** or **large circles** to the beginning or end of the stroke. The **Cap** and **Join** buttons provide flexibility in selecting the shape of line ends and determining how they connect with other paths, particularly useful when dealing with **complex shapes** or **paths**.

MODIFY THE SHEAR VALUE

You can modify the shear of a shape using the **Transform** panel. Skew and shear are synonymous terms: They both denote a slanted shape, allowing you to simulate a sense of perspective for the skewed or sheared element. This transformation proves valuable when aiming to craft a perspective effect on a page.

Follow these straightforward instructions to skew a shape:

1) Select a basic shape, then navigate to **Window** > **Object & Layout** > **Transform**.
2) choose a value from the **Shear X Angle** drop-down list located in the lower-right corner of the **Transform** panel.

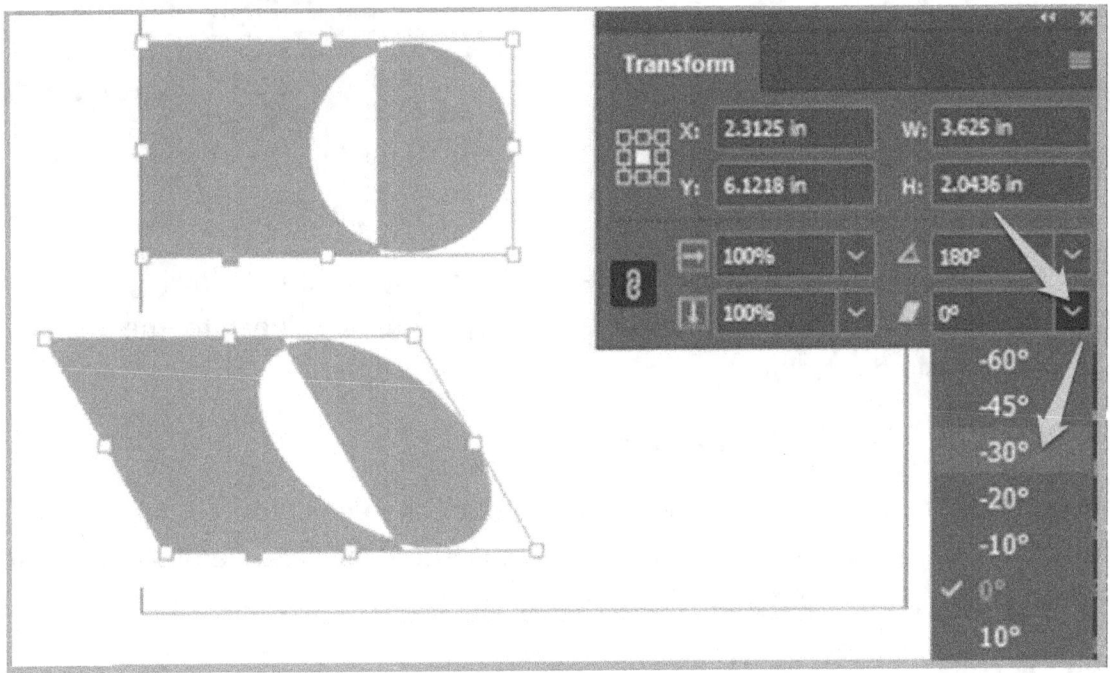

Once you choose a new value, the shape undergoes skewing or shearing, based on the selected value. Similarly, directly inputting a numerical value into this field will also result in skewing the shape accordingly.

ROTATING A SHAPE

To adjust the rotation of a shape, use the Transform panel. The procedure for rotating a shape is identical to that of skewing:

1) Select a basic shape, then navigate to **Window** > **Object & Layout** > **Transform**.

The Transform panel will open.

2) Choose a **different value** from the **Rotation** Angle drop-down list.

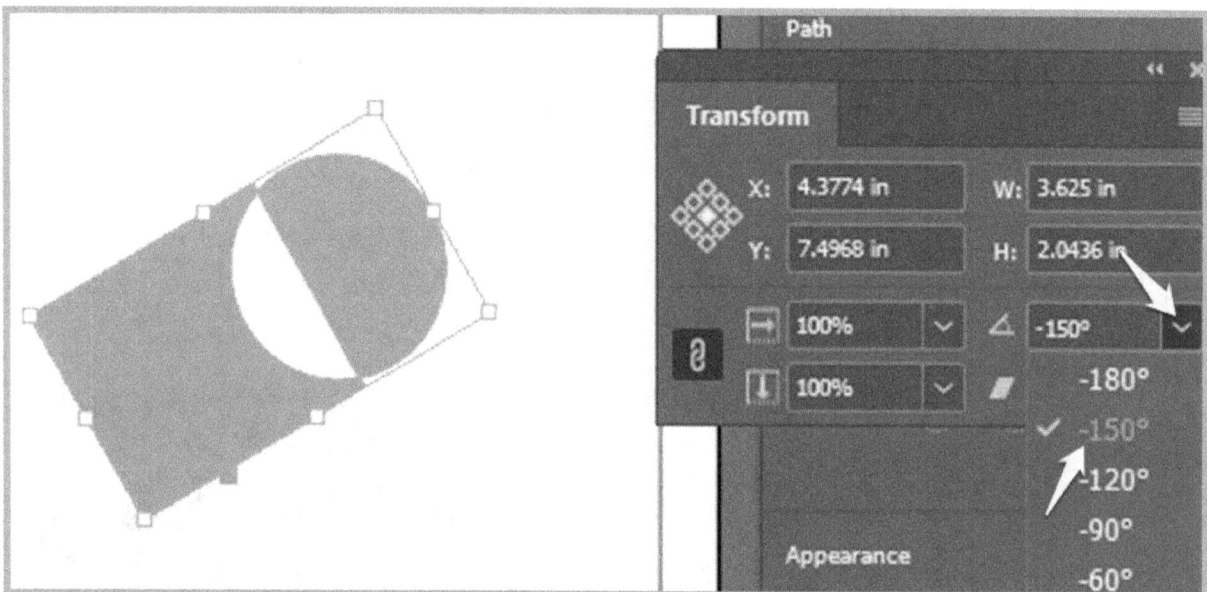

Upon selecting a new value, the shape automatically rotates following the specified rotation angle. Alternatively, you can manually input a value into the text field to achieve the desired rotation.

SKETCHING FREEFORM PATHS

Various tools are available to draw paths, including the Pencil tool for crafting freeform paths. Such paths often resemble lines, and both the Pencil and Pen tools facilitate the creation of straightforward or intricate paths.

EXPLORING THE PENCIL TOOL

When it comes to sketching freeform paths, the Pencil tool stands out as one of the most straightforward tools to utilize.

Start with these procedures:

1) Create a new document and Opt for the **Pencil** tool located in the **Tools** panel. Ensure you have set a stroke weight and color for your stroke.

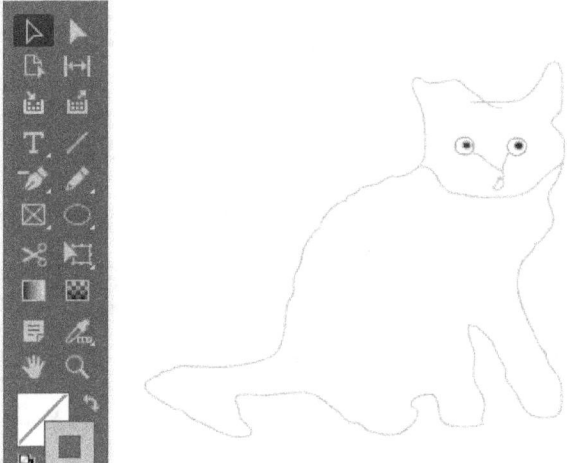

2) Move the cursor around the page to sketch a new path using the Pencil tool.

EXPLORING THE PEN TOOL

Distinguishing between the Pen tool and the Pencil tool is essential. Initially, the Pen tool might appear intricate, but once you become familiar with it, operating it becomes straightforward. The Pen tool utilizes points to craft specific paths, and you can modify these points to alter the segments connecting them. Mastering control over these points requires some practicing.

To create points and segments on a page, check the following instructions:

- Move to a new page and select the **Pen** tool in the Tools panel. Make sure a **stroke weight** and **Color** are indicated before using this tool.
- Click anywhere on the page, and then click a second location.

You've created a new path with **two points** and one segment joining them.

- **Command-click** (macOS) or **Ctrl-click** (Windows) an empty part of the page to deselect the current path.

After you deselect the path, you may create a new path or add new points to the path you just created.

To add a new point to a selected segment with the Pen tool:

- Select the segment, hover the mouse over the line, and click. This action displays a **small plus (+)** icon next to the Pen tool cursor.
- Alternatively, choose the **Add Anchor Point** tool from the menu that expands when you click and hold the **Pen** icon in the Tools panel.
- Repeat Step 5, but now, you are clicking on a new location along a line segment, after clicking, drag away from the line.

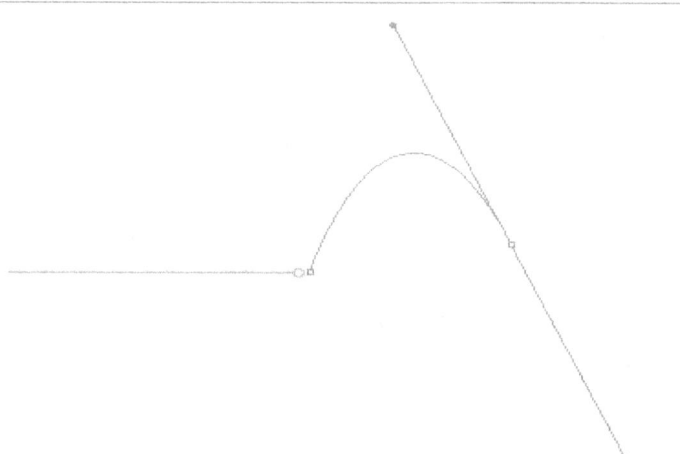

Note: By following this step, you generate a curved path. The segments of this path adjust and curve based on the positioning of the points along its length. The point that you've just created is referred to as a curve point.

Mastering the usage of Pen tool requires a lot of practice but you will be glad if you do.

MODIFYING FREEFORM PATHS

Skilled artists encounter occasions where adjustments or eliminations are necessary in their creations. Should errors arise or alterations become desired, stick to the procedures outlined in this section to effect modifications.

To modify a segment of a path, ensure it is deselected, then use the Direct Selection tool to select a point. A solid appearance denotes a pick point, while unpicked points appear hollow.

Once you have selected the point, you can use the handles that appear to adjust the segments accordingly. Check these instructions:

- press the **A** key or choose the **Direct Selection** tool from the Tools panel, and then click a point.

The selected point appears solid. If you select a curve point, handles will emanate from it.

When you select and manipulate them, curved points and corner points behave differently. Curve points are characterized by handles that extend from the point, whereas corner points lack such handles.

- Move the point to your desired location. To adjust a curve point, select and drag either end of the handle right or left. The path alters based on the direction of the handle movement.

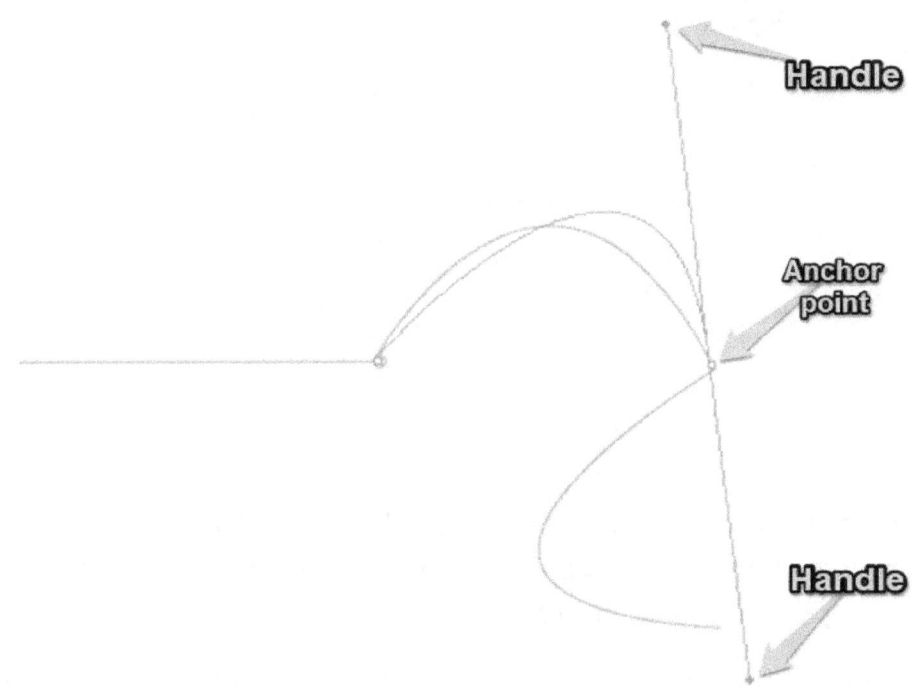

If you wish to convert a corner point into a curve point or vice versa, you can achieve this with the Convert Direction Point tool. To effectively use this tool, it's best to work with a path containing both straight and curved segments. Follow these steps to switch between a corner point and a curve point:

1) Begin by selecting the **Convert Direction Point** tool, which is located within a menu under the **Pen** tool in the Tools panel. To access it, hold down the mouse

button over the **Pen** tool icon until a menu appears, then choose the **Convert Direction Point** tool from the menu.

2) Click on a curved point using the **Convert Direction Point** tool. This action transforms the selected point into a corner point, thereby altering the appearance of the path.

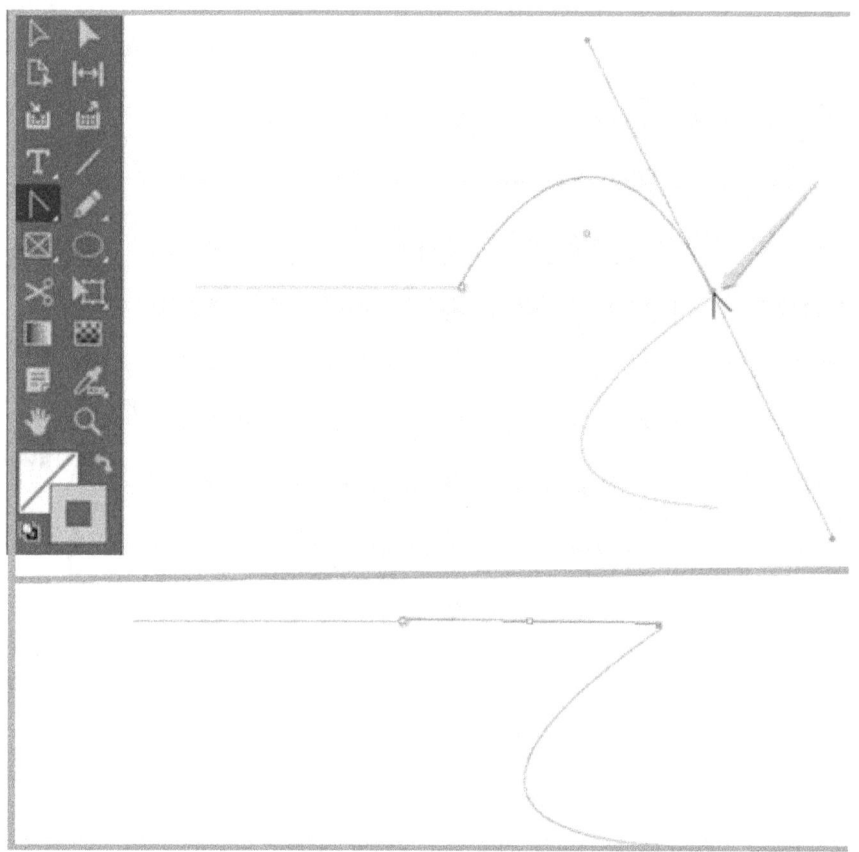

3) To convert a corner point into a curved point, click and drag the corner point using the **Convert Direction Point** tool. As you drag, the point transitions into a curve point, resulting in a change in the path's appearance.

This tool proves useful for adjusting the direction of a path. If you need to manipulate a point differently, consider modifying its type using the Convert Direction Point tool.

ADJUSTING FRAME CORNERS

You can enhance the appearance of basic shapes by applying corner effects, which offer a personalized touch to their overall look. These effects are particularly handy for adding visual interest to borders, allowing for several creative possibilities by applying effects to various shapes or layering multiple effects onto a single shape. Follow these steps to create a corner effect on a rectangle:

1) Start by selecting the **Rectangle** tool and drawing a new rectangle anywhere on the page. Hold down the **Shift** key while using the **Rectangle** tool if you wish to create a perfect square.
2) Once the shape is drawn, switch to the Selection tool and select the shape. Then, navigate to **Object > Corner Options**.

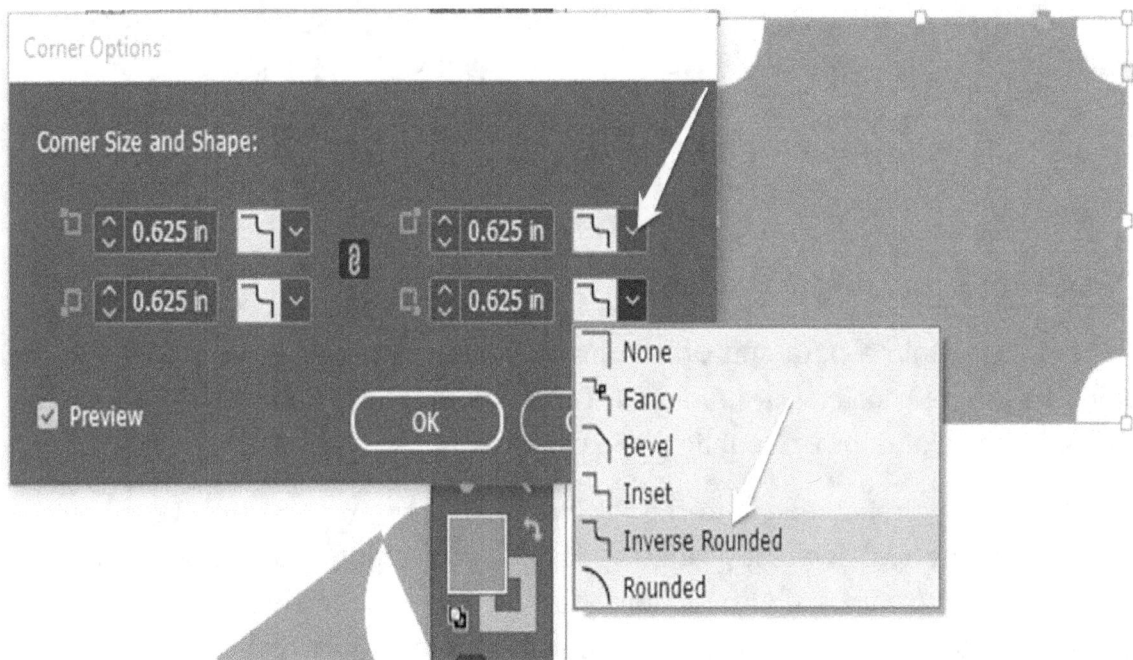

The Corner Options dialog box will appear, offering various options for corner styles. Alternatively, if you prefer to use the **Properties** panel, access it by choosing **Window > Properties** and clicking on the **Corners** button to reveal the same **Corner Options** window.

3) Select the **desired type of corner** effect from the options provided, then click **OK** to apply it to the shape. Ensure that the "**Make All Settings the Same**" chain icon is selected if you want to apply the same corner effect to all corners of the shape.

To visually adjust corner effects, use the **Selection** tool to click and select a **frame**. Once the frame is selected, locate the **yellow** box positioned towards the upper right edge of the frame. Upon clicking this **yellow** box, each corner handle transforms into a yellow color, enabling horizontal dragging either left or right to adjust the corners accordingly.

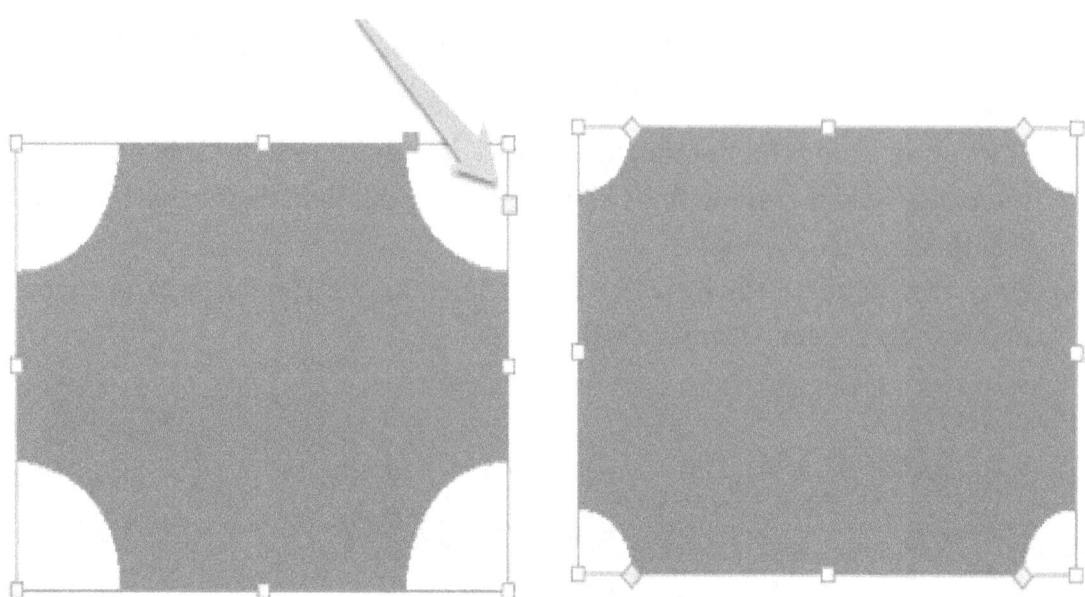

EXPLORING FILLS

A fill resides within a path and offers the ability to fill paths and shapes with various colors, transparent colors, or gradients. Fills serve multiple purposes, including artistic effects, illusions of depth, or enhancing page designs.

You might have already encountered fills while working with shapes. Within the Tools panel, you'll find two swatches: one for strokes (represented by a hollow square) and another for fills (represented by a solid box). A shape either has a fill, indicated by a color in the Fill box or lacks one if the Fill box displays a red line through it.

CREATING BASIC FILLS

To create a basic fill, check the following instructions:

1) Begin by crafting a new shape on the page using a shape tool. Drag the tool across the page to generate the desired shape, which automatically fills with the chosen fill color.
2) If the **Properties** panel isn't visible, navigate to **Window** > **Properties** to reveal it. Click on the **Fill** option within the panel in the Appearance section and select your preferred color from the **swatches**, **Color Picker**, or **Gradient** options.

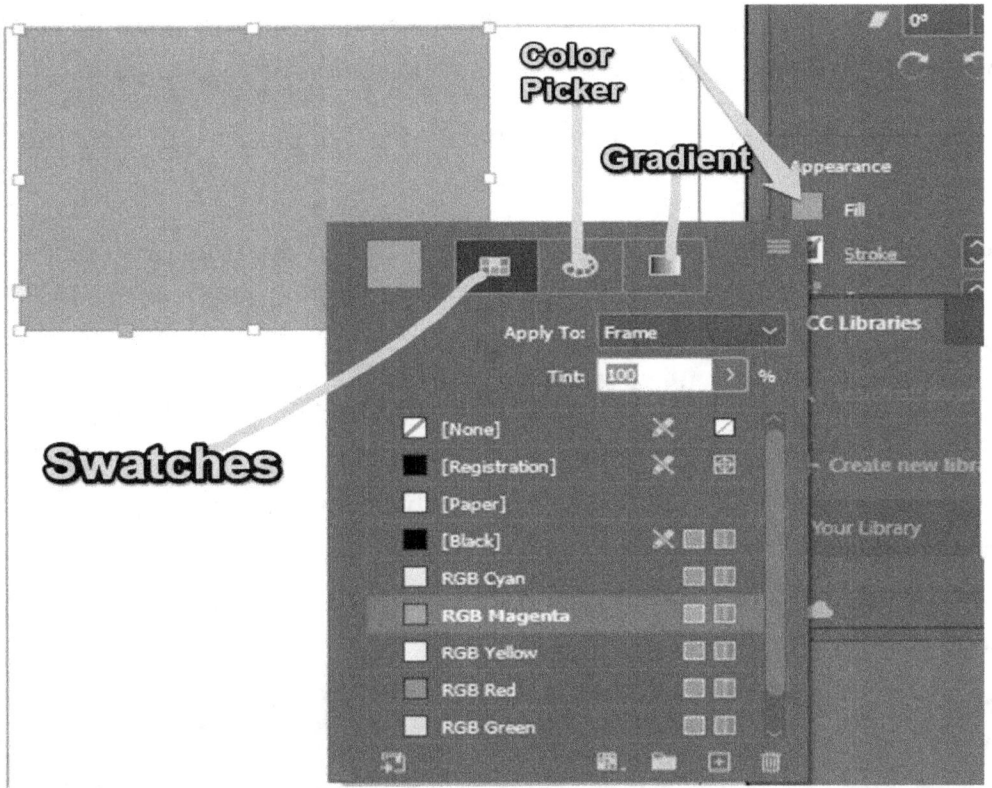

3) Choose a color from the Color panel by entering values into the **RGB (Red, Green, Blue) or CMYK (Cyan, Magenta, Yellow, Black)** fields manually or via sliders.

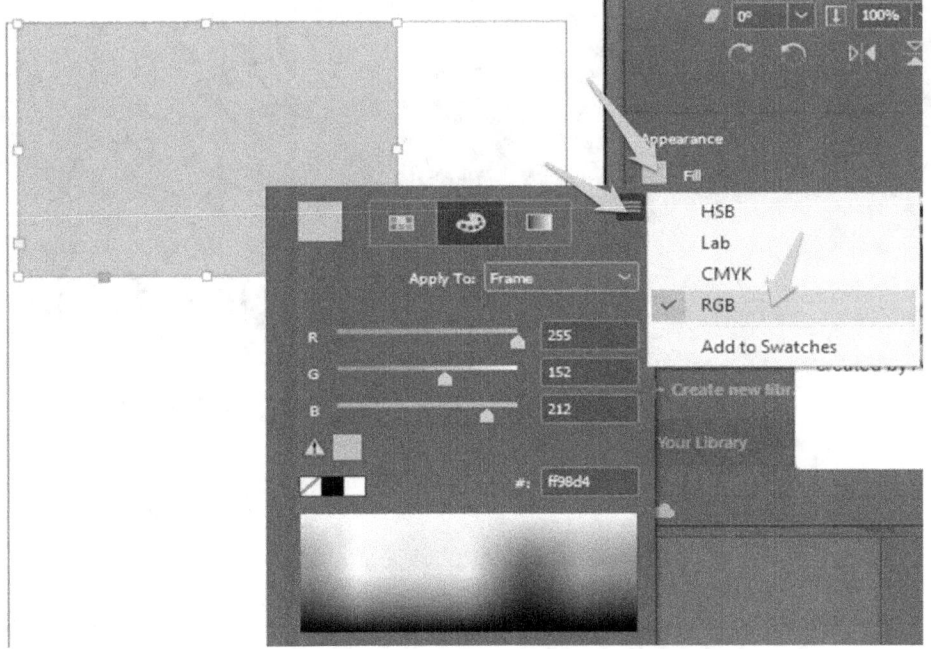

Alternatively, use the **Eyedropper** tool to pick a color from the **Color Picker** located at the bottom of the Color panel.

Upon selecting a **color** in the **Properties** panel, the **Fill** box in the Tools panel updates accordingly.

Similar to other Creative Cloud applications, you can create tints of a color constructed with **CMYK** by holding down the **Shift** key while dragging any color slider. This action causes all color sliders to adjust proportionally.

You have the option to use color swatches for selecting fill colors through the **Swatches** panel. To access the Swatches panel, navigate to **Window** > **Color** > **Swatches**. Here, you can create a new color swatch by clicking the "**New Swatch**" button located at the bottom of the panel. Double-clicking on the newly created swatch enables you to define its **properties** using sliders to adjust **CMYK or RGB** color values or by directly entering values into the text fields.

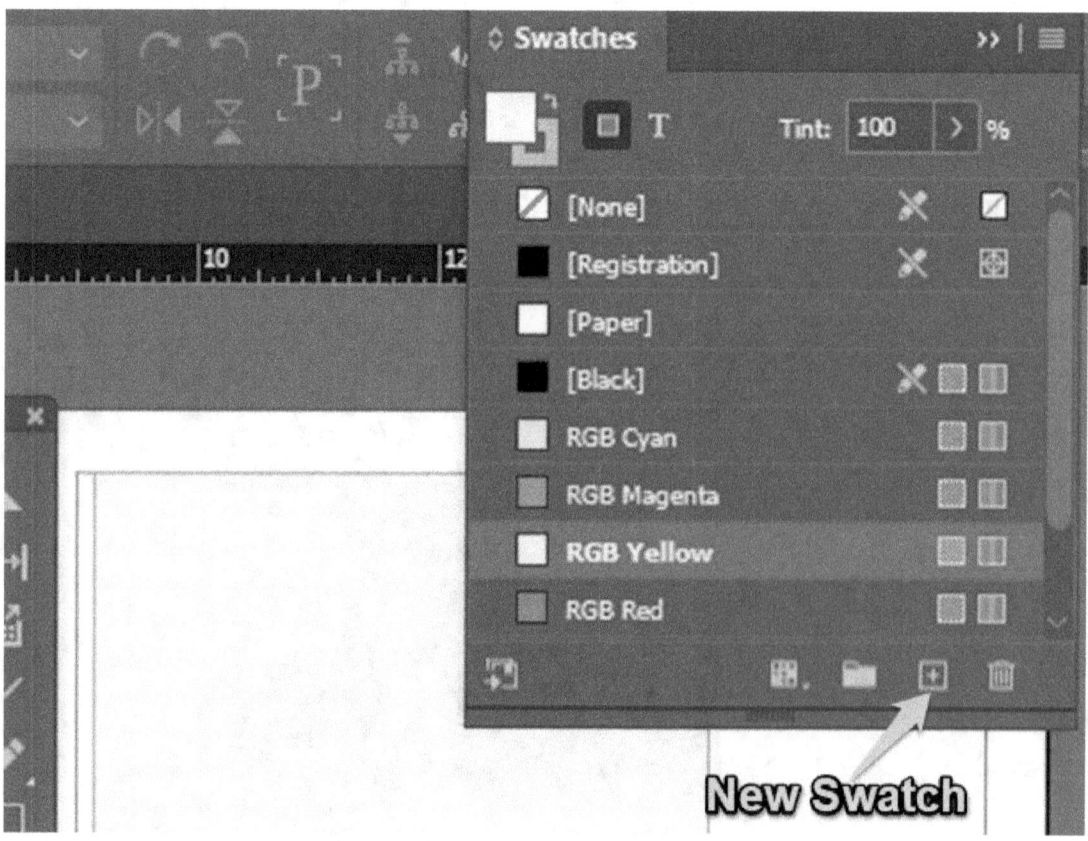

Note: If you have a shape without a fill and wish to add one, or if you intend to change the color of an existing fill, simply select the shape and click on the **Fill** color in the **Windows** > **Properties** panel. Then, choose a new color from the list of swatches.

Furthermore, you can apply a fill color to a shape on the page by dragging and dropping a swatch color, even if the shape isn't currently selected. Open the Swatches panel via **Window** > **Color** > **Swatches**, and then drag the desired color swatch onto the shape. Release the mouse button, and the fill color will be automatically applied to the shape.

CREATING TRANSPARENT FILLS

To create visually appealing layouts, consider creating partially transparent fills. Applying transparency to multiple elements on the page and layering those elements can produce intriguing effects, enhancing the overall depth and stacking illusion of your document's design.

The following steps show you how to apply transparency to an element on your page:

1) Use the **Selection** tool to choose a **shape** that already contains a fill color on the page. Upon selection, a bounding box will appear around the chosen shape.
2) If the Properties panel isn't visible, access it by selecting **Window** > **Properties**.
3) Adjust the **transparency** of the shape by using the **Opacity** slider in the Appearance section. You can either click the arrow to open the slider or directly enter a value into the text field using the keyboard. The transparency effect will be immediately applied to the selected shape.

 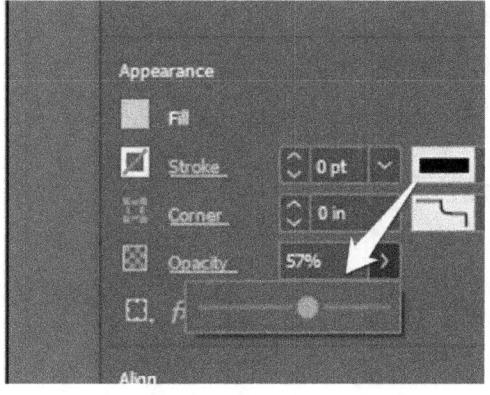

4) Click to open the **Apply Effects to Object** menu and designate which element you wish to apply the transparency to, as shown below

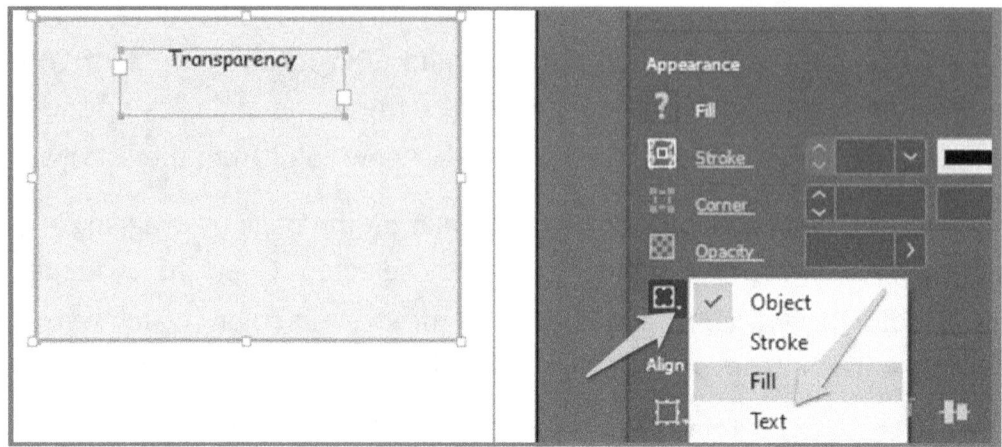

GRADIENT FILLS

Gradients denote the transition of color from one color (or the absence of color) to another. They can consist of two or more colors in the transition, offering diverse effects including 3D effects, glowing effects, or simulating the impact of light on a surface.

In InDesign, two types of gradients are available: **radial and linear.**

- ✓ Radial gradients include a transition of colors in a circular manner from a center point outward.
- ✓ Linear gradients display a transition of colors along a straight path.

Gradients can be applied to strokes, fills, or even text. To apply a gradient to a stroke, simply select the stroke instead of the fill.

Note: Applying gradients to the stroke of live text may result in printing challenges. Exercise caution and use these features carefully to avoid complications in the printing process.

To apply a gradient fill to a shape, follow these steps:

1) Use the Selection tool to choose the object to which you want to apply the gradient. Then, go to **Window > Color > Swatches** to open the Swatches panel.
2) From the drop-down of the **Swatches** panel's menu, select "**New Gradient Swatch**".

This action prompts the opening of the New Gradient Swatch dialog box.

3) Enter a descriptive name for the swatch in the **Swatch Name** field.

Providing a clear name can help identify the purpose of the swatch.

4) Choose either "**Linear**" or "**Radial**" from the Type drop-down list.

This selection determines the type of gradient that the swatch will create each time it is used. In the example, "**Radial**" was selected from the drop-down list.

5) Adjust the gradient stops positioned below the **Gradient Ramp** to position each color in the gradient.

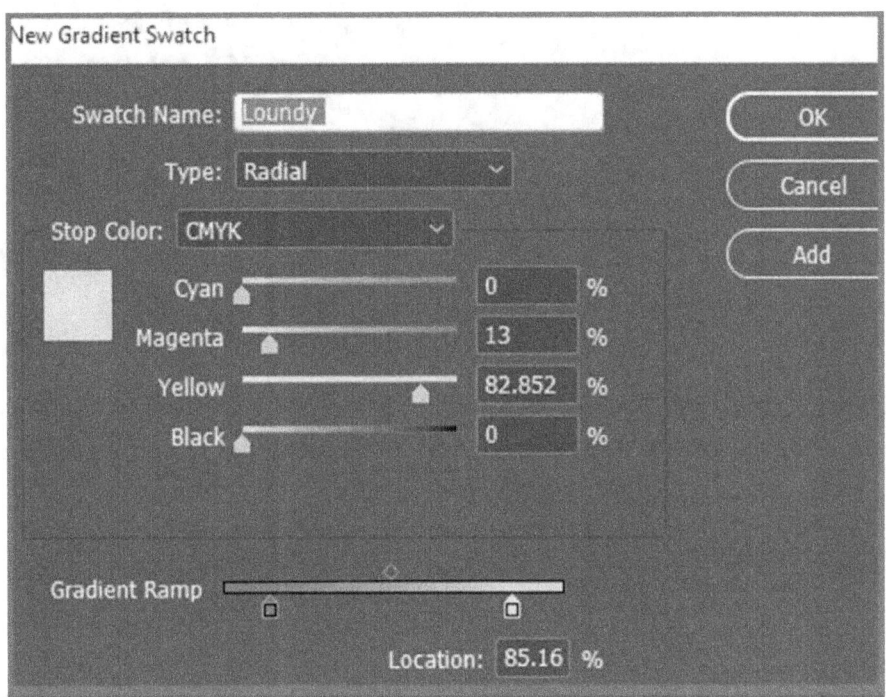

Gradient stops, represented by color chips below the **Gradient Ramp**, can be manipulated by moving the diamond shape above the Gradient Ramp to regulate the center point of the gradient. Each gradient stop can be selected to modify the color and rearranged to edit the gradient. When a gradient stop is selected, the color values in the Stop Color area can be altered using sliders or by entering values into each **CMYK** text field. If a list of swatches appears and you prefer the **CMYK** sliders, choose "CMYK" from the Stop Color drop-down menu. To add a new color to the gradient, click the area between gradient stops and then edit the new stop as desired. To remove a gradient stop, simply drag it away from the Gradient Ramp.

6) After completing the gradient creation process, click "**OK**." This action generates the gradient swatch and applies it to the selected object.

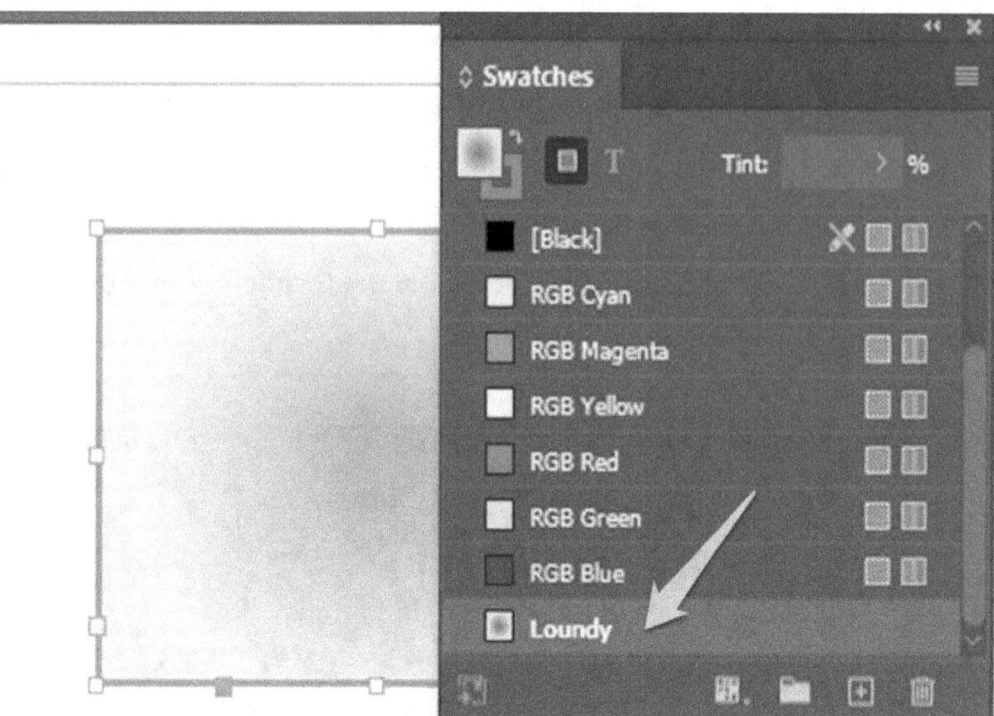

You can edit a gradient by double-clicking the **gradient's swatch** in the **Swatches** panel. This will open the **Gradient Options** dialog box, enabling you to modify the settings established in the New Gradient Swatch dialog box.

REMOVING FILLS

Removing fills is a straightforward process as shown below:

1) Begin by selecting the **shape** using the **Selection** tool, which will display a bounding box around the shape.
2) Locate and click the **Fill** box in the Tools panel.
3) Click the "**Apply None**" button positioned below the **Fill** box.

This button is identifiable by its white color with a red line through it. Upon clicking, the fill is removed from the selected shape, and the Fill box indicator changes to "No Fill". The same thing applies to Stroke.

Additionally, the "None" fill becomes visible in both the Swatches and Color panels.

Note: If you're utilizing a single-row Tools panel, you may not initially see the "**Apply None**" button. In this case, you need to click and hold down the "**Apply Gradient**" (or "**Apply Color**") button to reveal it.

EXPLORING LAYERS

Layers in InDesign function similarly to transparent sheets placed over one another. The addition of layers enables the creation of a layered appearance where graphics are stacked over one another. The Layers panel serves as the command center for managing layers, allowing users to add new layers, remove unnecessary ones, or rearrange them to adjust the stacking order. Moreover, it's possible to duplicate an InDesign file and manipulate layers to generate alternative versions of the document.

Here's a step-by-step guide on working with layers in InDesign:

1) Open the **Layers** panel by going to **Window** > **Layers**. This panel provides options for creating, deleting, and organizing layers
2) Use a **shape** tool to draw a shape on the page.

Ensure the shape is sizable enough to accommodate another shape stacked above a portion of it.

3) Click the "**Create New Layer**" button located at the bottom of the Layers panel to generate a new layer.

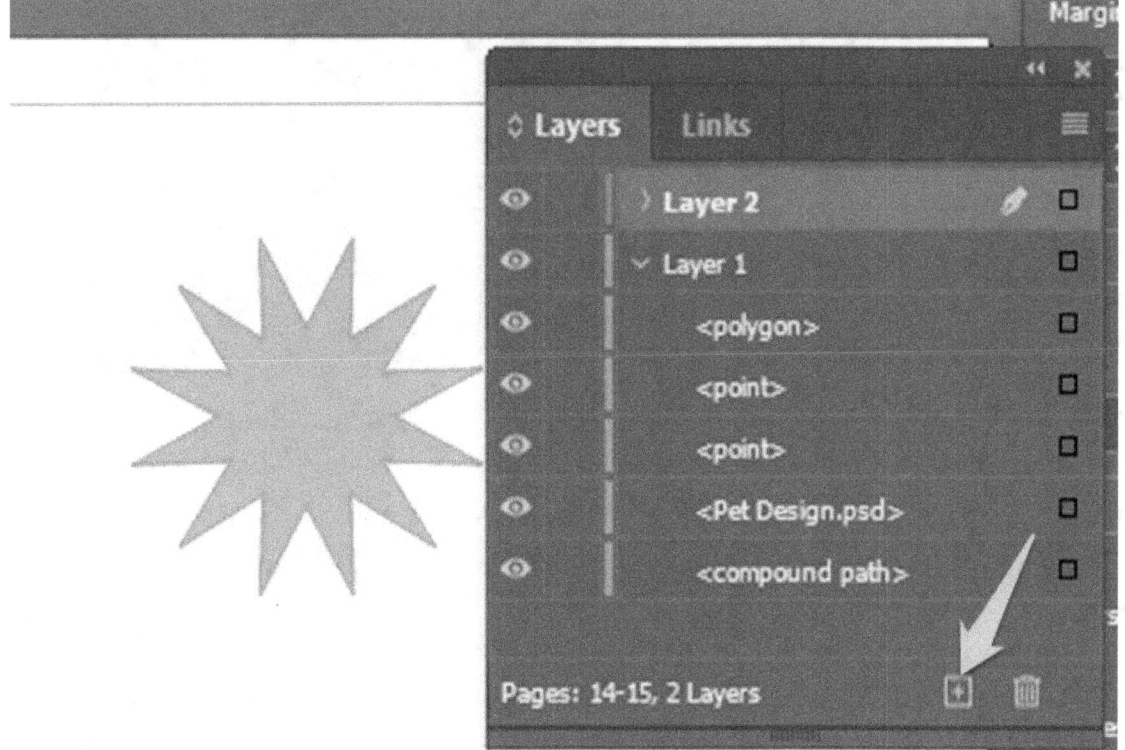

The new layer is positioned atop the selected layer and becomes the active layer. To assign an appropriate name to the layer, double-click it. Alternatively, hold down the **Option** (macOS) or **Alt** (Windows) key and click the "**Create New Layer**" button to open the Layer Options dialog box before the layer is created.

Before modifying the layer, ensure the intended layer for content creation is selected. The selected layer is highlighted in the Layers panel. This precaution prevents inadvertently adding content to the wrong layer. If content is mistakenly added to the wrong layer, it can be corrected by cutting and pasting items to the correct layer.

4) Confirm that a **shape** tool is still selected, then create another shape on the new layer by dragging the cursor to overlap part of the previously created shape. This action results in the new shape being stacked on top of the initial shape.

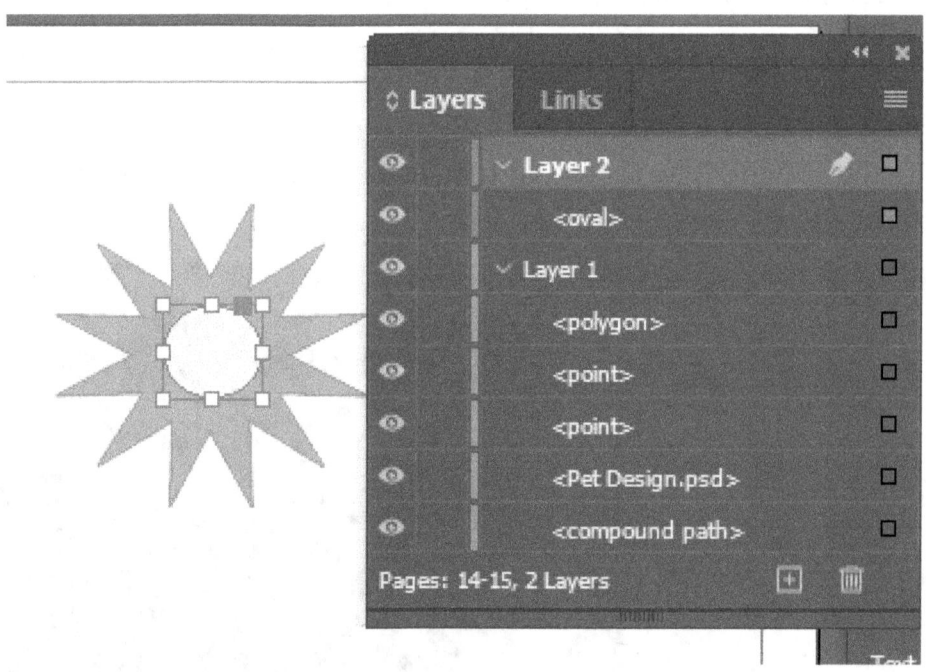

GENERATING QR CODES

InDesign provides you the capability to both generate and customize QR code graphics. QR codes function as a type of barcode capable of storing various forms of data such as text, URLs, or numerical information. When a QR code is scanned by a device equipped with the necessary software, such as a smartphone camera, the encoded data is used, whether it's opening a webpage, identifying a product, or tracking a package. InDesign allows for the encoding of hyperlinks, text, email messages, or even business card information.

QR codes within InDesign are treated as graphics, offering flexibility in scaling and color modification like any other artwork in your document. Interestingly, you can transfer them into Illustrator by copying and pasting.

To integrate a QR code into your InDesign document, follow these steps:

1) Use the **Rectangle Frame** tool to create an empty frame on the page.
2) With the newly created frame selected, navigate to **Object** > **Generate QR Code.**
3) The Generate QR Code dialog box will appear, with the **Content** tab active. Choose the type of data you want to encode from the **Type** menu, such as Web Hyperlink, Plain Text, Text Message, Email, or Business Card. The content area below the menu adjusts based on your selection.
4) Enter the relevant data to be encoded in your QR code.

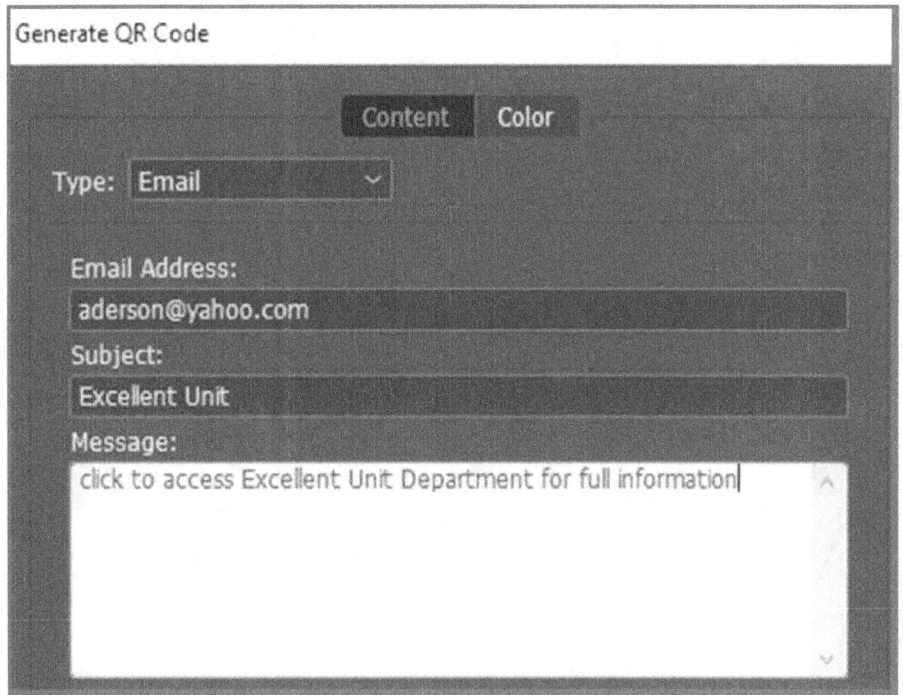

Depending on the chosen Type, different fields will be provided. For instance, if you select Email, you'll need to input an address, subject, and message.

5) Switch to the **Color** tab and select a **color swatch**.

This determines the color of your QR code, impacting its appearance on the page. You can further adjust the color after placing the QR code by modifying the Fill and Stroke features of the selected frame.

6) Click **OK** to finalize the process. The QR code will be embedded within the selected frame. If further editing is required, simply select the text frame containing the QR code and choose **Object** > **Edit QR Code**.

CHAPTER SIX
EXPLORING COLOR

Color holds significant importance in life. Advertisements frequently leverage color to convey brand identities or convey impactful messages; consider the delivery company recognized by its brown identity or the soft drink brand distinguished by its red cans and bottles. Using effective color can amplify your message and, when applied consistently, contributes to building a recognizable brand identity. It is essential for the colors you use to be precise, whether in print or online display. Within this chapter, you will delve into the fundamental principles of working with color and receive basic guidelines on preparing documents for printing.

CHOOSING COLOR WITH COLOR CONTROLS

When working within InDesign, you are presented with various color modes and choices to explore. Within this user guide, you will learn how to incorporate color into your illustrations using the Color panel. This section will guide you through the process of selecting colors from the Color panel and applying them to objects within your page. Additionally, you will uncover the method of saving colors as swatches, enabling convenient reuse in your projects.

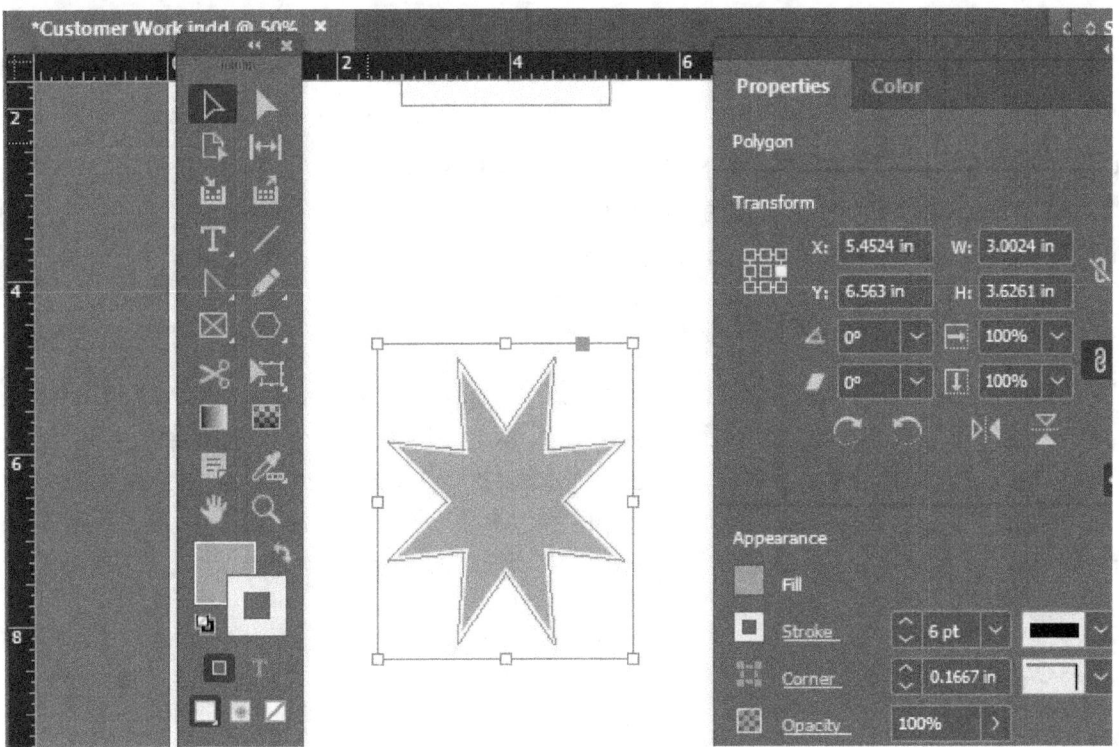

It's advisable to use swatches whenever feasible as they utilize named colors, this facilitates easier matching by others. While an unnamed color can impersonate the appearance of any other swatch, the essence of a swatch lies in establishing a connection between the color on the page and its designated name, such as a Pantone color number. For further insights into this type of color management, check the later section titled "**Exploring Color Swatches and Libraries**"

In your document, you have access to several color controls for making selections as shown below:

- ✓ **Stroke color**: This control allows you to pick colors for strokes and paths within InDesign. The Stroke color control is represented by a hollow box.
- ✓ **Fill color:** This control is used for selecting colors to fill shapes. It is indicated by a solid square box within the Fill color control.

Within the Tools panel, you can easily switch between the Fill and Stroke color controls by clicking on the **Swap Fill and Stroke** button. Alternatively, pressing the "**X**" key on the keyboard toggles between the selected controls.

- ✓ **Text color**: When working with text, a separate color control becomes active. The Text color control is visible and displays the chosen text color. Text elements can have both strokes and fill colors.

To add colors to your selections, you can click the "**Apply color**" button situated under the color controls in the Tools panel. Alternatively, you can choose and click a **color swatch**.

In InDesign, the default colors consist of a black stroke and no fill color. You can easily revert to these defaults at any point by pressing the "**D**" key. This shortcut is universally applicable across all tools except for the **Type** tool.

GETTING TO KNOW COLOR MODELS

In InDesign, you have the flexibility to use three primary color models: **CMYK (Cyan, Magenta, Yellow, Black), RGB (Red, Green, Blue),** and **LAB** colors (**Lightness, and A and B** for the color-opponent dimensions of the color space). A color model serves as a system for representing each color through a group of numbers, letters, or both. The optimal color model to employ depends on your intended method for printing or displaying your document.

- ✓ When creating a PDF intended for electronic distribution and unlikely to be printed, opt for the RGB color model. RGB corresponds to how colors are shown on a computer monitor.
- ✓ If your project involves process color, it is required to use the CMYK color model. Rather than having inks that precisely match specified colors, the CMYK model includes four ink colors layered to replicate a particular color. It's important to note that the colors displayed on the monitor may differ from those printed. using sample swatch books and numerical references can assist in determining which colors are necessary to match the printed output accurately.
- ✓ If professionals handle the printing process and determine each color beforehand, whether you use CMYK, RGB, or Pantone colors becomes less critical. However, in numerous instances, CMYK colors offer a more precise representation of the final printed output because RGB colors often appear more intense and brighter on computer monitors.

EXPLORING COLOR SWATCHES AND LIBRARIES

Using the Swatches panel and swatch libraries facilitates the selection, preservation, and application of colors within your documents. The range of colors used in your documents can be diverse. For instance, one publication crafted in InDesign might entail a newsletter or bulletin characterized by just two colors, while another might entail a catalog printed using CMYK in addition to a distinct spot color. Tailoring the available swatches for each document enables you to operate well.

USING THE SWATCHES PANEL

From the Swatches panel, you can create, apply, and modify colors. Moreover, you can create and save solid colors. Access the Swatches panel by going to **Window** > **Color** > **Swatches** to open or expand it.

To create a new color swatch that you can use within a document, check the following instructions:

1) Select the **panel** menu dropdown situated in the top-right corner of the **Swatches** Panel, then opt for "**New Color Swatch**".

The New Color Swatch dialog box will appear.

2) Keep the "**Name with Color Value**" checkbox selected to assign a name to your new color swatch, or deselect it to leave the name field blank.
3) Pick the color type from the **Color Type** dropdown list.

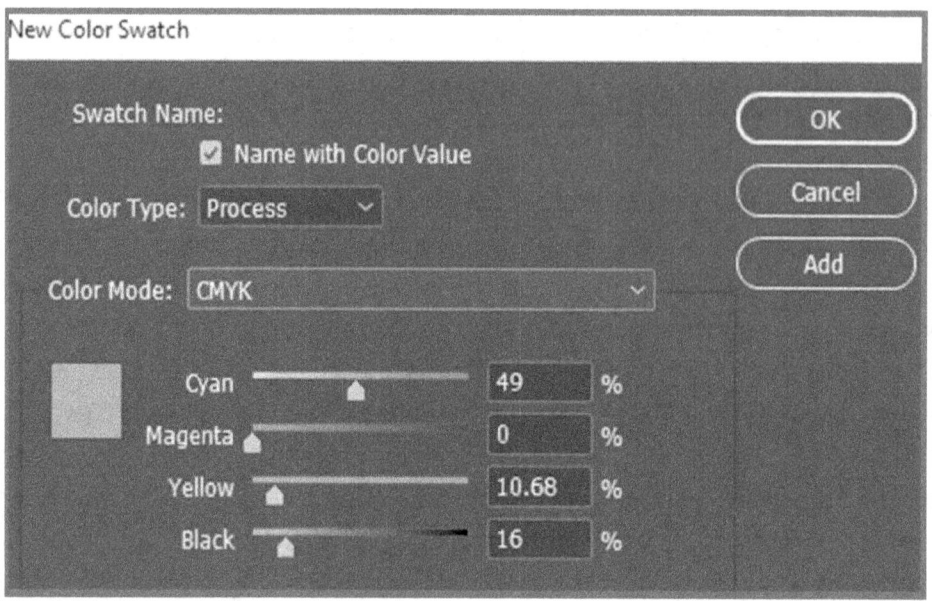

By default, colors in the Swatches panel are named based on their color values. When you input a name for a color, it appears next to the color swatch within the panel.

If you are using a spot color, such as Pantone, or opting for Process color, which involves printing with Cyan, Magenta, Yellow, and Black (CMYK)?

4) Select the **Color Mode**.

choose a color mode on the Color Mode drop-down list. In this instance, we're using **CMYK**. You'll notice various other options representing inbuilt color libraries for different systems.

5) Use the **Color sliders** to create the color

Keep in mind that if you start with Black, you'll need to slide it to the left to reveal other colors. If you opt for a spot color like Pantone, you'll see a list of available color swatches instead of sliders.

6) Click "**OK**" or "**Add**" to confirm your changes.

Note: Choose **Add** if you're adding more colors to the Swatches panel or **OK** if this color is the only one you're adding. The colors will be added to the Swatches panel. If you click **Add**, hit **OK** when you're finished adding color swatches.

You can edit a swatch by selecting it in the **Swatches** panel and then selecting **Swatch Options** from the panel menu, or simply double-clicking it in the Swatches panel.

UTILIZING SWATCH LIBRARIES

Swatch libraries, also called color libraries, are accepted sets of named colors designed to simplify color selection. They include commonly used color swatches, they spare you the effort of mixing your own colors, which can be challenging. For instance, InDesign provides swatch libraries for Pantone spot colors and Pantone process colors, which are particularly helpful when working with these color sets. If you missed it, you might want to review the earlier section "Getting to Know Color Model" where we explain the distinction between spot and process colors.

To choose a swatch from a swatch library, check these instructions:

1) Open the **Swatches panel** menu and select **New Color Swatch.**

This action opens the New Color Swatch dialog box.

2) From the **Color Type** drop-down list, choose the color type you wish to work with.

Options include **Process** or **Spot Color types**.

Process color creates your color using a mix of CMYK colors (Cyan, Magenta, Yellow, and Black). Using spot colors adds a distinct solid color to your document, which can be particularly useful for professional printers utilizing a CMYK press to precisely reproduce specific ink colors.

Note: In the CMYK color model, 'K' stands for black, signifying its importance as the Key color.

3) Choose a color library on the **Color Mode** drop-down list.

This list provides various color swatch libraries to select from, including options like Pantone Process Coated or TRUMATCH. Upon selection, the chosen swatch set opens within the dialog box. In this example, we opted for **Trumatch**, which is a standard choice. This set is convenient for accessing the standard numbered Pantone colors. Upon selection, the Trumatch library of swatches becomes available.

4) Select a **swatch** from the library.

If you have a specific trumatch number provided, enter it into the designated **TRUMATCH** textbox. Many organizations maintain predetermined Trumatch or Pantone colors to ensure consistency across various printing or display platforms. Alternatively, you can scroll through the library's list of colors and click on the desired swatch.

5) Press the "**Add**" button.

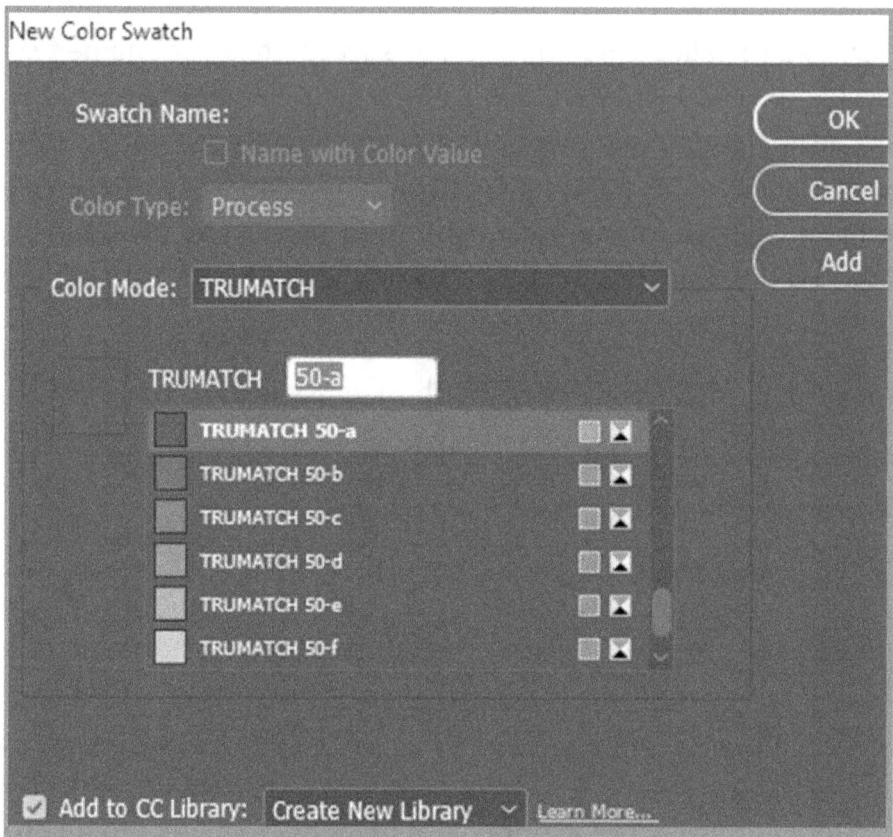

This action incorporates the selected swatch into your collection of color swatches within the Swatches panel. Feel free to include as many color swatches as needed.

6) Upon completing the addition of swatches, click "**OK**".

Once a new color is added, it integrates into the roster of swatches within the panel, ready for immediate utilization in your project. Verify the inclusion of the newly added colors by inspecting the **Swatches** panel.

CHAPTER SEVEN

CLIPPING PATHS, OBJECT MANIPULATION, AND ALIGNMENT

Next, you'll explore various techniques for manipulating and arranging objects within a page layout. You'll learn how to utilize the Transform panel along with other tools in the Tools panel to modify objects effectively. In InDesign, there are multiple approaches to applying transformations to objects, and we'll illustrate a few methods to accomplish the same task.

Aligning and distributing objects plays a crucial role in organizing elements logically on a page. Throughout this chapter, you'll discover how to align objects using the Align panel. Additionally, while Chapter 5 briefly covers paths, this chapter delves deeper into clipping paths. We'll guide you through the process of creating a new path to serve as a clipping path for an image within your document.

GETTING STARTED TRANSFORMATIONS

In Chapter 5 of this guide, you learn the art of transforming graphic objects using the Free Transform tool. In InDesign, the possibilities for manipulating objects are vast. You can start a transformation by selecting an individual object and accessing the Transform panel, found under **Window > Object & Layout > Transform**. Alternatively, you can visually adjust objects using the **Free Transform** tool. Moreover, resizing a selected object can be effortlessly accomplished via the Properties panel.

EXAMINING THE TRANSFORM PANEL

The Transform panel and the Properties panel prove helpful when adjusting the scale, rotation, or skew of selected objects. For certain modifiers, you have the option to select from a preset range of values or input your own manually. As the Properties panel offers greater accessibility, we'll delve into its features in more depth first.

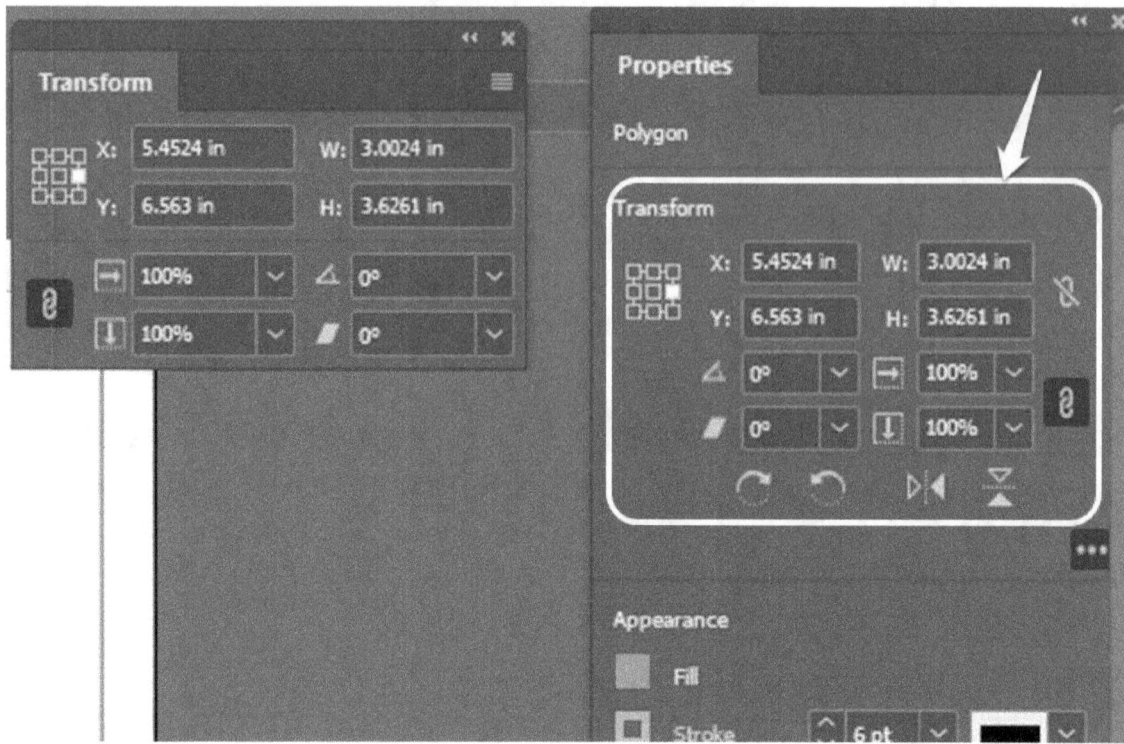

Both the Transform and Properties panels provide essential information and tools for adjusting objects in your design:

- ✓ **Reference point:** This indicates which handle serves as the reference for any transformations you apply. For instance, resetting the **X** and **Y** coordinates will position the reference point accordingly. The reference point is located in the top-left corner, denoted by the solid square as shown below.
- ✓ **Position:** Adjust these values to reset the **X** and **Y** coordinate positions of the selected object.
- ✓ **Size**: Use the **W** and **H** text fields to modify the current sizes of the object.
- ✓ **Scale**: Specify a percentage or select from the **Scale X Percentage** and **Scale Y Percentage** drop-down lists to resize the object along each axis.
- ✓ **Constraining proportions**: Enable the Constrain Proportions button to preserve the current proportions of the object during scaling.
- ✓ **Shearing**: Enter a negative or positive number to alter the shearing angle (skew) of the selected object.
- ✓ **Rotation angle:** Define a negative value to rotate the object clockwise and a positive value to rotate it counterclockwise.

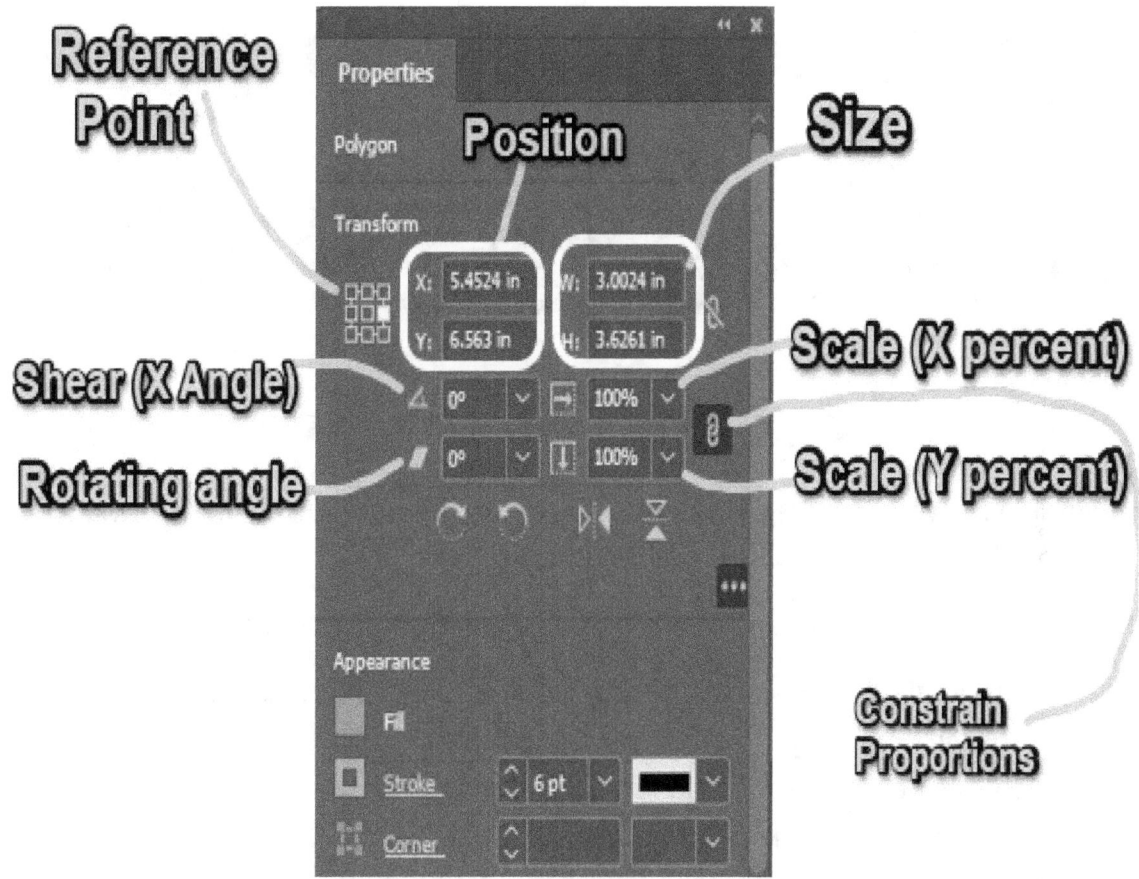

When you resize, rotate, or shear an object within your layout, it alters according to the chosen reference point found in the **Transform** panel. For instance, in the case of rotating an object, InDesign takes the center point as the reference. To adjust this, simply click on a different reference point square within the Transform panel to align the graphic with the corresponding bounding box handle of the selected object.

MAKING USE OF THE FREE TRANSFORM TOOL

With the versatile Free Transform tool, you can speedily alter objects in various ways. It enables you to effortlessly move, shear, rotate, mirror, and resize objects. Here is how to use the Free Transform tool:

1) To manipulate any illustration, select the **object(s)** you want to transform with the **Selection tool** and then click on the **Free Transform** tool in your **Tools** panel.
2) In InDesign, the **Free Transform Tool** offers various functions represented by different cursors, as illustrated below.

If you're concerned about the clarity of your images, you can check if they're displaying in high quality. Simply right-click on the image and choose "**Display Performance**" from the menu that appears, as shown below.

The following steps show how to move an object with the Free Transform tool:

1) Start by selecting an **object** on the page using the **Selection tool**. You can choose an existing object or create a new shape using the drawing tools. Once selected, you'll see handles around the edges of the object.
2) Next, select the **Free Transform tool** from the Tools panel. You'll notice the cursor change to the Free Transform tool icon.
3) Hover the cursor over the middle of the selected object. It will change appearance, indicating that you can drag to move the object. If you move the cursor outside the object's edges, it will switch to other tools like rotate, scale, and shear.

4) Now, simply drag the object to the desired location on the page. It will be moved accordingly.

ROTATING OBJECTS

To rotate objects, you have a few options: you can either use the Rotate tool, the Free Transform tool, or the Transform panel. If you want to specify the exact degree of rotation, the Transform panel is your go-to. However, if you prefer a more visual approach, the Free Transform tool allows you to directly manipulate the object on the page.

Here's how you can rotate an image using the Free Transform tool:

1) Start by selecting the **object** you want to rotate using the **Selection tool**. Once selected, **handles** will appear around its edges, indicating that it's ready for manipulation.
2) Next, grab the **Free Transform tool** from the Tools panel and position it near one of the handles outside the object's bounding box. Pay attention to the cursor, which will change to indicate that you're in rotation mode. Make sure to keep the cursor just outside the object.
3) Once the cursor changes to the rotation icon, drag it to rotate the object to your desired angle. You can visually adjust it until it's just right.

Alternatively, you can opt for the Rotate tool:

1) With your object selected, locate the **Rotate tool** in the Tools panel. You can find it by clicking and holding the arrow in the lower corner of the **Free Transform** tool. When you move the cursor near the object, it will resemble a crosshair.
2) Click anywhere on the page near the object to set the rotation point. This point will act as the center of rotation for the object.
3) Drag the cursor away from the object to start rotating it. If you want to rotate in increments of **45 degrees**, hold down the **Shift** key while dragging.

Note: for exact rotation where you can type the value of rotation, make use of the Transform panel. we have treated this in one of our previous lessons.

SCALING (OR RESIZING) OBJECTS

To resize objects, you have a few options such as the Free Transform panel, Transform panel, or Scale tool. With the Transform panel, you can precisely set the width and height dimensions you desire, similar to setting percentages for rotation.

Here's how to resize with the Free Transform tool or Scale tool:

1) Select the **object** on the page, and you'll see a bounding box around it.
2) Choose either the **Free Transform tool** or the **Scale** tool from the Tools panel.
3) Hover your cursor over a corner handle; it will turn into a double-headed arrow.
4) Drag outward to increase the object's size or inward to decrease it. If you want to maintain proportions, hold down the **Shift** key while dragging.
5) Release the mouse button when the object is scaled to your desired size.

For resizing using the **Transform** panel:

1) Select the object and enter new values into the **W (width)** and **H (height)** fields in the panel.

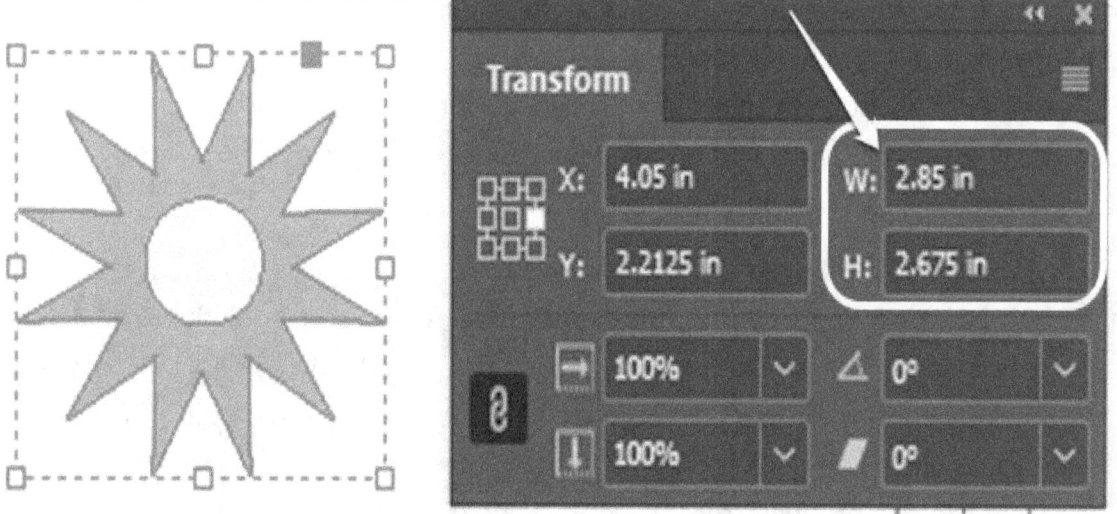

2) The object will resize to those particular dimensions.

SHEARING (SKEWING) OBJECTS

To shear an object means to tilt it horizontally, giving it a slanted appearance either to the left or right. This adjustment can add a sense of perspective or depth to the object. To achieve this effect, utilize the Shear tool, as illustrated in the next steps:

1) Begin by selecting the object on the page. This action will display a bounding box around the selected object.
2) Next, access the **Shear** tool located in the **Tools** panel by clicking and holding the **Free Transform** tool. Upon selection, the cursor will transform into a crosshair. Click on the corner of the object from which you wish to shear, and a crosshair will appear.

3) Then, click anywhere below or above the object and drag. The direction in which you drag will determine the direction of the shear. Hold down the **Shift** key while dragging to shear the object in **45-degree** increments.

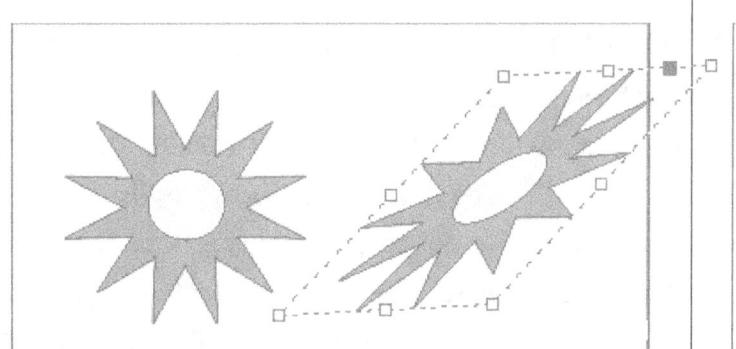

Alternatively, to shear objects using the **Free Transform** tool, begin dragging a handle and then hold down **Command + Option (macOS)** or **Ctrl + Alt (Windows)** while dragging.

For precise adjustments, you can input exact values into the **Transform** panel. Select the **object**, and then input a **positive or negative value** representing the desired amount of slant in the panel.

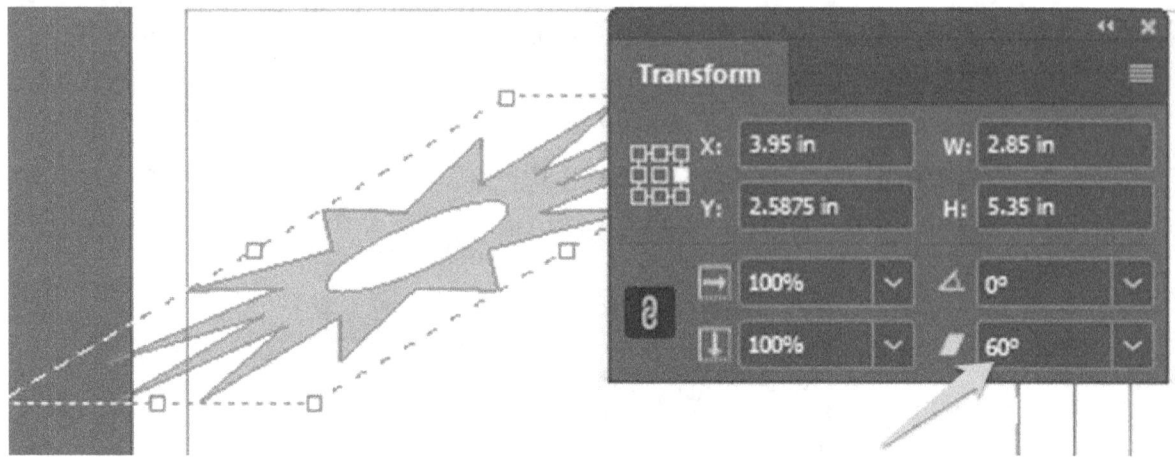

Another method is to apply shear by selecting **Object** > **Transform** > **Shear**, which will prompt the display of the Shear dialog box. From there, you can adjust the Shear accordingly.

REFLECTING OBJECTS

To create mirror images of objects, you can use the Transform panel menu. This menu offers various options for adjusting objects. Here's how to reflect an object:

1) Begin by selecting the object on the page. Then, navigate to **Window** > **Object & Layout** > **Transform** to access the Transform panel, or simply open it from the **Window** menu. This action will display the object's bounding box and handles, along with the current values in the Transform panel.
2) Next, click on the panel menu located within the Transform panel. This action will unveil a plethora of options for altering the selected object.
3) From panel the menu, choose **"Flip Horizontally"** As a result, the object on the page will flip along its vertical axis. You can also experiment with other reflection options available in the menu, such as **"Flip Vertically"**.

Additionally, you can achieve object reflection using the Free Transform tool. Simply drag a corner handle of the object past its opposite end. This action will cause the object to reflect along its axis.

GETTING TO KNOW CLIPPING PATHS

Clipping paths are a powerful tool in image editing, enabling you to precisely define a boundary that isolates or crops a specific area of an image, typically used for removing backgrounds. Whether you create a custom shape within InDesign or import an image already equipped with a clipping path, the versatility of this feature is invaluable. Additionally, InDesign effortlessly integrates with existing alpha or mask layers from programs like Photoshop, treating them as clipping paths.

These paths prove particularly handy when you need to mask portions of an image, allowing text to stylishly wrap around the remaining visual elements.

In InDesign, creating a clipping path is straightforward. Simply use drawing tools like the Pen tool to outline a shape, then insert the image into this defined area on the page. For future-proofing and ease of reuse, it's advisable to construct the clipping path directly within Photoshop and save it alongside the image file.

To swiftly remove a background using InDesign:

1) Select **File** > **Place** and navigate to the desired image.
2) Use the **Pen** tool to trace a path directly over the image, ensuring it encompasses the desired area.

3) Using the **Selection** tool, click on the image, then go to **Edit** > **Cut**.

4) select the previously drawn shape and select **Edit** > **Paste Into.**

The image will neatly fill the selected shape, as sketched by the **Pen** tool.

If you've got an image with a clipping path already set, when you're placing it into your InDesign layout, you can opt to use it by selecting **"Show Import Options"**. On a macOS, just hit the **Options** button to access this feature.

If the image has multiple paths, you can pick which one to use by going to **Object** > **Clipping Path** > **Options**, and then selecting either **Clipping Path** or **Alpha Channel** from the **Type** menu, depending on what's in the image.

Now, let's say the image you're bringing into your layout is an image against a solid light-colored or white background, like a product photo for a catalog. You can have InDesign create a clipping path for it. Here's how:

1) Import the image with a solid background into your document. Use the Selection tool to click and select the image.
2) Go to **Object** > **Clipping Path** > **Options.**
3) In the Clipping Path dialog box, choose **Detect Edges** from the **Type** drop-down menu. Adjust the **threshold** slider until the background disappears.
4) Click **OK**.

Note : Now, the path is set up, removing the background and keeping the image visible. You can place this image over any other object, and it'll reveal whatever is behind it.

Just a heads-up: for the clipping path to reveal objects behind it, make sure it's at the topmost layer or the topmost object within its layer. You can check this by selecting the object, then going to **Object** > **Arrange** > **Bring to Front.** You can also use the layers panel by selecting **Window** > **Layers**.

ALIGNING OBJECTS OVER THE PAGE

In InDesign CC, aligning objects visually is a breeze, requiring no additional tools or panels. With Smart Guides enabled (typically on by default), simply select and move objects using the **Selection** tool, and guides will automatically appear. These guides signal alignment with other objects on the page or with the page itself. If these guides become distracting, you can easily disable them by navigating to **InDesign** > **Preferences** > **Guides & Pasteboard** (macOS) or **Edit** > **Preferences** > **Guides & Pasteboard** (Windows) and toggling off the options under the Smart Guide Options heading.

Alternatively, you can utilize the Align panel to align objects on your page. Access it through **Window**> **Object & Layout** > **Align**. This panel offers precise control over how elements align with one another or with the overall page layout. Each button in the Align panel corresponds to a specific alignment function, with tooltips providing descriptions of their actions upon hovering. If unsure about a button's function, refer to its icon, which often provides visual cues regarding its alignment behavior.

These are the instructions for arranging elements on your page:

1) use the **Selection tool** to choose several objects. You can hold down the **Shift** key while clicking each object to select several at once. If you don't have enough objects on your page, you can quickly create some using the drawing tools.

2) Go to **Window** > **Object & Layout** > **Align**. This will open up the **Align** panel, where you can fine-tune the alignment of your selected objects.
3) Once the Align panel is open, you can choose the type of alignment you prefer for your selected objects. **For instance**, you can try clicking on the **Align Vertical Centers** button, which will align all the selected objects to the vertical center point of the page.

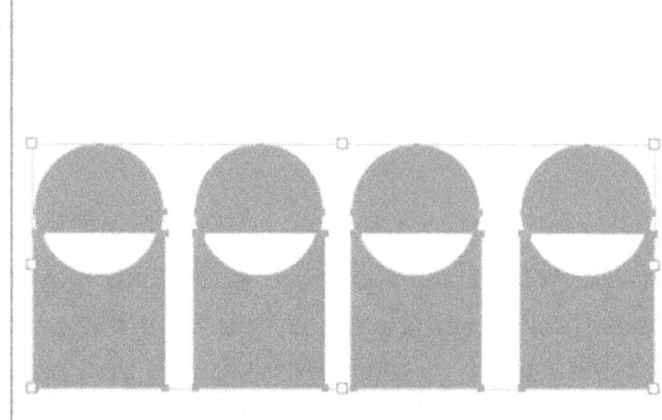 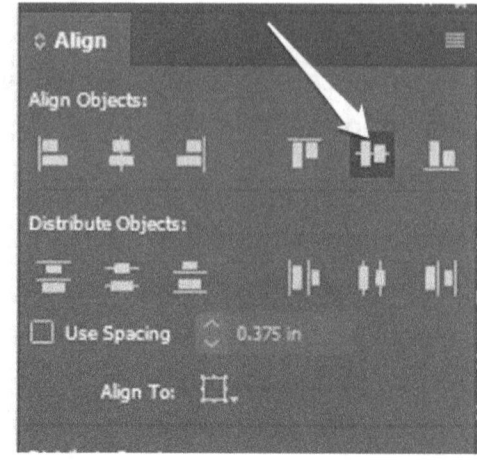

DISTRIBUTING OBJECTS

In the previous section, you learned about aligning objects on a page, but what if those objects aren't evenly spaced? Picture this: you've got some objects lined up with their centers aligned, but there's a big gap between two of them and a smaller one between the others. In such cases, you need to distribute and align the objects properly. Distributing objects means spacing them relative to the page or each other in various ways. Here's how you can do it:

1) Start by selecting the objects on the page that aren't aligned or evenly distributed. To do this, use the **Selection** tool while holding down the **Shift** key. As you click on each object, it will be added to the selection group, and they'll all align with each other on the page.
2) If you don't see the **Align** panel, go to **Window > Object & Layout > Align** to open it up.
3) Now, click on the "**Distribute Horizontal Centers**" button, followed by the "**Align Vertical Centers**" button directly above it on the **Align** panel. This will ensure that your objects are not only aligned but also evenly distributed both horizontally and vertically on the page.

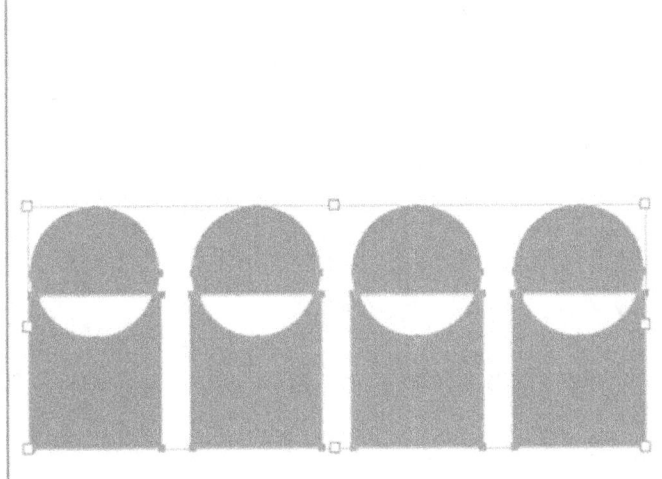 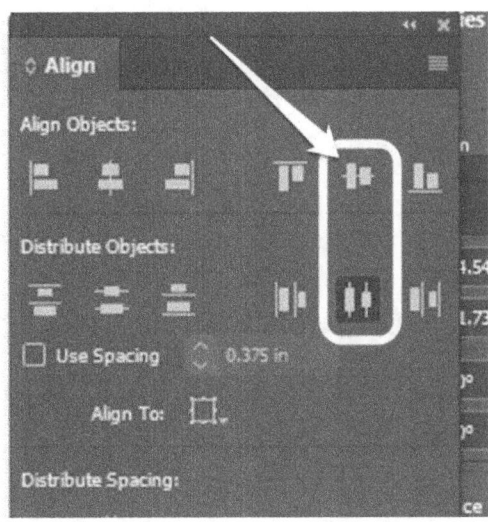

Make sure not to overlook the fantastic **Multiple Place** feature: It allows you to effortlessly distribute and align images on the go! Give this convenient option a try to insert multiple images at once:

1) Select **File** > **Place**.
2) While holding down **Command** (macOS) or **Ctrl** (Windows), pick **multiple images**, and click the **Open** button.
3) Before placing the images, hold **Command + Shift** (macOS) or **Ctrl + Shift** (Windows). Be patient as the grid loads.
4) Your cursor will display as a grid as shown here. Click and drag to draw the rectangle for aligning and distributing your images within.

The images will automatically align and distribute, similar to what is shown below:

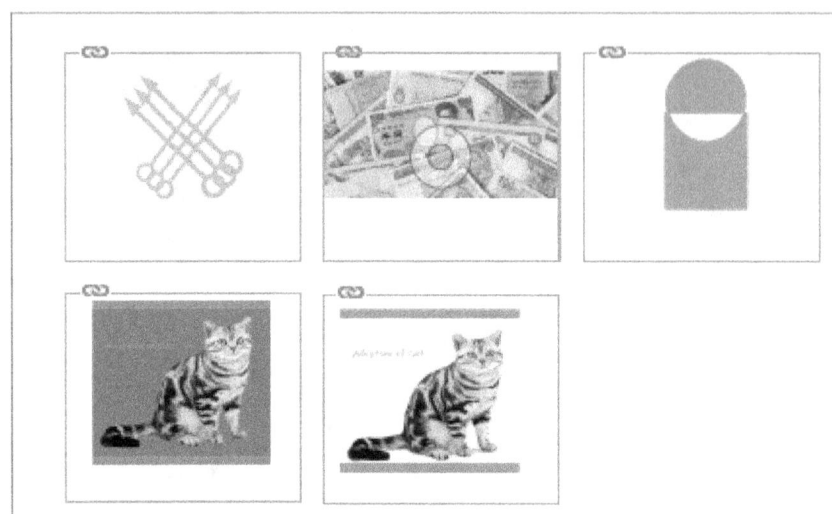

CHAPTER EIGHT
EXPORTING YOUR PUBLICATION

Aside from simply printing your document, you have the option to export InDesign files into various file formats. This chapter delves into the steps required to prepare your file for delivery to a print vendor and explores the diverse array of electronic files you can generate from an InDesign document. Before sending your document to print, it's essential to ensure everything is in order, which is why we'll begin by examining the preflight option.

PREPARING YOUR DOCUMENTS FOR PRINTING WITH PREFLIGHT

The Preflight feature in InDesign serves as a vital tool to ensure that all necessary elements for printing your document are in place and ready. It offers valuable insights into your document, such as listing the fonts, print settings, and inks utilized. By using Preflight, you can identify potential issues like unlinked images or missing fonts before sending your document to print. Here's how to utilize the Preflight option effectively:

1) Open any InDesign document, especially the one with missing fonts and images.

2) With the file open, navigate to **Window > Output > Preflight**. This action will open the **Preflight** panel.
3) Ensure that the **On** checkbox is checked, and the **Profile** is set to **[Basic] (working).** These settings offer a fundamental preflight analysis, confirming the availability of all necessary fonts and images for printing.
4) If any errors are identified within the document, click on the **page number** associated with the error listed in the preflight window to view more details. Common errors, such as **missing fonts or overset text**, are conveniently listed within the **Preflight** panel and can usually be rectified with some attention. It's crucial to address these errors before proceeding with printing to ensure a smooth printing process.

When you activate the **Preflight** option, a small circle appears in the bottom-left corner of the document window, either **green or red**. A **green circle** indicates that the document has been p**reflighted** without any reported errors, while a **red circle** signifies a potential error. To investigate any possible **errors**, simply click on the **errors** drop-down located in the same corner of the **Document** window to open the **Preflight** panel.

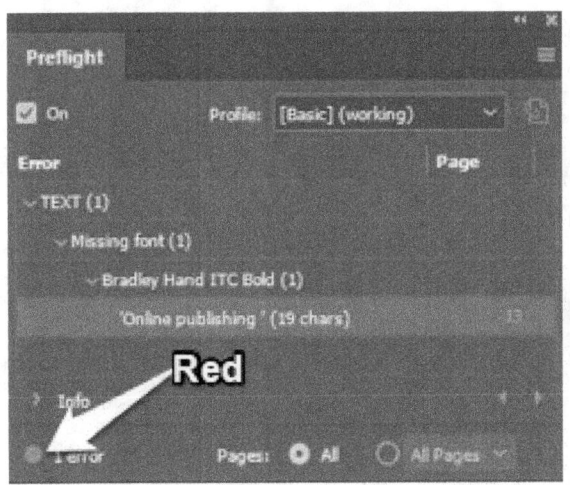 

You'll notice that there's a missing image and some text overflow in this particular InDesign document I am currently using. Follow these steps to rectify the errors:

1) Open the **Links** panel by selecting **Window > Links**.

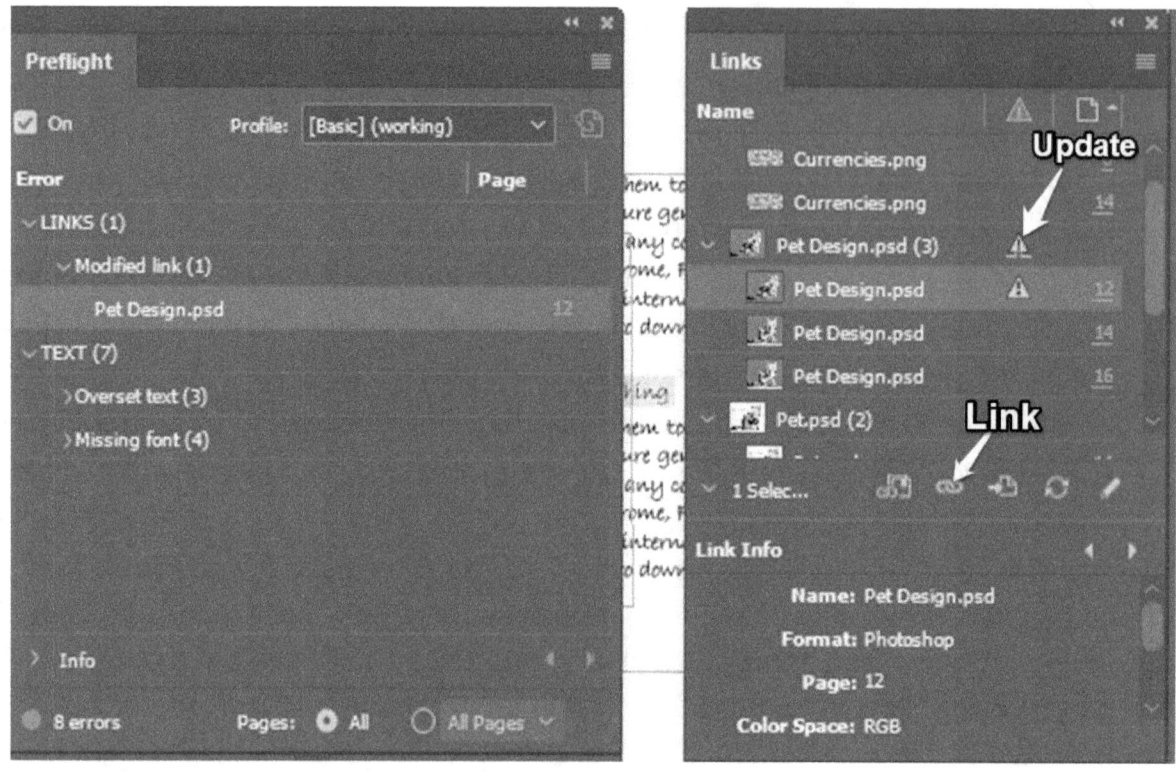

2) Click on the **Relink** icon for the missing image issue, browse the folder you initially linked it with, and then click **OK** to relink it. This action resolves the image error.

3) To address the text-overflow, simply expand the text box by dragging the middle handle at the bottom until the text fits appropriately.

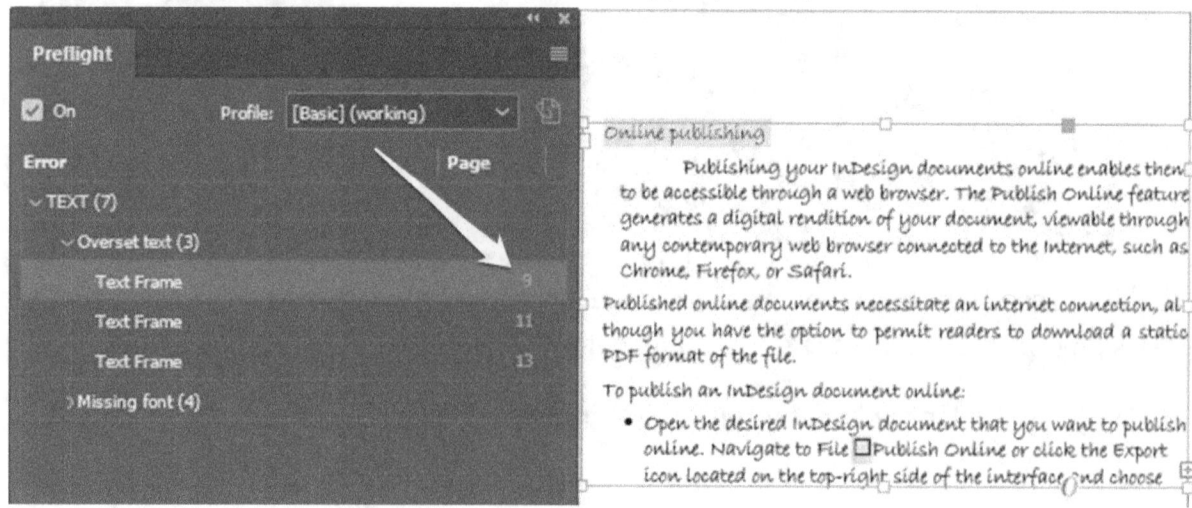

Note: If you prefer the text to continue onto another page, you can also click on the red plus (+) icon in the lower-right corner of the text box. Once the cursor changes to indicate loaded text, you can click and drag to create a new text area or click on an existing one. This allows the text flow to continue effortlessly from the overflow into the new text box.

PREPARING YOUR DOCUMENTS FOR DELIVERY

When it comes to delivering your documents to a print service provider or another designer, ensuring that you provide everything they need to continue their work on the InDesign file is crucial. This is where the Packaging command proves invaluable. Packaging assembles copies of all images and fonts utilized in the document, along with a duplicate of the InDesign file itself, which is consolidated into a single folder for convenient delivery. This option can also be used for archiving completed projects, ensuring that all essential elements are stored together. Here's how to utilize the Packaging feature effectively:

1) Go to **File** > **Package**. This action opens the Package dialog box, where the Summary screen displays all current images and fonts in the document based on an analysis of the file.
2) Select "**Fonts**" from the list on the left side of the dialog box. Any fonts used in the document are listed here. You can select fonts from this list and click the "**Find/Replace Font**" button to locate them. Clicking the **"More Info"** button reveals the path to the font. These fonts are automatically saved into the package folder upon completion.

Package

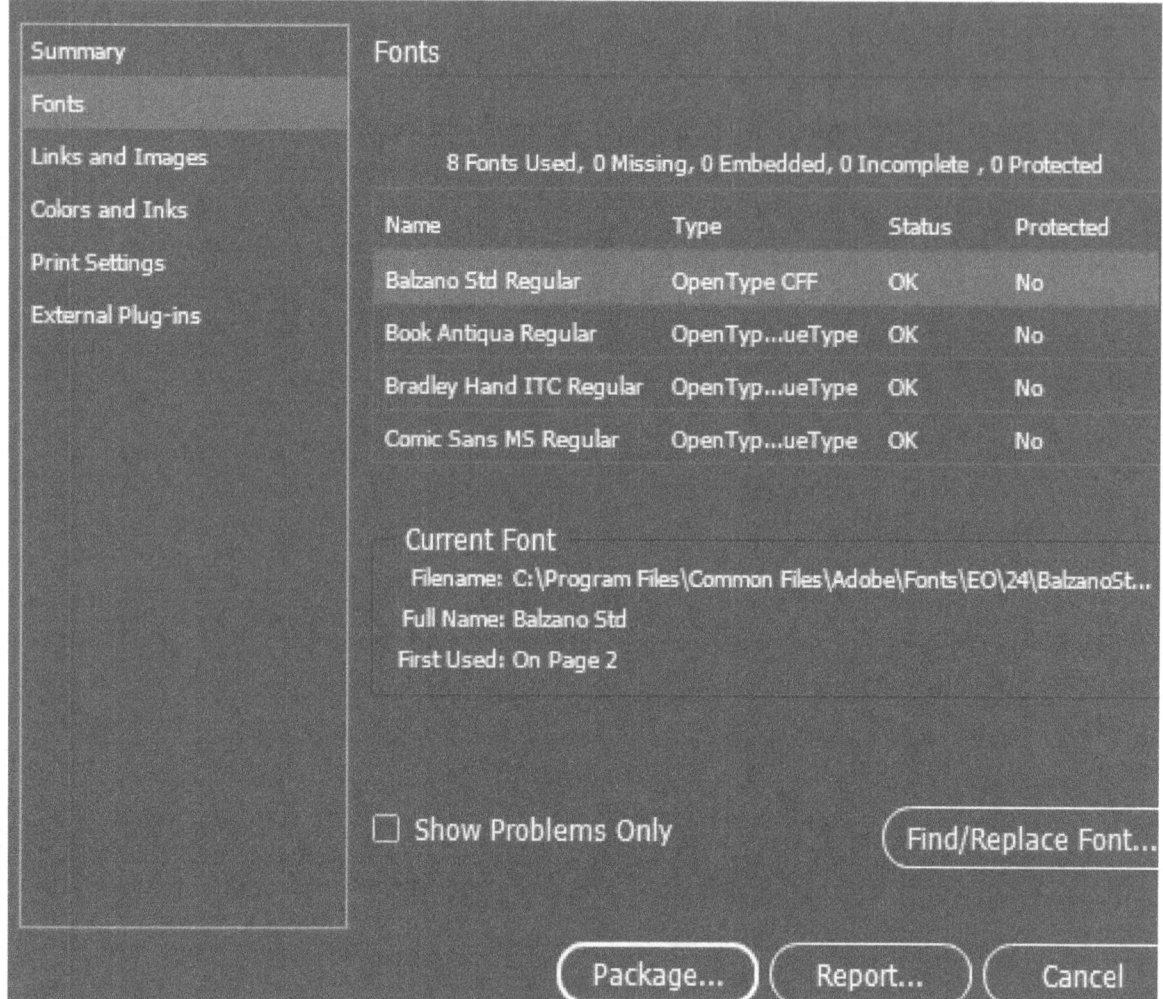

3) Click on "**Links and Images**" in the list on the left side of the dialog box. This screen displays the images within your document. If any images are not properly linked, your document will be incomplete and may print with missing pictures. Ensure that all images are properly linked and update them, if necessary, before proceeding with packaging.

4) Once you've addressed any issues, click the "**Package**" button at the bottom of the dialog box. Your document and all connected files will be saved into a folder. You'll have the opportunity to name the folder, indicate a location on your hard drive, and add any instructions for printing.

Note: If you're delivering a file to a professional print service provider, you can provide them with either the original InDesign document or a high-quality PDF file suitable for printing. It's advisable to inquire about the preferred file type from your print service provider, as different vendors may have their preferences. Providing an InDesign file allows the printing service to fine-tune the document before printing, while a PDF document limits the editing capabilities. Effective communication with your print service provider is essential to ensure a smooth printing process.

GETTING TO KNOW FILE FORMATS

The choice of file format for exporting depends entirely on your specific requirements. Firstly, consider where you intend to use the exported file. For instance, you might need to:

- ✓ Send the entire document to someone who lacks InDesign but prefers to receive it via email.
- ✓ Display an image of your InDesign document or page on the internet.
- ✓ Prepare a particular file format for printing elsewhere.
- ✓ Incorporate the content into another software program like Adobe Animate or Illustrator.

Exporting InDesign documents enables you to make them "portable," allowing for versatile usage, whether it's for the web or integration into another program. With InDesign offering support for numerous file formats, you have the flexibility to choose the most suitable one for your needs, with control over various settings related to the files you generate.

Several file formats are available for export from InDesign. Format like PDF, JPEG, and EPS can be exported from InDesign and subsequently imported into other software applications. These images can be utilized for print purposes after importation into a different graphics program, or they can be used on the web, depending on the document setup and export settings you apply.

Once you've decided on the appropriate file format for exporting your file, delve into the process of exporting and familiarize yourself with the various settings you can manage. The remainder of this chapter guides exporting various file formats from InDesign.

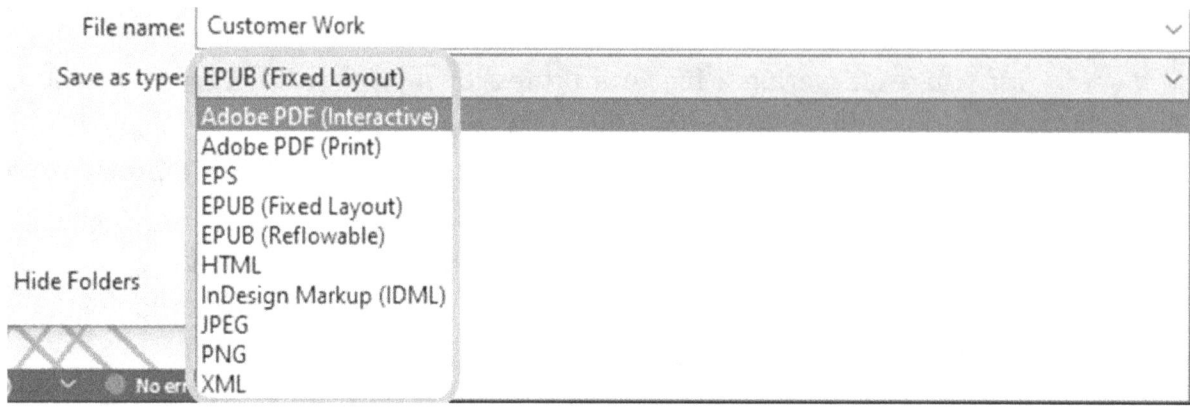

JPEG (JOINT PHOTOGRAPHIC EXPERTS GROUP) AND PNG (PORTABLE NETWORK GRAPHICS)

These are commonly used formats for compressed images. They are ideal for creating a picture of an InDesign page to be posted on the internet, such as a thumbnail image representing a document. However, they are not suitable if you want someone to read the InDesign file on the web; for that purpose, exporting to PDF is recommended. These formats serve as picture previews of document pages.

EPS (ENCAPSULATED POSTSCRIPT)

EPS is a self-contained image file that includes high-resolution printing information for all text and graphics used on a page. It is often used for high-quality printing when an image of an InDesign page needs to be incorporated into another document, such as a book cover created with InDesign appearing in a promotional catalog. Using an EPS of the book cover in your layout ensures quality printing results.

XML (EXTENSIBLE MARKUP LANGUAGE)

XML allows you to separate content from layout, enabling repurposing of content in various ways, whether online or in print. Companies frequently use XML to store large amounts of information, such as product data in catalogs containing thousands of items.

PDF (PORTABLE DOCUMENT FORMAT)

PDF is widely used for exchanging documents across different computer systems and operating systems. It is widely used for distributing files like e-books and brochures, either to a broad audience or to a service provider for printing. PDFs can be designed for printing, in this case, select (**PDF Print**) or if the file includes hyperlinks and multimedia for online distribution, select (**PDF Interactive**). A user with Acrobat Reader installed can also view your document on his/her computer.

TEXT FORMATS

Rich or Plain text files offer options for exporting content with or without formatting. Text files provide a simple means to export content, useful for incorporating or sending text from documents elsewhere. Exporting as text may be preferable when sharing with individuals who do not have InDesign.

EPUB

EPUB is used to create electronic books compatible with e-book readers like the Nook or iPad, and any other e-book reader software. With additional conversion, EPUB files can also be read on the Amazon Kindle.

HTML HYPER TEXT MARKUP LANGUAGE

HTML export converts documents into HTML format, suitable for viewing in web browsers. Usually, this option requires HTML editing for formatting and design, which can be done using Adobe Dreamweaver.

IDML INDESIGN MARKUP LANGUAGE

IDML (InDesign Markup Language) allows exporting InDesign documents in a format readable by earlier versions of InDesign. This is useful for collaboration when different versions of InDesign are being used, ensuring compatibility across versions.

EXPORTING PUBLICATIONS

To export publications, access the Export dialog box by selecting File > Export. Within this dialog box, you have the flexibility to choose the desired file format, specify a name and location for the exported file, and then click Save to proceed. Upon clicking Save, a new dialog box emerges, enabling you to adjust settings tailored to the chosen file format. Below, we explore some of the most commonly used file formats for export.

EXPORTING PDF DOCUMENTS FOR PRINTING

If you aim to ensure that viewers see your document precisely as you've created it, even without InDesign, generating a PDF file is the ideal choice. Additionally, PDF files restrict editing capabilities, reducing the likelihood of alterations to your document. When exporting a PDF document, you have numerous customization options at your disposal. These include controlling compression levels, configuring marks and bleeds directly within InDesign, and setting security measures for the document's protection.

Follow these instructions to export to PDF:

1) Begin by selecting **File** > **Export**. This action opens the **Export** dialog box.
2) Choose a location to save the file and enter a new filename.

Navigate to a location on your hard drive using the **Save As text** field (for macOS users). Or the **File Name** drop-down list (for Windows users). Enter the desired filename in the **File Name** text field.

3) Select **Adobe PDF (Print)** from the **Format** (macOS) or **Save As Type** (Windows) drop-down list at the bottom of the Export window.

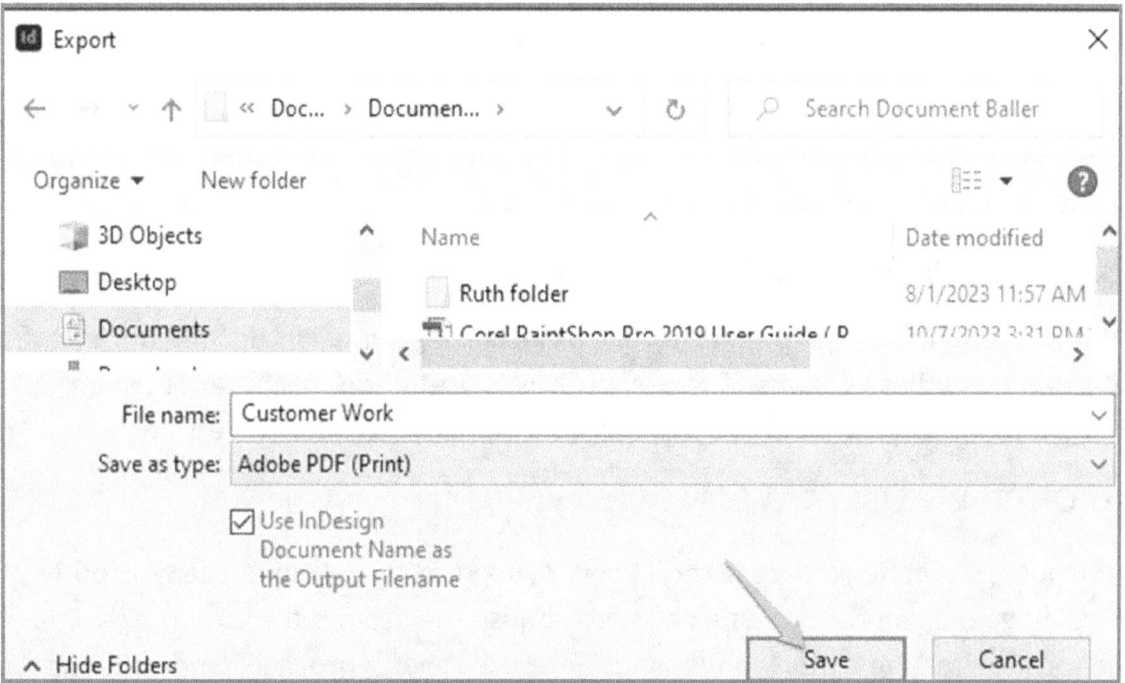

4) Click **Save**. This action opens the **Export Adobe PDF** dialog box, with the General options screen visible.
5) Choose a **preset** from the **Adobe PDF Preset** drop-down list.

These presets simplify the process. They function similarly to Adobe Acrobat and Adobe Distiller functions. For instance, you can choose **High-Quality Print** if you plan to print with a home printer or **Press Quality** if you wish to get PDF professionally printed.

6) Leave the Standard drop-down list at None.

Unless you're familiar with PDF/X standards for sharing advertisements, there's no need to change this setting.

7) Specify a range of pages to export, if needed, by entering the start and end page numbers in the **Range** text box by separating them with a hyphen. Nonconsecutive pages can be exported by separating the page numbers with a comma. Note that all pages will be exported by default.
8) Select a compatibility setting for the PDF from the **Compatibility** drop-down list. This setting indicates which reader is required to view the document. Choosing compatibility for **Acrobat 5 (PDF 1.4)** ensures broader accessibility.

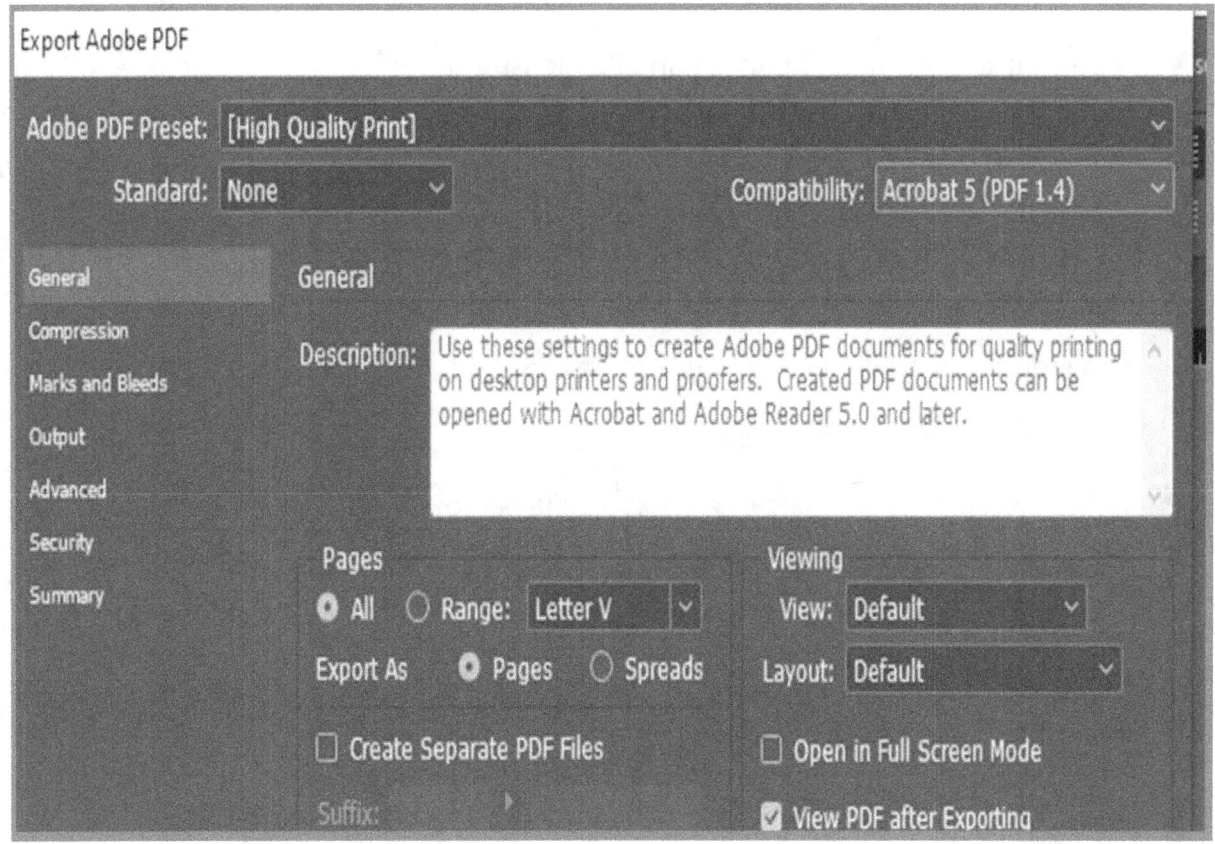

9) Decide whether to embed thumbnails, optimize the document, and select which elements to include in the file by checking the appropriate boxes in the **Include**

section. Other settings, such as bookmarks and links, and other elements can also be specified here. Except you have added any elements, you wouldn't need to bother selecting these options. You may intend to embed thumbnail previews, but acrobat generates thumbnails when the file is opened automatically, and thus, this may add to the file size unreasonably.

Click Security in the list on the left of the Export Adobe PDF dialog box to summon the Security screen. Here, you can set passwords for opening, printing, or altering the PDF file.

10) Finally, click the **Export** button to export the file. The file will be saved to the location specified.

EXPORTING EPS FILES

InDesign allows you to export EPS (Encapsulated PostScript) files, which are invaluable for importing into various other programs. EPS files are single-page graphics files, meaning that each exported InDesign page is stored as an individual EPS file.

It's important to note that exporting an EPS file isn't necessary for placing one InDesign file into another. If you're working on classified pages or any page containing other InDesign pages, you can streamline the process by selecting **File** > **Place** and choosing the desired InDesign file. InDesign can effortlessly import InDesign files into a layout, as well as PDFs. Therefore, the primary reason for exporting to EPS is to create a picture for older software or databases that do not support newer file formats.

Here's a step-by-step guide on how to export EPS files:

1) Begin by selecting **File** > **Export**.

This action triggers the opening of the Export dialog box.

2) Choose a location on your hard drive to save the EPS files, enter a new filename, and select **EPS** from the **Format** (macOS) or **Save As Type** (Windows) drop-down list. Then, click **Save**.

This prompts the Export EPS dialog box to appear.

3) Select the **range of pages** you wish to export.

Opt for the All-Pages option to export all pages or choose the Ranges option and specify the desired page range. If you prefer spreads to export as a single file, check the Spreads radio button.

When creating multiple EPS files, each page of your InDesign document is saved with a filename followed by an underscore and the respective page number. For instance, if you export page 9 of a document named "**Customer work .indd**" file, it would be saved as **"Customer work-9 .eps"** in the specified location.

   4) Choose a color mode from the **Color** drop-down list, and specify font embedding from the **Embed Fonts** drop-down list.

Choose "**Leave Unchanged**" to maintain the color mode used in your InDesign document. You can also opt for **CMYK (Cyan, Magenta, Yellow, Black), Gray (grayscale), or RGB (Red, Green, Blue)** modes. Refer to Chapter 6 for more details on color modes.

From the **Embed Fonts** drop-down list, choose "**Subset**" to embed only the characters used in the file. Selecting **"Complete"** loads all fonts in the file when printing, while **"None"** writes a reference to the font's location into the file.

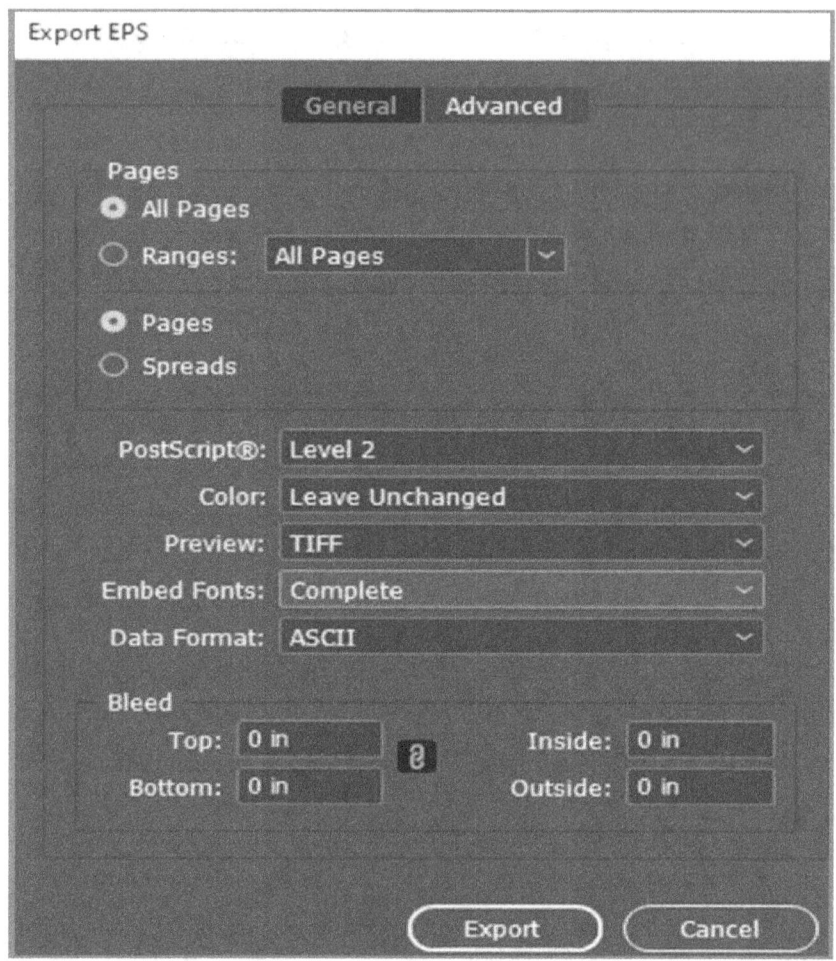

5) Decide whether to generate a preview for the file by selecting an option from the **Preview** drop-down list.

Previews, small thumbnail images, are helpful when EPS files cannot be displayed directly. For instance, when browsing a library of images, a preview allows you to visualize the content before use or opening on your computer. Choose "**TIFF**" to generate a preview, or "**None**" to skip creating a preview.

6) Click the **Export** button to begin the export process.

The files will be saved to the location specified.

EXPORTING PNG AND JPEG FILES

InDesign allows you to export PNG and JPEG files, popular formats extensively used in web publishing. These formats are particularly handy when you need to insert an image of an InDesign document or page online. Whether you're exporting a single image or entire pages and spreads as a PNG or JPEG. PNG and JPEG files offer efficient compression for full-color or black-and-white images, to ensure optimal presentation on the web.

To export a JPEG or PNG image, check these instructions:

1) Begin by selecting an object on a page or ensure that no object is selected if you intend to export a page or spread.
2) Choose **File** > **Export** to open the Export dialog box.
3) Specify a filename, designate the location for saving the file on your hard drive, and from the **Format** (macOS) or **Save As Type** (Windows) drop-down list, select either **JPEG** or **PNG**. Then, click **Save** to proceed.

The Export JPEG or PNG dialog box will appear.

4) Determine whether to export a page or a selected object:
    - ✓ If exporting a page, select the **Pages** radio button and enter the page number in the **Range** text field.
    - ✓ If exporting a selected object, ensure that the **Selection** option is chosen. Note: The Selection option is available only if an object was selected in **Step 1**.
5) Customize the image quality and format by selecting options from the **Quality** and **Format Method** drop-down lists:

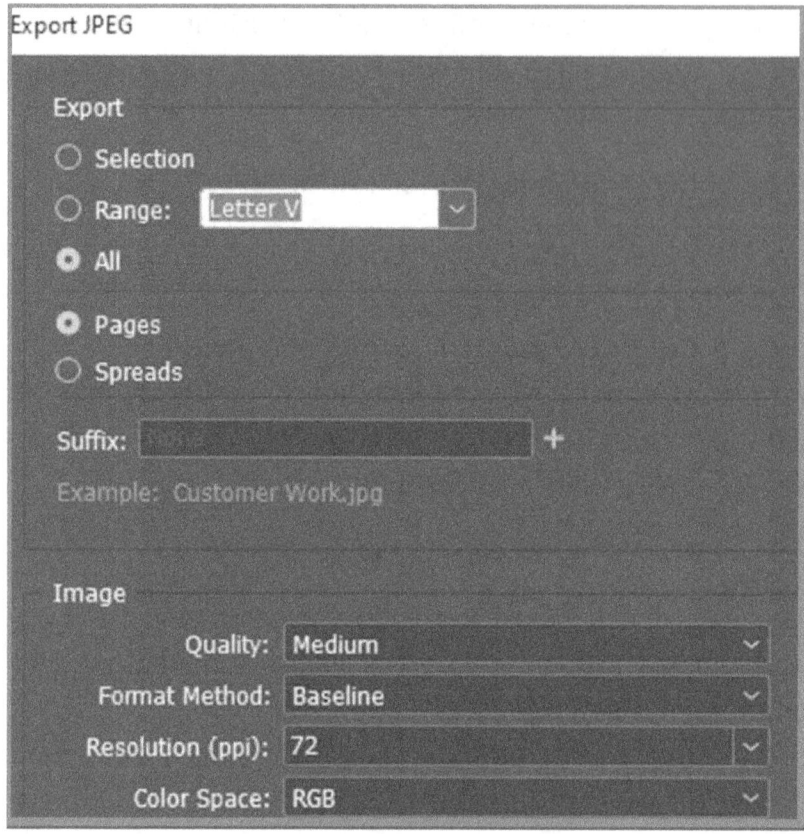

The Image Quality drop-down list allows you to adjust compression levels as explained below:

- ✓ **Maximum**: Highest quality with a larger file size
- ✓ **High**: High quality with a larger file size
- ✓ **Medium**: Medium quality with a medium file size
- ✓ **Low:** Smaller file size with lesser quality

For the Format Method, choose Baseline to download the entire image before display in a web browser, or Progressive to display the image progressively as it downloads.

6) Click the **Export** button to initiate the export process.

The file will be exported and saved to the location specified.

EXPORTING TEXT FILES

InDesign offers the capability to extract text from your document for editing or use in other applications. The exported text formats may vary slightly based on the content of your document. Here's how to export text:

1) Begin by selecting the **Text tool** from the toolbox and highlighting some text within a text frame in your document. Alternatively, position the cursor within a text frame where you intend to export all the text. Note: The cursor must be within a text frame for text export.

2) Next, choose **File** > **Export** to open the Export dialog box.

3) provide a filename, specify the location to save the file, and from the **Format** (macOS) or **Save As Type** (Windows) drop-down list, select **Text Only**. Then, click **Save** to proceed. This action triggers the opening of the **Text Export Options** dialog box.

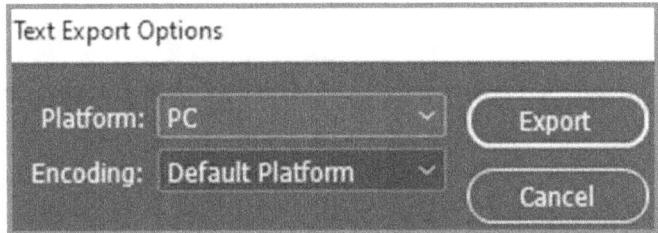

4) Customize the export settings by selecting a platform and encoding:
   - ✓ Choose either **PC** or **Macintosh** from the **Platform** drop-down list to set compatibility with the respective operating system.
   - ✓ From the **Encoding** drop-down list, select an encoding method appropriate for the chosen platform. Options include **Default Platform** or **Unicode**. Unicode, a universal character-encoding standard, ensures compatibility across major operating systems. Encoding determines how characters are represented in digital format, basically defining character rules set representation through specific code sequences.

5) Finally, click the **Export** button to start the export process.

The file will be exported and saved to the location specified.

PRINTING YOUR PUBLICATION

Printing your work from an InDesign document offers various options and methods, accommodating different printers and processes. Whether using a home or office printer or opting for a professional printing service, each option provides varying levels of production quality.

The subsequent sections delve into setting up a document for printing and addressing potential issues confronted during the process.

GETTING TO KNOW BLEED

To achieve an image or color span extending to the edge of a page, devoid of white margins, it's necessary to bleed it off the document's edge. Bleeding entails extending the print area slightly beyond the page's edge into the section slated for cutting during printing. Professional printers often employ this technique by printing documents on a larger page size, subsequently trimming off the excess paper.

You can implement bleeding in your work. During the design phase, enabling crop and bleed marks helps identify where trimming is required to ensure the image extends adequately beyond the page's edge. Further details on this topic will be covered in the subsequent section.

SELF-PROOFING AND PRINTING AT THE OFFICE OR HOME

When you're taking charge of printing and proofing either at home or in the office, it's essential to understand the options available in InDesign. Despite the range of settings, they're designed to be intuitive rather than overly complex. Here's a breakdown to guide you:

- ✓ Begin by selecting **File** > **Print** to access the Print dialog box.
- ✓ From the **Printer** drop-down menu, choose the specific printer you're using. Alternatively, if you're not printing directly, opt for **Microsoft Print to PDF** from the menu to follow along with the instructions provided below.

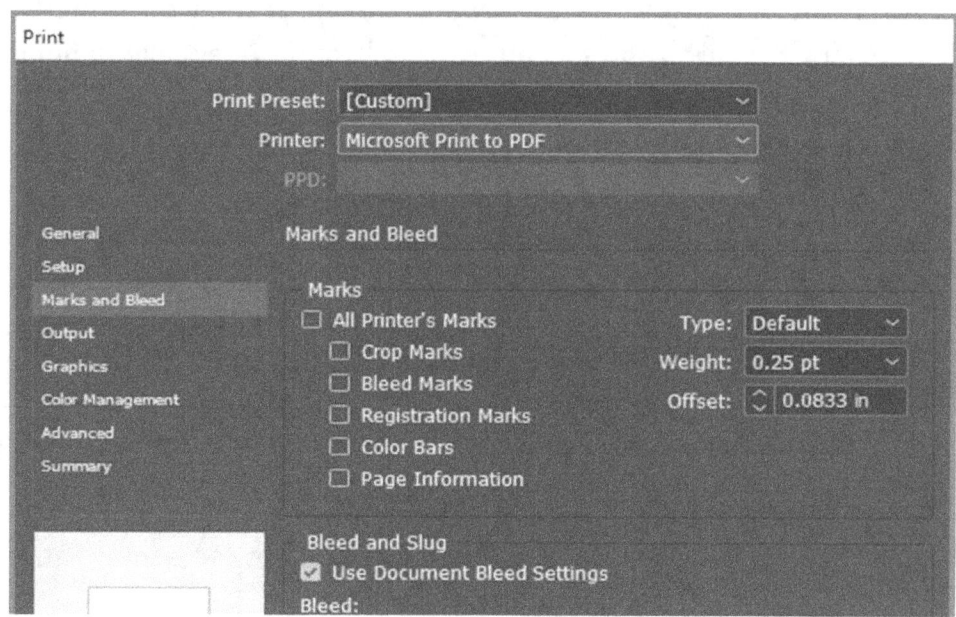

Explore the various printing options listed on the left side of the Print dialog box. Clicking on each option will reveal the specific settings you can adjust based on your requirements.

Explore each of the sections below to gain a comprehensive understanding of these commonly used printing options:

- ✓ **General:** This section allows you to specify the number of copies you wish to print and the range of pages to include. You can even opt to print in reverse order or select specific sequences like even or odd pages only on the **Sequence** drop-down menu. If your document contains spreads that need to be printed on a single page, you can choose the Spreads option.
- ✓ **Setup:** Here, you can define important aspects such as paper size, orientation (portrait or landscape), and scale. You have the flexibility to scale your page up to 1000% or down to 1%. Additionally, you can maintain the aspect ratio by constraining the width and height scales (this is optional). The Page Position dropdown is handy when dealing with larger paper sizes, ensuring your document is centered correctly.
- ✓ **Marks and Bleed:** In this section, you can toggle various printing marks such as crop, bleed, and registration marks on or off. These marks are helpful, especially when dealing with bleeds that extend beyond page boundaries, indicating where to crop each page. Additionally, you can preview how the page will appear when printed and choose to include page information like filename and date.
- ✓ **Output**: This section allows you to specify how pages should be printed, whether as separations or composites and which inks to use (applicable for separations). You can also enable trapping if necessary. InDesign provides the capability to separate and print documents as plates, which is commonly used in commercial printing. Note that the availability of separation options may vary depending on the printer selected.
- ✓ **Graphics:** This section allows you to control how graphics and fonts are printed. The "Send Data" drop-down determines the amount of bitmap image data sent to the printer. Here are the available options:
    - o **All:** Sends all bitmap data for high-quality printing, but may increase printing time for jobs with high-resolution images.

- **Optimized Subsampling**: Sends as much image data as the printer can process, useful for maintaining image quality.
- **Proxy:** Prints lower-quality images for preview purposes.
- **None**: Prints placeholder boxes with an X, useful for quickly proofing layout designs.

✓ **Color Management**: Here, you can specify how colors are handled during output. If you have color profiles loaded for your output devices, you can select them here. Color management is crucial for commercial print vendors and those with precise color requirements, though it's a complex topic beyond the scope of this overview.

✓ **Advanced:** This section allows you to indicate how images are sent to the printer, including options like Open Prepress Interface (OPI). OPI enables the swapping of low-resolution images with high-resolution versions during output, often used by commercial print vendors dealing with numerous images.

✓ Flattening; If your design includes drop shadows, feathered objects, or transparency, flattening needs to be addressed. This ensures proper rendering during printing. Use preset resolutions like Medium for desktop printers and High for professional press output.

✓ **Summary:** Provides an overview of all print settings without the ability to make modifications.

Note : Once you've adjusted your settings to your liking, don't forget to hit the "**Save Preset**" button if you want to keep those changes. This can be a real time-saver if you anticipate using the same settings for future documents. When you click "**Save Preset**," a dialog box will appear, allowing you to give your preset a new name. Then, the next time you print a document, you can simply select your saved preset from the drop-down list in the Print dialog box. Finally, when everything is set up the way you want, just click the "**Print**" button at the bottom of the dialog box to print your document.

CHAPTER NINE

USING EPUB TO CREATE DIGITAL DOCUMENTS AND PUBLISH ONLINE

Beyond crafting traditional printed materials, InDesign offers the versatility to create captivating digital documents and eBooks, effortlessly shareable in digital formats. With its user-friendly tools, InDesign empowers you to design dynamic flyers, brochures, and books without the complexities of coding.

These digital versions enable continuous access for others, regardless of whether they possess InDesign software. Moreover, they're compatible across a spectrum of devices, from smartphones and tablets to conventional computers. Depending on your content and its intended usage, InDesign facilitates the creation of various digital file types. In this chapter, we delve into three distinct methods for disseminating digital documents from InDesign."

- ✓ **Publish Online:** Opt for this method to effortlessly share documents accessible to readers with internet connectivity, allowing them to view content online.
- ✓ **EPUB:** The go-to standard for electronic books, EPUB offers versatility for both online and offline viewing. Choose the reflowable format for text-heavy content, while the fixed layout option suits intricately designed documents, offering room for animations and interactivity.
- ✓ **PDF:** Ideal for maintaining precise formatting across diverse devices and operating systems, PDF stands out as a reliable choice for widespread distribution.

Next, we shall explore how to craft documents tailored for distribution using these three prominent digital publishing formats."

SELECTING THE APPROPRIATE DIGITAL FORMAT

When sharing files electronically, it's essential to opt for the most suitable file format based on the document's requirements or the nature of its content. Refer to the Table shown below for guidance in determining the optimal formats for files you intend to distribute digitally.

Type of Documents	EPub Reflowable	EPub Layout	Fixed	PDF	Publish Online

It demands formatting that can't be altered		↓	
Includes multimedia or interactivity			↓
Extensive content, intended to read just as a book	↓	↓	
A downloadable document available offline	↓	↓	↓

STRATEGIZING LAYOUTS FOR DIGITAL DISTRIBUTION

As part of your planning process, if a document is exclusively meant for digital sharing, you can tailor its layout for specific devices or orientations. For instance, you can choose an iPad horizontal layout during the document's creation phase.

Before digitally sharing a document, it's beneficial to contemplate the devices viewers will use, their intended actions with the file, and the most user-friendly orientation for reading. For example, while your printed documents may be designed for letter-sized paper, digitally, they may need to be viewed on a tablet or phone in a horizontal position. This strategic planning enables you to create and distribute documents that better cater to your audience's needs.

ADAPTING PRINT DOCUMENTS FOR DIGITAL SHARING

If you've got a document designed for print but need to share it digitally, tweaking it for online viewing is essential. Start by saving a duplicate of the original InDesign file and tailor it to suit the digital audience better.

To transform your print document to a digital layout, follow these steps:

1) Open the existing document, then select **File** > **Save As** and give the duplicate a name indicating it's for digital distribution. Click **Save**. Opt for a name that hints at its online purpose, perhaps adding terms like "**eBook**" or " **Online** " to distinguish it from the print version.

If you're converting a text-heavy book into an EPUB format, jump to Step 6 after this, as you won't need to specify layout details. For other documents, including EPUBs with complex layouts, continue with Steps (2-5).

2) To let InDesign adjust object sizes and positions for the new layout, go to **Layout** > **Margins and Columns**, and then enable the **Adjust Layout** checkbox, and hit

OK. If you prefer manual layout adjustment for the new size, skip this step. To create various document sizes for different platforms, explore liquid layout rules in this chapter.

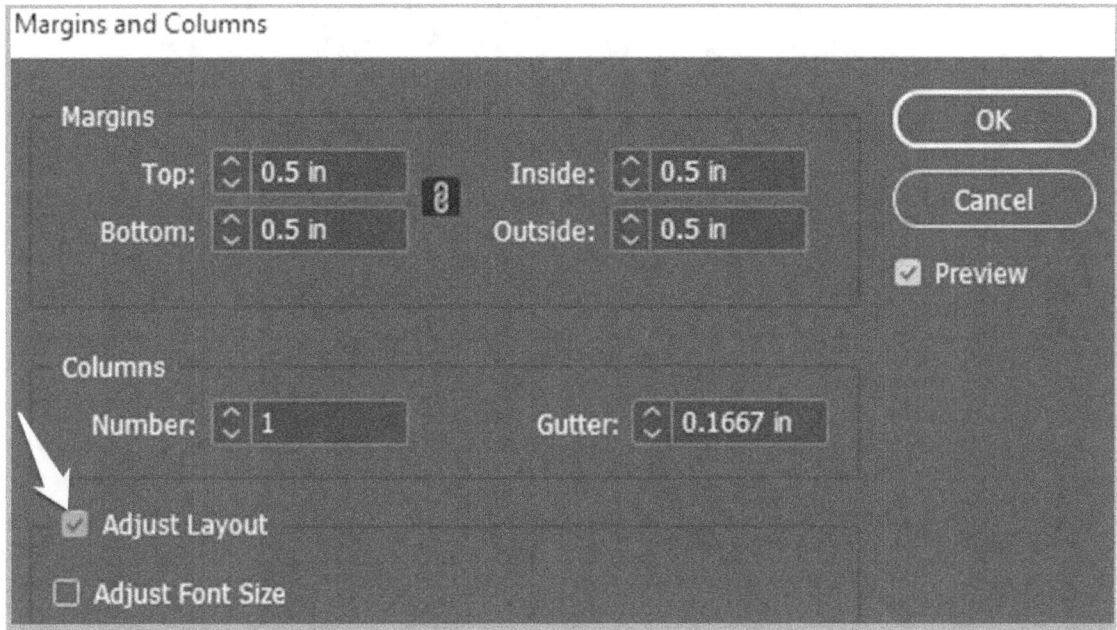

3) Go to **File** > **Document Setup**.
4) In the **Document Setup** window, tailor your document for different screen sizes: opt for "**Mobile**" for smaller screens or "**Web**" for larger ones. Then, select your preferred **Page Size** and **Orientation** (vertical or horizontal), and finally, click **OK**.

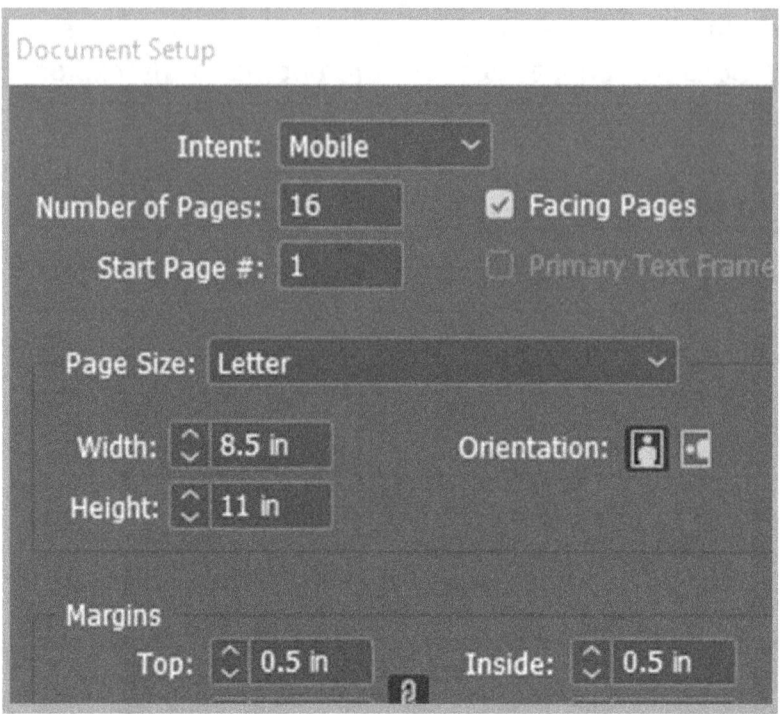

5) Go through your document, carefully adjusting the layout manually. Ensure you're satisfied with any automatic adjustments made. Relocate objects with the **Selection tool** and the **Pages panel** to add or remove pages as necessary. Once done, navigate to **File** > **Save** to preserve these changes.
6) Access the **Articles** panel by selecting **Window** > **Articles**. Here, you can organize the content for your **EPUB or HTML** file. Drag items from your layout into the Articles panel to establish the desired order of display. Exclude any elements you don't wish to include in the digital version by refraining from placing them in the **Articles** panel or deleting them from the layout. For images related to specific text sections, ensure they're anchored appropriately to ensure they appear adjacent to the text rather than at the end.
7) Once you've arranged all elements intended for export into the **Articles** panel, remember to save your document again to finalize the process.

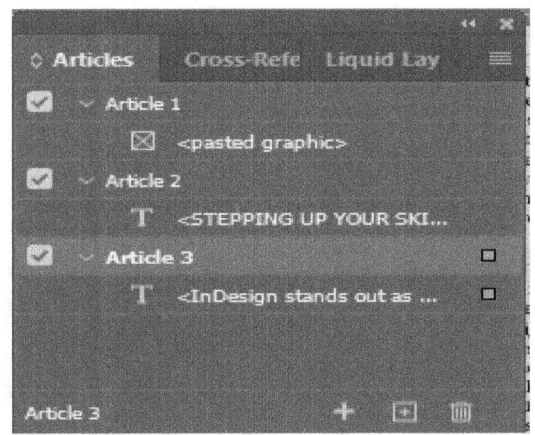

CRAFTING LIQUID LAYOUT RULES FOR ALTERNATIVE LAYOUTS

When crafting layouts of various sizes within a single project using InDesign, the Liquid layout feature offers a more efficient workflow. It reduces the need for extensive manual adjustments between various versions, such as print and online formats. This functionality works hand in hand with alternative layouts, enriching the design process before converting documents to different dimensions. begin the process by defining liquid layout rules to govern the adaptation of page elements to new layouts. These rules dictate how content will flexibly adjust when altering page sizes. Once the liquid layout rules are established for each page, you can freely modify page sizes or create alternative layouts. While both liquid layouts and alternative layouts provide valuable flexibility for accommodating different page sizes and destinations, they remain optional elements in the design process. They streamline content adaptation but are not mandatory for preparing documents for digital publishing. If you prefer manual adaptation over automated tools for adjusting content to different document sizes, you can opt out of using these features.

Follow the instructions provided here to create Liquid layouts:

1) Start by selecting the **Page tool** and clicking on the desired page to apply liquid layout rules.
2) Navigate to **Layout** > **Liquid Layout** to access the Liquid Layout panel.
3) Within the Liquid Layout panel, opt for a **Liquid Page Rule** for each page, as shown below. Choose any of these options:
    - ✓ **Scale:** Resizes the entire page proportionally, potentially leaving white space.
    - ✓ **Re-center**: Keeps content unchanged but centers it in the new page size.

- ✓ **Guide-based:** Allows content to adapt to custom liquid guides set by users with the help of the Page tool.
- ✓ **Object-based:** Empowers users to define specific rules for each object on the page, including adjusting dimensions and positioning.

4) Repeat the selection process for each page, setting individual rules tailored to their content.

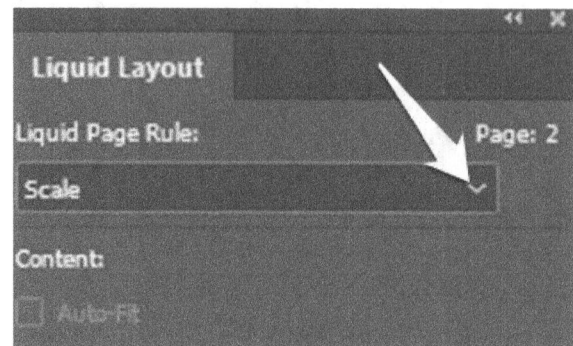

5) Test the liquid layout functionality by selecting the **Page** tool and dragging the page handles. Observe how objects dynamically adjust their positions based on the liquid layout settings and page size alterations.

CRAFTING ALTERNATE LAYOUTS

Once, you have decided how you intend the pages to change with the Liquid Layout rules, there is flexibility to create different vertical and horizontal layouts for your document.

Follow the instructions provided here to create alternative layouts:

1) Go to the **Layout** menu and select **Layout > Create Alternate Layout** to generate a new layout variation based on your current design. For instance, if you have a vertical print layout (**portrait**), you might also want a horizontal layout (**landscape**) for digital viewing.
2) Give your alternate layout a descriptive name and indicate its attributes as shown below:
   - ✓ **Name:** Provide a name for the alternate layout.
   - ✓ **From Source Pages**: Decide whether to base the alternate layout on a single page, a range of pages, or all pages.
   - ✓ **Page Size**: Specify the dimensions and orientation (portrait or landscape) for the alternate layout.

- ✓ **Liquid Page Rule**: Choose whether to **Preserve Existing** rules or indicate a rule to apply to whichever pages for which an alternate layout has been created.
- ✓ **Link Stories:** Use this option to connect text between the original and new layouts. If you revise text in the original layout, this feature simplifies updating it in the new layout through the Links panel.
- ✓ **Copy Text Styles to New Style Group**: Choose this if you're utilizing text styles and want to duplicate them for variation in the alternate layout without impacting the original styles.
- ✓ **Smart Text Reflow:** This feature eliminates manual text formatting like forced line breaks from the original source layout.

Once configured, click **OK** to confirm your choices.

3) After creating the alternate layout, locate it in the **Pages** Panel and adjust the page content as necessary.

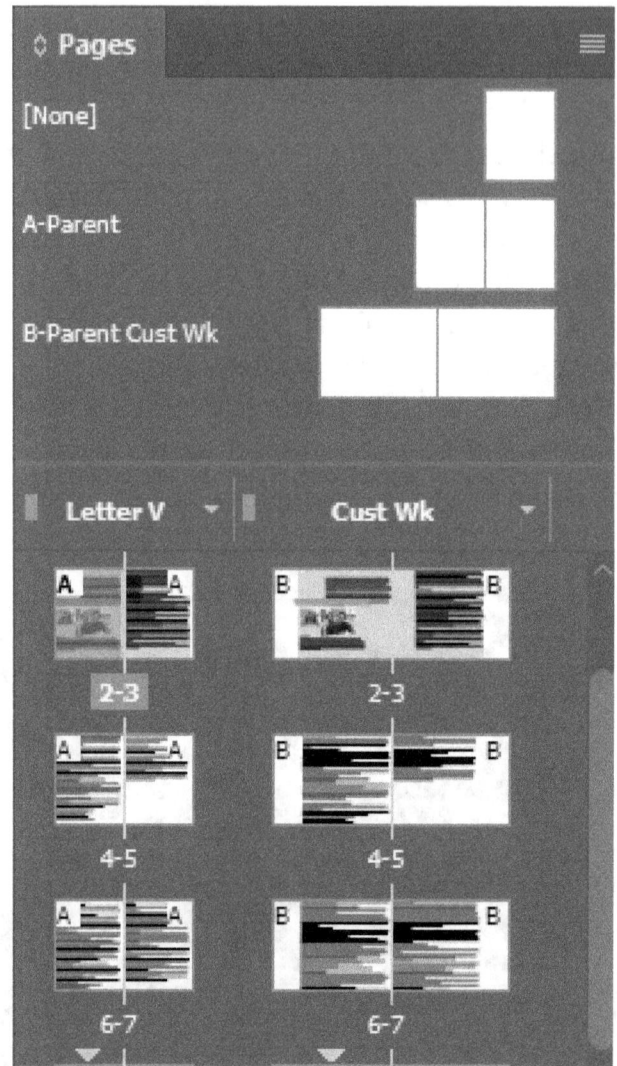

Note : While Liquid Layout helps adapt content to new page sizes or orientations, it doesn't replace your role as a designer. You'll likely need to finalize the design and review any changes in the new alternate layout after its creation.

Note that frames duplicated onto the alternate layout may display a link icon, signifying that the text and images within the alternate layout are linked to the original. Changes made to items in the original layout reflect on the alternate layout. If an item in the alternate layout differs from the original, a yellow triangle displays in the place of the link symbol. Double-click the yellow triangle to synchronize the item in the alternate layout with the original. Any alterations made to an alternate layout won't affect the original layout.

ADD INTERACTIVITY TO DIGITAL DOCUMENTS

To make your digital documents interactive, you have various options depending on how you plan to export them. For interactive PDFs, buttons and forms work well, while animations are great for documents intended for online publishing.

Here's how to add interactivity using InDesign:

- ✓ **Animation Panel:** Utilize the Animation panel to add movement to objects on your pages. For instance, you can make an object fade in or out as the page loads. Access this panel by going to **Window > Interactive > Animation**. Choose individual objects and select an animation from the Preset drop-down menu to add animation.

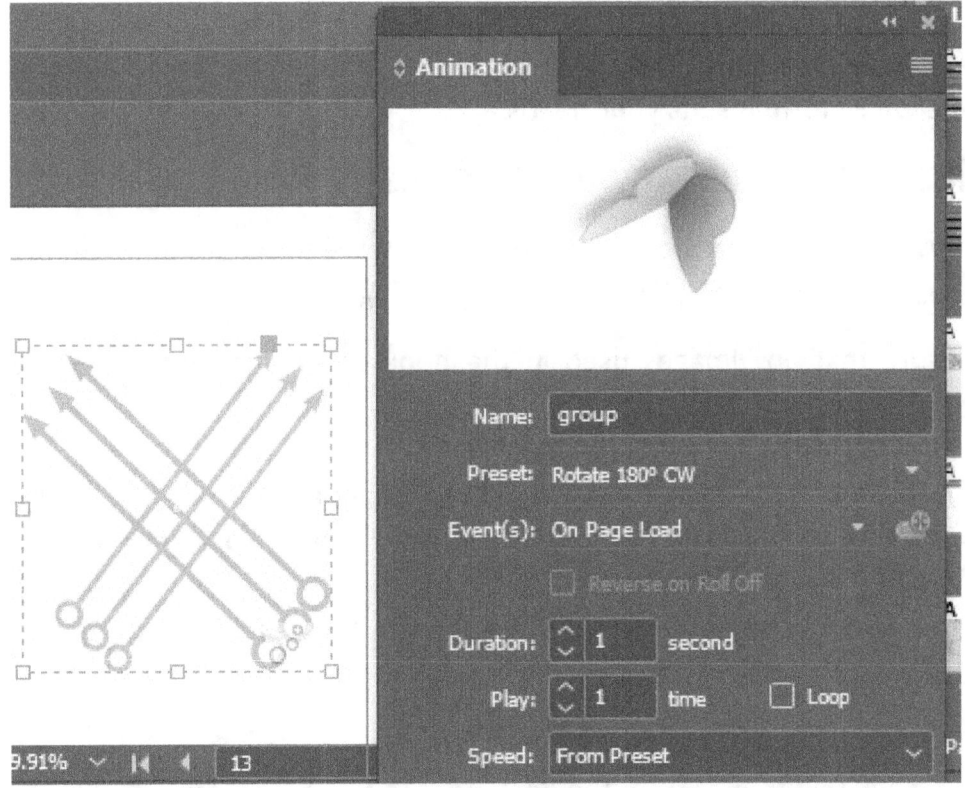

- ✓ **Timing Panel:** Adjust the timing of animations using the Timing panel, which you can access through **Window > Interactive > Timing**. Specify when an animation should occur using the **Event** drop-down list, and set delays if needed before the animation begins using the **Delay** option.
- ✓ **Buttons and Forms:** Convert text or images into interactive buttons using the Buttons and Forms panel. This feature is handy when exporting to formats like modern EPUB or PDF. Access the panel through **Window > Interactive > Buttons**

and Forms. Buttons can trigger various actions when clicked, such as playing media, navigating to a specific page, or playing an animation.

EXPORTING DIGITAL BOOKS AS EPUB

When it comes to distributing digital books through platforms like Google, Apple, and various other digital retailers, they often use the EPUB file format. This format allows users to read books on devices such as the iBooks app, Nook, Kobo reader, Sony eReader, and even Amazon's Kindle. Although Kindle uses a proprietary format, it undergoes an additional conversion process. So, if you're diving into the world of creating electronic books, understanding EPUB files is essential.

InDesign offers a way to convert your files to EPUB format, but there are decisions to make regarding the specific EPUB format you prefer—either reflowable or fixed layout. Next, we'll explore how to craft an EPUB file for your digital books with InDesign and determine which format suits your needs.

PREPARING EPUB (REFLOWABLE) BOOKS

The Reflowable EPUB format works best for text-heavy books, such as novels or biographies. To make a book file ready for exporting to EPUB, follow these steps:

1) Ensure that any images used in the book are anchored to the matching text. Here's how:
    a) Select the image using the **Selection** tool.
    b) Cut the image using the **Edit** > **Cut** command.
    c) Switch to the **Type** tool, click where the image should stay, and paste using **Edit** > **Paste**.

The precise location of the image in InDesign matters less, as EPUB adapts based on where the image is anchored to the text.

2) Access the **Articles** panel by going to **Window** > **Articles**.
3) Drag any text frames from the document to the Articles panel.
4) Rearrange the stories within the Articles panel to specify their sequence for EPUB creation.

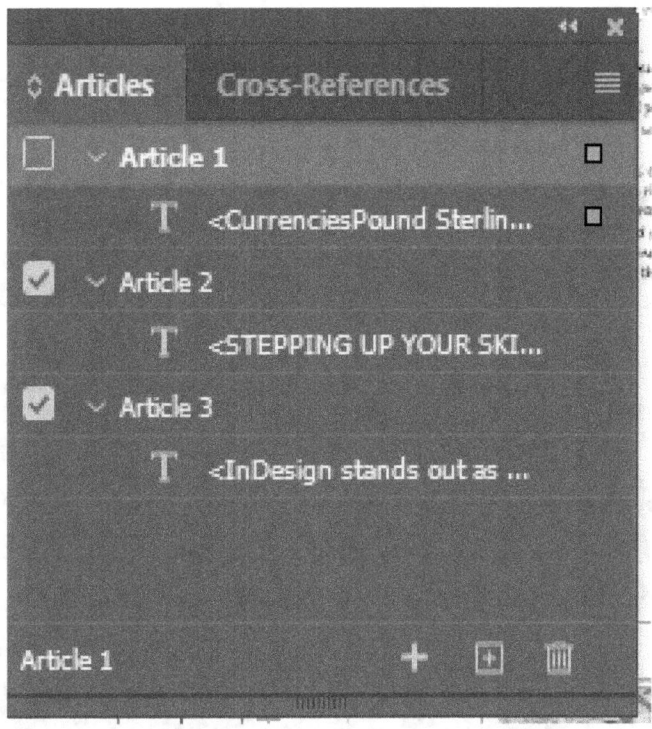

The flow of content in a reflowable EPUB file follows the order set in the Articles panel.

EXPORTING EPUB (REFLOWABLE) BOOKS

Exporting an EPUB transforms the file from an InDesign format into a format compatible with digital book readers. Check these to transform a book into an EPUB reflowable format:

1) While having an InDesign document open, navigate to **File** > **Export**. This action will open the Export dialog box.
2) From the **Format** (macOS) or **Save as Type** (Windows) drop-down list, opt for **EPUB (Reflowable).** Choose a location on your computer or network to save the document, and **assign a name for the EPUB file** in the **File Name** section of the Export dialog box.
3) Click the **Save** button.
4) In the **EPUB Reflowable Layout Export** Options dialog box, customize the options suitable for your book. The **General** tab shown below is one of eight tabs available for specifying EPUB options.

Here's a summary of the essential settings in the General tab when creating an EPUB:

EPUB - Reflowable Layout Export Options

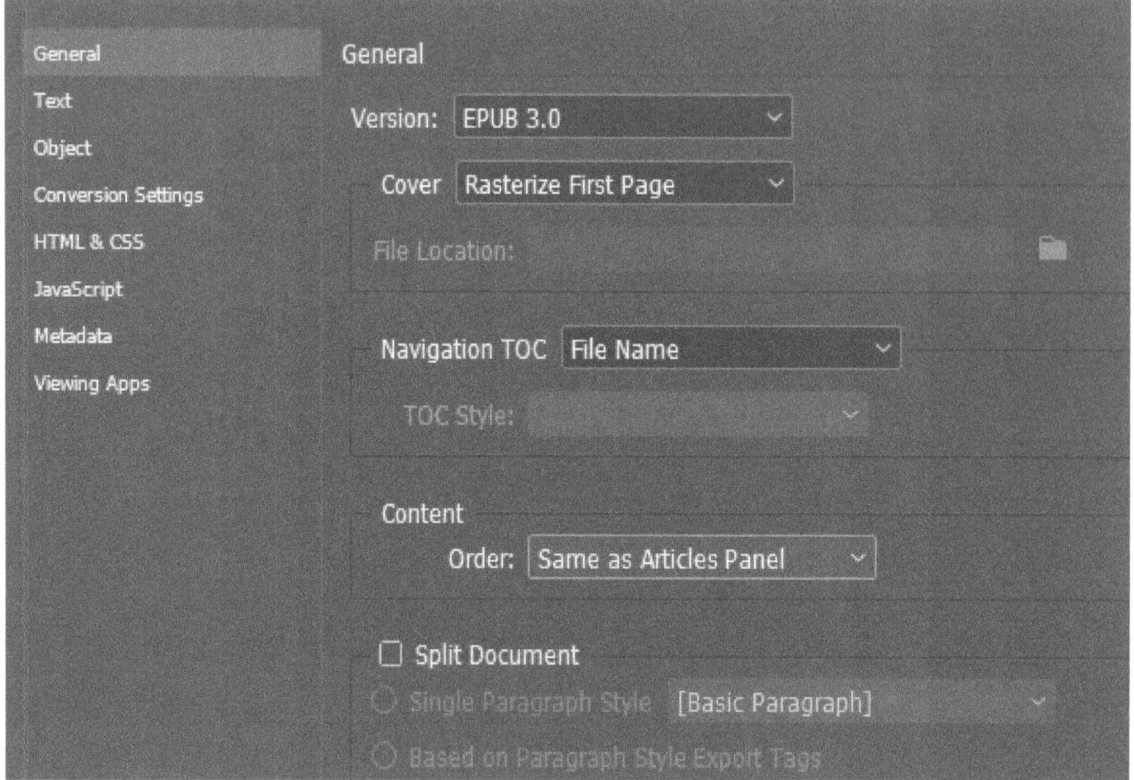

- ✓ **Version:** By default, **EPUB 2.0.1** is selected, allowing readers on older devices to access your reflowable content. If the files will only be read on modern devices, consider switching to **EPUB 3.0.**
- ✓ **Cover:** Choose whether InDesign should create the cover image for the EPUB using the first page (Rasterize First Page) of the document or opt for a specific image file. The cover image is shown in digital libraries and bookstores.
- ✓ **Navigation**: Select Multi-Level (TOC Style) if you desire InDesign to automatically create a table of contents for easier navigation within the EPUB file.
- ✓ **Content:** For Order, opt for Same as Articles Panel. This ensures that your content flows based on how you arranged your images and stories in the Articles panel, as explained in the preceding section

5) In the **Text and Objects** tab located on the left side of the dialog box, you'll find additional options to tailor how your text (including bullets and numbering lists) and graphics (with fixed or relative size) are displayed.

6) To customize the resolution of images created for the EPUB format, navigate to the **Conversion Settings** tab on the left side of the dialog box. If you opt for the

Automatic format, InDesign will determine whether to save images as **JPG, GIF, or PNG files.**

7) Before generating the EPUB, make the necessary adjustments as shown here:
    - ✓ **Metadata:** Head to the **Metadata** tab to input essential information such as book title, publisher, and ISBN. Additionally, you can enter further document metadata in the Document Information field accessed via **File > File** Info.
    - ✓ **HTML & CSS**: Select the **HTML & CSS** tab to add Cascading Style Sheets (CSS) if you've created them to control EPUB formatting. You can include a style sheet by selecting **Add Style Sheet**.
    - ✓ **Viewing Apps**: Choose the preferred app on your computer for viewing EPUB files post-export.
    - ✓ Enabling the **View EPUB after Exporting** option ensures that the EPUB opens automatically in the default EPUB reader once generated. Various free EPUB readers are available, such as iBooks for Mac and Adobe Digital Editions for both macOS and Windows. Previewing the EPUB on multiple e-readers is recommended to ensure cross-device compatibility.
8) Click the **OK** button to generate the EPUB. If you've selected the **View EPUB after Exporting** checkbox, the EPUB file will open using your default EPUB reader.

If the EPUB Options dialog box resembles the HTML Export window, it's because EPUBs utilize HTML as their foundation. Electronic book readers function as specialized browsers tailored to display HTML and CSS formatted books. All the HTML and CSS content for an EPUB file is included within the compressed folder bearing the EPUB file extension.

EXPORTING EPUB (FIXED-LAYOUT)

For a book that includes intricate designs, graphics, or interactive elements crafted using InDesign. Consider using the EPUB (Fixed-Layout). This option is ideal for cookbooks, picture books, or any publication requiring specific formatting that needs to be retained when transformed into a digital book format. The following are the instructions for creating a Fixed Layout EPUB from InDesign:

1) Open your InDesign document and navigate to **File > Export**. This action brings up the Export dialog box.

2) In the dialog box, select **EPUB (Fixed-Layout)** from the **Format** (macOS) or **Save as Type** (Windows) dropdown menu. Then, designate a location on your hard drive or network to save the file. Enter a name for the **EPUB** in the **File Name** field.

3) Once you've set the location and named the file, click the **Save** button to finalize the export process.

4) In the **EPUB Fixed Layout Export** Options dialog box, you can tailor the **General** settings for your book, as shown below. Here's a breakdown of the key options on the General tab for creating a Fixed Layout EPUB:

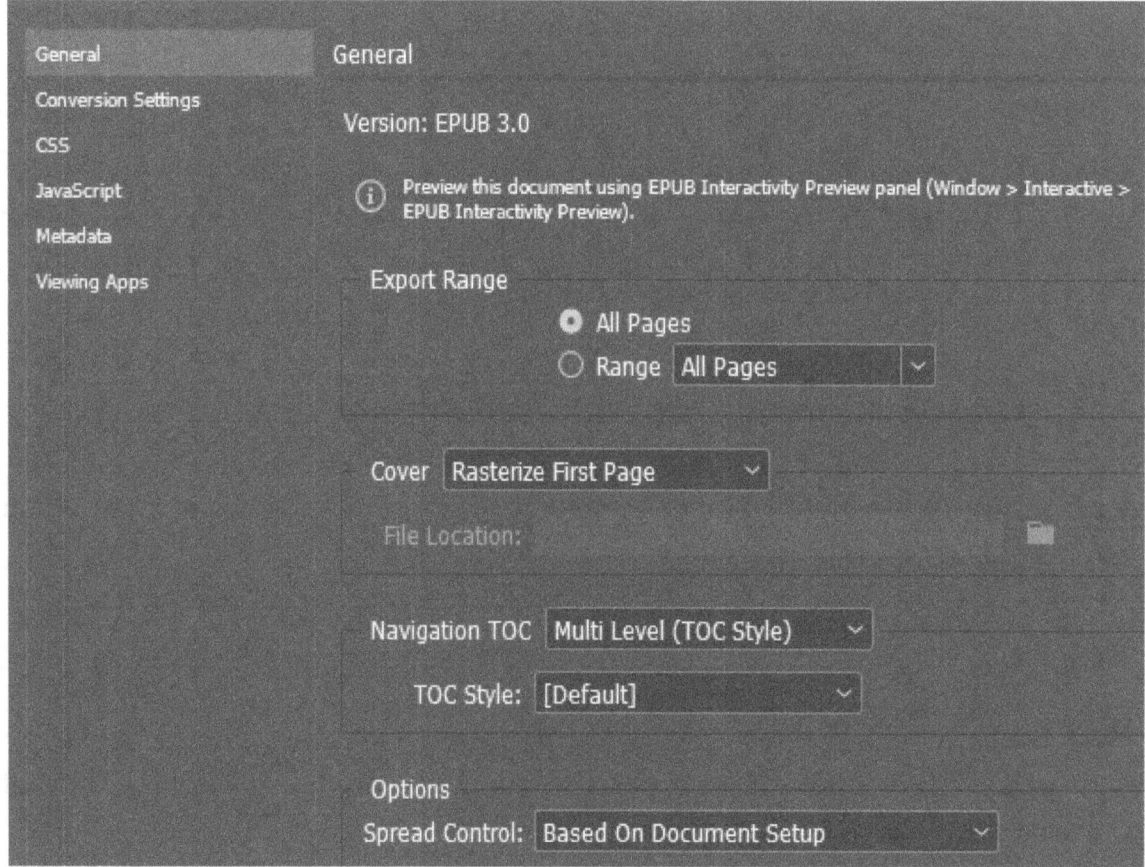

✓ **Version:** By default, EPUB 3.0 is selected, and for a fixed layout, this option remains the only choice.

✓ **Navigation:** Opt for Multi-Level (TOC Style) to have InDesign automatically create a table of contents for easier navigation within the EPUB. However, for image-rich books like children's books, selecting **none** ensures the table of contents won't clutter the reader's sidebar.

- ✓ **Options**: for Spread Control, based on whether you used Facing Pages in your document setup, you can control how pages display in the reader. Choosing **Based on Document Setup** lets InDesign output pages as single or double spreads, based on your initial setup in the **Document Setup** Dialog Box.

5) To customize Conversion Settings, CSS, JavaScript, Metadata, and Viewing Apps further, go to the **Additional Export Layout** Tab options. Detailed definitions were provided previously in Export Reflowable.
6) Finally, click **OK** to save your settings.

Both EPUB formats use HTML and CSS. While HTML and CSS from an EPUB Reflowable can be easily modified using web editors like Dreamweaver or Sigil, making changes to an EPUB (Fixed Layout) file is best done by returning to the original InDesign file, making your adjustments, and reexporting the file. The complexity of HTML and CSS in fixed-layout EPUBs makes direct modifications challenging.

PUBLISH DOCUMENT ONLINE

Share your InDesign creations with the world by publishing them online for easy viewing in any modern web browser like Chrome, Firefox, or Safari. With Publish Online, your document becomes a digital version accessible to anyone connected to the internet. While viewing requires an internet connection, you can also provide readers with the option to download a static PDF version for offline access.

This dynamic publishing tool offers interactive features such as forms, buttons, and animations, enhancing the viewer experience. When you publish using Publish Online, your document is uploaded to Adobe's server, and you receive a unique URL to share with others. However, keep in mind that because the files exist on Adobe's servers, this option may not be suitable if you prefer to host content on your own website.

To publish your InDesign document online, follow these steps:

1) Open your desired InDesign document and navigate to **File** > **Publish Online** or click the **Export** icon located at the upper-right corner of the interface, then select **Publish Online**.

2) In the Publish Your Document Online interface, provide a **Title** and **Description** for your document. You can also choose to export as Spreads if your document contains left and right pages meant to be viewed together. Additionally, decide whether to allow viewers to download the document as a PDF for offline viewing. If you want to restrict embedding on unauthorized websites, select the **Hide the Share and Embed options** checkbox.

3) To access more options, go to the **Advanced** button within the **Publish Your Document Online interface**. From there, you can indicate whether you want to publish all pages or only specific ones. Additionally, you can choose which page or image will serve as the thumbnail representation of the document. If wanted, you can adjust the image quality and, if PDF download is enabled, you can also select the quality of the PDF, which will impact its file size.

4) Once you've configured your preferences, click **Publish** to make your document available online. InDesign will display a progress bar as it converts and uploads the document to Adobe's servers. Once the upload is complete, you can either click "**View Document**" to open it in your web browser or copy the URL to share it with others.

COLLABORATE AND GET FEEDBACK WITH SHARE FOR REVIEW

If you're working on a project that requires input from others, the "Share for Review" feature in InDesign can be incredibly handy. It allows you to create an online version of your document, similar to the "Publish Online" feature, but with added options for receiving comments and feedback from reviewers.

Here's how you can share an InDesign document for review:

1) Start by opening the InDesign document you want to share for review. Look for the **Export** icon at the upper-right corner of the interface and click on it. From the options, choose "**Share for Review**".

2) In the **Share for Review** panel, click on "**Create**". This action will upload your file to Adobe's servers for online viewing and remarking.

3) Once the file is uploaded, provide a title for the document under review. You can also choose who can access the document – whether it's specific individuals or anyone with the link. If you're restricting access, use the **"Add People"** option to invite specific individuals to view and comment on the project. They'll receive an

email invitation and can directly comment on the published file. If you make changes later, you can click **Update Link** to update the link accordingly.

4) Next, either click on the provided link to view the published file online or copy the link using the **Clipboard** icon and paste it into a web browser. You can now add new comments or respond to comments made by collaborators, which will appear on the right side of the web browser window.

5) Switch back to the InDesign document you have shared for review. Any comments made online will be directly shared within the InDesign document through the Review panel. If you can't find the Review panel, you can open it by selecting **Window** > **Comments** > **Review**. Inside the **Review** panel, you can click on the **eye** icon to show or hide comments within the InDesign document. As you address the comments and make updates to the document, you can change the status of each comment by selecting the ellipsis **(...)** next to it.

Sharing documents for online review is beneficial when all reviewers have internet access to make comments. However, if a reviewer needs access to the document offline, creating a PDF might be a better option. Comments added to a PDF version of the document using Adobe Acrobat annotation tools can be imported into InDesign with the **PDF Comments** panel, to open this go to **Window** > **Comments** > **PDF Comments**.

CHAPTER TEN
NAVIGATE YOUR WAY FASTER WITH INDESIGN SHORTCUTS

Exposing the true speed of navigation often relies on shortcuts and mastering them is the key to quickly progress. But, without knowing these shortcuts or where to find them, their potential remains untapped.

This principle is true, especially with InDesign. It's widely acknowledged that using keyboard shortcuts rather than relying solely on mouse clicks significantly enhances productivity and efficiency

Here's a handy guide to essential shortcut keys enabling rapid adjustments to effects, strokes, swatches, links, and layers without the need to constantly reach for the mouse. With these shortcuts at your fingertips, achieving desired effects becomes a breeze, saving you valuable time otherwise spent searching through menus and options.

PANEL SHORTCUTS

USES	WINDOWS	MACOS
Swatches	F5	F5
Pages	F12	F12
Stroke	F10	F10
Preflight	Ctrl + Alt + Shift + F	Command + Option + Shift + F
Align	Shift + F7	Command + Shift + F7
Links	Ctrl + Alt + Shift + D	Command + Shift + D
Layers	F7	F7
Info	F8	F8

| Control | Ctrl + Alt + 6 | Command + Options + 6 |

OBJECT SHORTCUTS

If you need to fit the frame to the content or content to the frame, group and ungroup, drop shadow, and so on. Below are the shortcuts for them.

USES	WINDOWS	MACOS
Make Compound Path	Ctrl + 8	Command + 8
Drop Shadow	Ctrl + Alt + M	Command + Option + M
Clipping Path	Ctrl + Alt + Shift + K	Command + Option +Shift + K
Fit Content Proportionally	Ctrl + Alt + Shift + E	Command + Option + Shift + E
Fit Frame to Content	Ctrl + Alt + C	Command + Option + C
Fit Content to Frame	Ctrl + Alt + E	Command + Option + E
Text Frame Options	Ctrl + B	Command + B
Unlock Position	Ctrl + Alt + L	Command + Option + L
Lock Position	Ctrl + L	Command + L
Ungroup	Ctrl + Shift + G	Command + Shift + G
Group	Ctrl + G	Command + G
Send Backward	Ctrl + [	Command + [
Bring Forward	Ctrl +]	Command +]
Send to Back	Ctrl + Shift + [	Command + Shift + [
Bring to Front	Ctrl + Shift +]	Command + Shift +]

CHARACTER SHORTCUTS

USES	WINDOWS	MACOS
Drop caps & nested styles	Ctrl + Alt + R	Command + Option + R
Paragraph Justification	Ctrl + Shift + Alt + J	Command + Shift + Option + J
Paragraph rule	Ctrl + Alt + J	Command + Option + J
Redefine styles	Ctrl + Alt + Shift + R	Command + Option + Shift + R
Underline	Ctrl + Shift + U	Command + Shift + U
Superscript	Ctrl + Shift + =	Command + Shift + =
Subscript	Ctrl + Alt + Shift + =	Command + Option + Shift + =
Strikethrough	Ctrl + Shift + /	Command + Shift + Control + /
All Caps	Ctrl + Shift + K	Command + Shift + K
Small Caps	Ctrl + Shift + H	Command + Shift + H

TYPE SHORTCUTS

These keys allow you to align type to center, left, right, or justify on a page with a few keys on your keyboard

USES	WINDOWS	MACOS
Apply Normal	Ctrl + Shift + Y	Command + Shift + Y

Apply Bold	Ctrl + Shift + B	Command + Shift + B
Apply Italic	Ctrl + Shift + I	Command + Shift + I
Justify All lines	Ctrl + Shift + F	Command + Shift + F
Justify all but the last line	Ctrl + Shift + J	Command + Shift + J
Align to Baseline Grid	Ctrl + Shift + Alt + G	Command + Shift + Option + G
Align Left	Ctrl + Shift + L	Command + Shift + L
Align Right	Ctrl + Shift + R	Command + Shift + R
Align Center	Ctrl + Shift + C	Command + Shift + C
Create Outlines without Deleting Text	Ctrl + Shift + Alt + O	Command + Shift + Option + O
Create Outlines	Ctrl + Shift + O	Command + Shift + O
Text Wrap	Ctrl + Alt + W	Command + Option + W
Auto Page Number	Ctrl + Alt + Shift + N	Command + Option + Shift + N
Paragraph Styles	F11	Command + F11
Paragraph	Ctrl + M	Command + Option + T
Tabs	Ctrl + Shift + T	Command + Shift + T

TEXT FRAME OR STORY SHORTCUTS

These keys help to navigate to the beginning of the story, end of the story, end of line, right one word or left one word with few keyboard keys

USES	WINDOWS	MACOS
Left one word	Ctrl + Left arrow	Command + Left arrow
Right one Word	Ctrl + Right arrow	Command + Right arrow
Start of Line	Home	Home
End of Line	Ctrl + End	Command + End
Beginning of Story	Ctrl + Home	Command + Home
End of Story	Ctrl + End	Command + End

LAYOUT SHORTCUTS

These are groups of favorite shortcuts, they help to carry out a group of things such as going to the last page, going to the next page, first page or previous page, and so on

USES	WINDOWS	MACOS
Add New Page	Ctrl + Shift + P	Command + Shift + P
Go Forward	Ctrl + Page Down	Command + Page Down
Go Back	Ctrl + Page Up	Command + Page Up

Previous Spread	Alt + Page Up	Option + Page Up
Next Spread	Alt + Page Down	Option + Page Down
Last Page	Ctrl + Shift + Page Down	Command Shift + Page Down
Previous Page	Shift + Page Up	Shift + Page Up
Next Page	Shift + Page Down	Shift + Page Down
First Page	Ctrl + Shift + Page Up	Command + Shift + Page Up

TOOLS SHORTCUTS

You can easily switch to each tool without necessarily looking across different tools in your tools panel. To conveniently access important tools for Windows and macOS, see the table below.

USES	WINDOWS	MACOS
Type Tool	T	T
Rectangle Tool	M	M
Pen Tool	P	P
Pencil Tool	N	N
Rotate Tool	R	R
Scale Tool	S	S
Line Tool	\	\
Zoom Tool	Z	Z
Hand Tool	H	H
Measure Tool	K	K
Type of Path Tool	SHIFT + T	SHIFT + T
Swap Fill and Stroke colors	X OR SHIFT X	X OR SHIFT X

Rectangle Frame Tool	F	F
Gradient Tool	G	G
Free Transform Tool	E	E
Ellipse Tool	L	L
Eyedropper Tool	I	I
Selection Tool	V	V
Direct Selection Tool	A	A

CONCLUSION

After going through this comprehensive user guide, it is evident that you have gained a wealth of knowledge about Adobe InDesign 2024. The guide has provided you with a thorough understanding of how to utilize the software effectively, regardless of the version you may be using.

With the step-by-step instructions and explanations provided in this user guide, learning how to navigate and utilize the features of Adobe InDesign has become as simple as reciting the alphabet. You have likely discovered that mastering this powerful software is within reach for anyone willing to invest their time and effort.

Now that you have experienced the benefits of this user guide firsthand, I encourage you to share your newfound knowledge with your friends and family. By recommending this guide to them, they too can enjoy the same level of understanding and proficiency in using Adobe InDesign.

Thank you for your time, and I hope to see you again in the future.

INDEX

A

ADD A PAGE JUMP NUMBER	51
ADD INTERACTIVITY TO DIGITAL DOCUMENTS	170
ADJUSTING AND LINKING TEXT FRAMES	46
ADJUSTING COLUMNS	43
ADJUSTING FRAME CORNERS	114
ADJUSTING TEXT INDENTATION	54
ADJUSTING TEXT WRAPS	88
ALTERING TABLE SETTINGS	64
Animation Panel	170
APPLYING PARENT SPREADS	92

B

Basic shapes and frame shapes	100
Buttons and Forms:	171

C

CLIPPING PATHS	140
COLOR CONTROLS	127
Color Management	162
Column	81
Column Guides	83
CONNECTING AND EMBEDDING IMAGES	76
Constraining proportions	134
Contour Options	86
Corner points	99
CRAFTING OWN CUSTOM SHAPES	105
CRAFTING TABLES:	62
CREATE A PARENT PAGE	93
CREATING BASIC FILLS	116
CREATING TABLE STYLES	67
Curve points	99

D

DIGITAL FORMAT	163

E

Embedding	76
ENABLING THE SNAP FEATURE TO A GUIDE OR GRID	26
EPUB	163
EXPLORING LAYERS	123
EXPLORING THE PANELS	22
EXPORTING EPS FILES	155

EXPORTING EPUB (REFLOWABLE) BOOKS	172
EXPORTING PDF DOCUMENTS	152
EXPORTING PNG AND JPEG FILES	157
EXPORTING TEXT FILES	158

F

FILE FORMATS	150
Fill color	128
Flowing	49
Font	35
Frame	35

G

Gutter	81

H

HANDLING TEXT FLOW	39
HTML & CSS	174

I

IMPORTING PICTURES	71
In port	49
INSERTING AND DELETING PAGES	90
INSERTING PLACEHOLDER TEXT	40

J

Jump Object	86
Jump to Next Column	86

L

Linking	76
Liquid Guides	84

M

Margin	81
Margin Guides	84
Marks and Bleed	161
Merge Cells	64
Metadata:	174
MODIFYING BASIC SHAPES	104

N

New Parent"	93
No Text Wrap	86

O

Offset	86
Out port	49
Output	161

P

Page	19
PAGE NUMBERING	91
Page Orientation	81
Page Size	81
PARAGRAPH STYLE	56
Parent pages	19
Pasteboard	19
Path	97
PATHS AND SHAPES	97
PDF	163
Point	98
POINTS AND SEGMENTS	98
Position	134
PREPARING EPUB (REFLOWABLE) BOOKS	171
PRINTING WITH PREFLIGHT	146
Publish Online	163

R

Reference point	134
REFLECTING OBJECTS	140
REMOVING FILLS	122
Rotation angle	134
Ruler Guides	84

S

Scale	134
Segment	99
SELECTING IMAGES	79
Shearing	134
SHEARING (SKEWING) OBJECTS	138
Size	134
Smart Guides	84
Spread	19
Story	49
Stroke	97
Stroke color	128
SWATCHES PANEL	129

T

Text	35
Text color	128
TEXT FRAME OPTIONS	41
TEXT ON A PATH	68
THE PAGES PANEL	24
The Pen tool	99
The Pencil tool	99
The toolbar	19
THE TRANSFORM PANEL	133
Threading	49
Timing Panel	170

U

USING CONTEXT MENUS	23
UTILIZING TEXT FRAMES	36

V

Viewing Apps	174

W

Wrap around Bounding Box:	86
Wrap around Object Shape:	86
Wrap Options	86
WRAPPING TEXT AROUND OBJECTS	85

www.ingramcontent.com/pod-product-compliance
Lightning Source LLC
Chambersburg PA
CBHW062103220526
45471CB00010B/3586